BOMBERS

REMOVE BEFORE FLIGHT

Times change, and so do the aircraft and the munitions, but smart weapons or not, every bombing mission still starts as it always did, with the work of the ground crews. The RAF armourers shown here are loading a laser-guided bomb on to a Tornado GR1 during the Kosovo crisis of 1999. (© British Crown Copyright/MoD)

BOMBERS

FROM THE FIRST WORLD WAR
TO KOSOVO

DAVID WRAGG

SUTTON PUBLISHING

First published in the United Kingdom in 1999 by
Sutton Publishing Limited · Phoenix Mill
Thrupp · Stroud · Gloucestershire · GL5 2BU

British Library Cataloguing in Publication Data
A catalogue record for this book is available from the British Library

ISBN 0 7509 2090 4

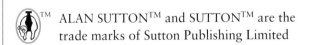 ™ ALAN SUTTON™ and SUTTON™ are the
trade marks of Sutton Publishing Limited

Typeset in 10/13 pt Sabon.
Typesetting and origination by
Sutton Publishing Limited.
Printed in Great Britain by
Butler & Tanner, Frome, Somerset.

CONTENTS

FOREWORD

One of the most controversial aspects of warfare has been, and to some extent remains, the role of the bomber. Yet the men who flew on these operations were human, often coping with great hardships and tremendous risks in the service of their country. Much of the controversy arises from the thought of aircraft being used to attack 'innocent' civilians, and there *were* cases of this happening, at Rotterdam and in the Channel Islands. Nevertheless, in most of the operations the 'innocent' civilians were factory workers and others whose contribution to the war effort was vital. Even so, as the reader will see, at the outset of the Second World War many on both sides went to great lengths to ensure that civilian casualties were avoided.

The bomber is also often portrayed as a blunt weapon, but as many of the operations recorded here show, it could also be very precise, and perhaps never more so than in the daring Mosquito raid on the prison at Amiens, described in Chapter Eight.

Unfortunately, war is sometimes a necessary evil, and we forget all too often that sometimes it is a lesser evil when the alternative is considered. It is important in such circumstances to recognize the great courage of so many.

I would like to thank all those who have helped with this book, and none more so than those who took the trouble to record their actions and emotions in the height of war.

David Wragg
Edinburgh
Summer 1999

INTRODUCTION

Although the bomber was a child of war, born during the First World War, the concept of aerial bombardment is several thousand years old. A Hindu epic poem, the *Mahabharata* of Dwaipayana-Vyasa, described a winged chariot, built by Krishna's enemies, which flew over the town of Dwarakha to bomb his followers. Later, in 1670, the Italian Jesuit Fr. Francesco de Lana de Terzi produced a design for an aerial ship, which was to be kept airborne by four hollow copper spheres, each of which was to contain a vacuum. He felt compelled to warn that the Almighty might not allow the construction of such a craft, in case it was used against an enemy, killing their men and burning their ships by means of 'artificial fireworks and fire balls'.

Sure enough, after the invention of the balloon by the Montgolfier brothers and their rival, Jacques Charles, in 1783, the idea of aerial bombardment was eventually tried. The only mystery is why it took so long, since it was not until 1849, during the siege of Venice by Austrian forces, that balloons were used to drop bombs on a city.

The Wright brothers, who were spasmodically very active in trying to interest the military in their new invention, believed that they had invented something which would make future wars impossible. This was high optimism, doubtless born of the belief that in future, movements of troops and of fleets would be impossible to hide, and it was based on assumptions which were far from correct. Even so, the military didn't take easily to the idea of flight. Aeroplanes involved in manoeuvres before the outbreak of war in 1914 were often regarded as a nuisance, and one British general is reputed to have complained that the 'aeroplanes completely spoilt the war', after war games in 1912.

The threat of the bomber was taken seriously enough for the Hague Convention of 1899 to prohibit bombing from balloons – this was four years before the first aeroplane or airship flights. In 1907, a second conference went even further, banning the bombardment of undefended places by land forces 'by any means whatsoever', whether this was from the air or by means of artillery. During the Italo–Turkish War of 1911, the Italians obtained and used aeroplanes for the first time, using these to bomb Turkish positions, prompting a protest that the Italian aviators had hit a hospital.

The optimism of the Wrights was echoed elsewhere by many who thought that bombing undefended towns and cities would not be allowed, and that in any event, no enemy would wish to attract the odium of such an action. Times and values change, and sometimes very quickly indeed!

THE FIRST WORLD WAR

The First World War had broken out in stages, with first Austro-Hungary declaring war on Serbia on 1 August 1914, followed by Germany declaring war on Russia, and then, on 4 August, the United Kingdom and France declaring war on Germany.

War found the opposing sides using the aeroplane primarily as a means of reconnaissance. There were exceptions, even at the outset, for the Royal Naval Air Service (RNAS) had already experimented with dropping bombs and torpedoes. The popular belief is that at first, the aviators of both sides behaved in a gentlemanly fashion, even waving to each other as they passed on their regular reconnaissance sorties, and that it took some time for aerial warfare to evolve. This is true to some extent, but the fact remains that as early as 6 August 1914 the first bombing raid of the war was conducted by the German Zeppelin *ZVI*, which dropped 13 bombs on one of the forts defending the Belgian city of Liège, failing to hit the target, but nevertheless killing nine civilians. The Zeppelin was fired upon, and crashed on return to its base at Cologne.

It took but another week for the first aeroplane to drop bombs, when a Rumpler Taube (ironically, the name means 'dove') dropped two small bombs on Paris. From this time onwards, aircraft of both sides would occasionally drop bombs on enemy formations or installations, the 'bombs' usually being hand-held artillery shells fitted with fins, and thrown over the side of an aircraft or airship. When the first RNAS detachment arrived in France shortly after the outbreak of war, a number of its Sopwith biplanes had already been modified as bombers, with racks fitted to the side of the fuselage, described by one observer, C.G. Grey, editor of *The Aeroplane*, as being:

> exactly like a pipe-rack fixed on the outside of the fuselage, handy for the pilot or passenger. They hung nose downwards and the stems of the bombs projected up through the holes in the pipe-rack arrangement. There a pin was stuck through each stem and rested across the hole. To the head of the pin a piece of string was tied, and when the bomber wanted to drop the bomb he pulled the string which pulled out the pin which let the stem of the bomb drop out of the pipe-rack, and the bomb fell.[1]

The threat was now so obvious that by September, the First Lord of the Admiralty, Winston Churchill, had volunteered the RNAS to defend the UK against attack by German Zeppelins or bombers.

Of course, the poor performance of the aircraft of the day meant that the threat was limited. On 22 September four Sopwith biplanes were sent against Cologne and Düsseldorf, where Zeppelins were known to be based. The raid on Cologne was unsuccessful because bad weather obscured the target, but one of the pilots found the main railway station, and bombed that instead. At Düsseldorf, there was better luck when the Zeppelin shed discovered there was bombed with two 20 lb bombs, destroying *ZIX*. This was not the first Zeppelin to be lost: two had already been destroyed over the Western Front, and another forced down in Russia. Given the small number of these craft available, the attrition rate was already appearing unsustainable. Drawing the same conclusions as the RAF would a quarter of a century later, the German Military Air Service decided to switch to night raids.

The British meanwhile pressed on with their attacks, fitting three of the new Avro 504 biplanes with mechanical bomb releases and sending them by sea and road to Belfort on the Franco–German border. On 21 November 1914 these three aircraft flew against Friedrichshafen, taking a circuitous route to make a surprise attack on the Zeppelin factory, seriously damaging one craft nearing completion, and incidentally destroying the town gasworks with a near-miss. As a result, the Germans removed troops and weapons

The initial air raids by the German military Air Service used the huge Zeppelin airships – here is L25 on the ground. (RAFM P146)

The largest man-made structures at the time included the airship sheds, vital to protect these lighter-than-air craft from the wind. This is L40. (RAFM P149)

The airships faced defensive measures, initially from the RNAS and then later from the RFC. This is all that remained of Zeppelin L33, which crashed at Little Wigborough in Essex. The crew of twenty-two, including Commander Becker, the captain, all survived and were made PoWs. (IWM HU54655)

from the front line – some 4,000 men in all – to provide anti-aircraft (AA) defences for the Zeppelin works. This in itself could be counted as a success for the bomber.

The Zeppelin night raids on towns on the East Coast of England had a similar effect. The Kaiser had ordered that only military targets were to be attacked, and that civilians and buildings of historic interest should be spared – hardly practical, given that the raids were at night and from a considerable altitude. The first of these raids was in February 1915, on the port of Yarmouth, in Norfolk. Later raids attacked towns as far north as Grimsby, and many reached London, with a total of 55 Zeppelin sorties throughout the year, leaving more than 700 dead and injured. Public opinion soon forced the authorities to divert men, guns and fighter aircraft to the defence of British cities.

Meanwhile, Frederick Handley Page, the aircraft manufacturer, convinced that the heavy bomber would be the war-winning weapon of the future, pressed ahead with a design which he intended would be a 'bloody paralyser of an aeroplane'.

GERMAN HEAVY BOMBERS ATTACK LONDON, 13 JUNE AND 7 JULY 1917

Faced with the limitations of the airship, both sides were developing heavy bombers. During 1916, the RNAS had started the first concerted bombing raids on Germany. German Gotha GIV bombers made their first raids on Folkestone in early 1917, before moving on to London itself.

The Aircraft

The Gotha GIV bomber was a twin-engined heavy bomber capable of an impressive altitude for its time, being able to reach 12,000 ft in 35 minutes, with a ceiling of 20,500 ft. This was a true strategic bomber, of the kind neglected by Germany during the Second World War. Two Mercedes DIVa six-cylinder water-cooled engines gave a maximum speed of 72 mph at 12,000 ft, and six 110 lb bombs could usually be carried. There was a nose gunner and a 'rear' gunner, although his position could really be described as 'mid-upper', being just aft of the trailing edges of the biplane mainplane.

The Action

The German Gotha bombers mounted their first major raid on London on 13 June 1917, when 20 Gotha bombers were sent against the capital, of which 17 found their way to the target to drop 6,600 lb of bombs. Attacking in broad daylight, they killed 162 civilians and injured another 432. No fewer than 92 aircraft were sent to intercept the raiders, but none of these managed to gain sufficient altitude to press home its attack, and one of them was forced down. The Gothas returned home without loss. The first true air raid on 13 June had caught the people of London unawares. Contemporary accounts tell of men and women standing, watching the huge aircraft which were no more than distant specks – even beautiful to some, with the sunlight glinting on their wings. There was no seeking shelter, no sense of imminent danger, even when they saw the leading machine fire a white flare, the signal to drop bombs.

One German crew member recalls:

With my telescope in one hand, I signal with the other to my pilot. Slowly long rows of streets pass the small orbit of the sight. At last it is time to drop. I give a signal and in less time than it takes to tell, I have pushed the levers and anxiously follow the flight of the released bombs. With a tremendous crash they strike the heart of England. It is a magnificently terrific spectacle seen from mid-air. Projectiles from hostile

The Gotha bombers attacked London and Folkestone – this is a Gotha GIII of the German MAS. (RAFM P012622)

batteries are spluttering and exploding beneath and all around us, while below the earth seems to be rocking . . .[2]

The attack started at 11.40, and in two minutes 72 bombs dropped within one mile of the centre of the target, Liverpool Street Station in the east of the City of London. Three landed on the station, two of these crashing through the roof, one of which was a dud, while the other exploded on the platform. The most damage was caused by the third, which hit an express train about to leave for King's Lynn and Hunstanton, wrecking the dining car and two coaches which were set on fire, trapping many of the victims inside.

The bombs were large for the day, with many in excess of 100 lb. Near Tottenham Court Road, a factory was burnt out, although generally, where there was no fire, damage was confined to the upper floors of buildings. There was more than one dud bomb, with another falling in the moat of the Tower of London, but the bomb which hit a workshop at the Royal Mint caused 34 casualties when it exploded.

Under intense political pressure, Maj Gen Trenchard, commander of the Royal Flying Corps (RFC), put two squadrons on fighter patrol over the Channel. He believed that this would simply encourage the Gothas to attack targets in France, which they did. After two weeks the patrols were stood down, and the Gothas resumed their attacks, first on Harwich and the Naval Air Station at Felixstowe on 4 July, when 18 out of 25 Gothas reached the target to drop 6,600 lb of bombs, and then, on 7 July, London.

The raid on 7 July saw 22 out of 24 aircraft reach the target, dropping 6,765 lb of bombs and killing 57 people, injuring another 193. One Gotha was shot down on this occasion, and another four crashed on landing on return to base, while two British aircraft were shot down and another was forced down. As in the Second World War, the politicians called for reprisal raids on Mannheim, although for practical reasons this had to be postponed. Meanwhile, Trenchard was told to find suitable bases for 40 long-range bomber squadrons to be based in France for attacks on German towns and cities. One US airman who had arrived in London in 1917 witnessed one of the first raids on the capital:

When we got down to the station it was already packed. We couldn't get down to the platform so camped on a landing halfway down. The air was as foul as the Black Hole of Calcutta and those people certainly were scared. We cheered the girls up and drank the whiskey and felt better.

Note the difference between the GIII and the later GVII, shown here. (RAFM P2966)

Everyone had brought campstools and it was sure a funny sight. I hadn't realized before how successful the raids are. It doesn't matter whether they hit anything or not as long as they put the wind up the civilian population so thoroughly. These people wanted peace and they wanted it quickly![3]

There was worse to come. December 1917 saw the use of larger bombs over London, including a 9 ft long 300 kg (660 lb) bomb of considerable penetrative power, since 60 per cent of its weight consisted of high explosive. On the night of 28/29 January 1918 the Staaken R-39 (a giant bomber) dropped one of these, hitting Odham's Printing Works in Long Acre, killing 38 Londoners seeking shelter in the basement, an officially designated public air raid shelter. Later, the first 1 ton bomb to land on England hit the North Pavilion of the Royal Hospital, Chelsea on 16 February 1918.

Before the end of the war, the Germans were planning raids using the new Elektron incendiary bomb. Had such a weapon been available a year or so earlier, it is interesting to speculate what might have been the outcome.

Comment

The heavy-bomber raids on London were far more concentrated than those of the Zeppelins. The impact on morale, the need to withdraw desperately needed units from France, and the casualties inflicted showed the clear potential for a sustained campaign. Nevertheless, the small number of aircraft available and doubtless poor availability meant that there would be no way the Gotha units could overwhelm English cities. A more concentrated effort, perhaps hitting fewer targets more often, could nevertheless have had a greater impact. While air raid shelters were made available, these were for the most part underground stations and cellars in buildings, the latter offering far less protection than the purpose-built shelters of the Second World War. Had even heavier German bombs or the Elektron bomb been available earlier, the damage would have been far worse, and the war could have been prolonged.

THE RFC IN FRANCE, APRIL–OCTOBER 1917

During 1917 the RFC squadrons in France received the new DH4 bomber, allocated to a number of squadrons, including 55 and 57 Sqns. This was regarded by many as the best bomber of the war, a fast, high-flying single-engined biplane. Observers also liked the dual controls, which gave them a sense of extra security if their pilot was injured, or worse, although one flaw was a fuel tank placed between pilot and observer, which hampered communication. Day-bombers seldom received escorts, as would be provided some twenty or more years later, but were sometimes accompanied by offensive patrols. The DH4s were expected to be able to look after themselves, using speed and altitude to escape the attentions of enemy fighters.

The Aircraft

The DH4, usually fitted with a 375 hp Rolls-Royce Eagle engine, was a reliable aircraft for the time, but shortages meant that some were built with the inferior Farnborough 3A engine. Other engines were tried as an alternative to the 3A, including a 260 hp Fiat engine which was notably noisy. The DH4 could carry one 230 lb bomb or two 112 lb bombs.

Designed by the then Superintendent of the Royal Aircraft Factory, Capt Geoffrey de Havilland, the DH4 has been called 'the best single-engined bomber of the war', although many crews disliked sitting behind the engine, suffering from the oil and smoke which was swept back over them, and preferred the earlier aircraft with pusher engines. Nevertheless, by the standards of the day, the aircraft marked a step forward. The Rolls-Royce Eagle engine gave a maximum speed of 125 mph, and a maximum altitude of 16,700 ft, while earlier bombers had managed just 90 mph.

The Action

On 5 April, 55 Sqn's DH4s were sent to bomb an assembly point at Valenciennes with 112 lb bombs. Afterwards, they were chased by a large formation of MAS Albatros scouts, but managed to outrun their opponents. Good fortune was not always on their side, however, and when four aircraft were sent on a raid on 8 April, three were shot down.

Another British bomber squadron was No. 57, whose members naturally enough called themselves the 'Heinz Varieties'. The squadron had been operating as a fighter unit within the RFC, having been formed in 1916, operating Royal Aircraft Factory FE2B biplanes. The members of the squadron were warned in May 1917 that their role was to change, and that they were to receive the DH4 single-engined biplane bomber.

The first raid by 57 Sqn was on 15 June, when they dropped several 20 lb bombs on the German airfields at Recken and Handzame, some 15 miles behind enemy lines. Although no aircraft were lost on the raids, the squadron's home airfield at Droglandt inflicted heavy losses and damage on the aircraft, being described as being 'quite inadequate for the comparatively large and heavy machines'. [4]

The squadron soon moved to Boisdinghem, near St Omer, which was regarded as an improvement, apart from being spoiled by 'some depressions 18 inches deep by 15 feet in diameter',[5] which were probably hastily filled shell craters. Raids included dropping 230 lb bombs on enemy billets in the village of Hooglede on 24 and 25 September 1917, and similar raids followed later in the softening-up process preceding the first Battle of Passchendaele on 12 October. Raids were interspersed with periods of training. An innovation, at least for this squadron, came during the raid on the airfield at Bissegem on New Year's Day 1918, when bombs were dropped on a signal from the formation leader, as was to become commonplace during the Second World War.

Not every unit could have the most up-to-date aircraft, and many laboured on with obsolete ones, or with designs which had been outclassed from the start. Aircraft design and development was still an imprecise art less than fourteen years after the first flights by the Wright brothers. Flying Sopwith 1½-Strutters on a raid against the railway junction at Tournai, one of 45 Sqn's flight commanders declared: 'Some say Sopwith two-seaters are bloody fine machines, but I say they're more bloody than fine.'[6]

Service aviation has often produced its eccentrics and characters, and the First World War was no exception. They were probably more noticeable in a society which was more restrained and concerned with correctness, and because the British Army and the Royal Navy were often harshly disciplined. On the other hand, some of the characteristics of civilian life followed the airmen. At first, German aircraft were not commanded by the pilots, who usually acted almost as flying chauffeurs for their superiors. One RFC bomber pilot, Lt W.R. 'Willie' Read, had a batman (officer's servant) who volunteered to become a Lewis gunner so that he could accompany his 'gentleman' on sorties. Having been a civilian valet in peacetime, he always boarded the aircraft carrying a small suitcase, 'in case we land on the other side, sir.'[7]

Flying military aircraft in combat has always been dangerous, and not for the faint-hearted. During the First World War this danger was heightened not just by the poor reliability and frail structures of the aircraft, but by the authorities' refusal to equip pilots with parachutes. True, the parachutes of the day had their failings, but the commanders' philosophy was that providing parachutes might encourage pilots to bale out prematurely rather than stay with their aircraft. Trenchard, in command of the RFC in France and later to be the RAF's first Chief of the Air Staff, did order 20 parachutes at one stage, but this was to drop agents in German-occupied territory, and even that plan was soon abandoned.

There were other problems. Flying at high altitude without oxygen often had adverse effects on aircrew, and the Germans were the first to fit their high-altitude aircraft with oxygen gear. Descending took some time, and great care had to be taken when throttling back the engines in case they went cold and stalled.

Comment

Military aviation was in its infancy, and in seeking to attack enemy airfields, the RFC was looking for aerial supremacy. Nevertheless, the pressures on any bomber commander to move onto other targets before the current targets had been suppressed must have been even more pressing during this conflict, due to the RFC's subjugation to the Army.

SUPPORTING THE ARMY: MESSINES AND YPRES, JUNE–JULY 1917

By June 1917 the RFC had 45 squadrons in France, plus five RNAS squadrons on loan, with a total of 881 aircraft. The front around Messines had 300 of these aircraft allocated to it, including 100 fighters. Just one squadron had the DH4, No. 55, and whereas before the battle at Arras many squadrons had their complement increased to 21 or even 24 aircraft, many had reverted to 18 aircraft because of delays in delivering replacements.

The Aircraft

The aircraft in this case were the DH4 (see pp. 6–7) and the SE5.

A product of the Royal Aircraft Factory, the SE5 was really a fighter rather than a bomber, although in this case it operated as a fighter-bomber. The twin-seat biplane was regarded as being one of the best of the war, and entered RFC service in large numbers. Propeller-synchronized Lewis guns were fitted, and Hispano-Suiza 'V' engines of 150 or 200 hp were used. An improved variant, the SE5a, entered service shortly before the Armistice.

The Action

Bombing included unescorted high-level raids by 55 Sqn's DH4s, and by 27 Sqn's Martinsydes with an escort of Sopwith Pups, both of which mounted daylight raids. Nevertheless, the most damage in the run-up to the battle for the Messines Ridge was caused by FE2bs of 100 Sqn, attacking at night. The DH4s also undertook photographic reconnaissance, flying as high as 21,000 ft, and the fighter squadrons also mounted strafing raids against ground forces. The campaign was marked by the mixture of old and new methods of warfare: 21 large mines were placed under the ridge, and of these, 19 detonated successfully at 03.10 on 7 June, with almost a million tons of high explosive, the sound being heard 130 miles away in London. Ten thousand Germans were estimated to have been killed, and another seven thousand were so badly stunned that they were easily captured. By 09.00, the Allies had taken the ridge, and a German counter-attack the following day was repulsed.

The attack by the British and French armies on the Ypres salient opened at dawn on 31 July 1917, leading to the Third Battle of Ypres. On the opening day, Lt R.A. 'Dick' Maybery of 56 Sqn took off at 04.45, crossing the lines at 500 ft, below heavy cloud. Smoke from the intense artillery barrage restricted his vision, so he diverted onto a south-easterly course, dropping first to 200 ft and then to 30 ft. He flew over Courtrai and on to the aerodrome at Heule. He was attacked by two Albatros fighters, at which he fired some machine gun bursts, but he had to avoid combat because of his bombload. He eventually found Heule, climbed to 200 ft and circled to find a target:

'I then flew east, turned and came back along the line of the southernmost sheds and dropped my first bomb, which hit the third shed from the east and exploded. This caused immense excitement . . .'. Turning first to the left, he flew along the line of the easternmost sheds and dropped another bomb, which hit the first shed from the south and exploded. He next flew straight at the sheds at the town end of the aerodrome and dropped his third bomb, which went through either the roof or the door of another of the sheds: he could see smoke, and he felt and heard the explosion.[8]

He was attempting to drop his fourth bomb when he came under ground fire. Pulling the bomb release as he approached from the north, his bomb failed to drop. By this time he was over the town railway station, so he tried again, and the bomb dropped between a goods train and a shed, where it exploded. He then went on to strafe the aerodrome, silencing the machine-gunner who had fired at him, and making two further runs over the aerodrome before making his way to Ceurne and machine-gunning the aerodrome there. Not content with this, he machined-gunned horsemen and an infantry column before returning to base in his SE5.

Comment

This is a good example of the state of tactics and AA defences during the First World War. In the Second World War, repeated runs across enemy airfields were discouraged: each run became progressively more dangerous because AA gunners were alerted and aware of the altitude of the aircraft, so that their aim became better. To achieve what he did, 'Dick' Maybery showed skill and courage, and enjoyed considerable luck.

C H A P T E R   T W O

DISTANT THUNDER: THE BOMBER BETWEEN THE WARS

At the outbreak of the First World War in August 1914 the RFC had 100 aircraft; by November 1918 the newly created Royal Air Force (RAF) had 22,677 aircraft in 188 squadrons, half of them in France.

The RAF had been created as a result of the Smuts Report of August 1917, which recommended:

That an Air Ministry be instituted as soon as possible, consisting of a Minister with a consultative board on the lines of the Army Council or Admiralty Board, on which the several departmental activities of the Ministry will be represented. This Ministry to control and administer all matters in connection with aerial warfare of all kinds whatsoever, including lighter-than-air as well as heavier-than-air craft . . . That the Air Ministry and Staff proceed to work out the arrangements necessary for the amalgamation of the Royal Naval Air Service and the Royal Flying Corps and the legal constitution and discipline of the new air service, and to prepare the necessary draft legislation and regulations . . . That the air service remain in intimate touch with the Army and Navy by the closest liaison, or by direct representation of both on the Air Staff, and that, if necessary, the arrangements for close co-operation between the three services be revised from time to time . . . Air power can be used as an independent means of war operations. Nobody that witnessed the attack on London on 7 July, 1917, can have any doubt on that point. Unlike artillery, an air fleet can conduct extensive operations far from and independently of both Army and Navy. As far as can at present be foreseen there is absolutely no limit to the scale of its future independent war use. And the day may not be far off when aerial operations with their devastation of enemy lands and destruction of industrial and populous centres on a vast scale may become the principal operations of war, to which older forms of military operations may become secondary and subordinate.'[1]

The creation of an autonomous air arm for the UK was far sighted, and the RAF was the first such air force in the world. It was to take another thirty years for the USA to follow suit, with not just heated debate in the mean time, but broken careers as well, at least in the case of Billy Mitchell. The unfortunate side effect of Smuts's recommendations was that the role of organic air power for the Army and the Royal Navy was not given its due consideration, and this was to cause many difficulties at the outset of the Second World War, with the Royal Navy having the right ships, at least on order, but lacking both high-performance carrier-borne aircraft and senior officers with a practical view of naval aviation. Nevertheless, between the wars the RAF applied itself to the creation of strategic air power in a way which was denied the Luftwaffe, and this was to be a vital element in the long, hard campaign for victory.

The new RAF had many problems from the start. Some were relatively trivial, including debate over the titles of the respective ranks. In effect, up to Air Commodore (the equivalent of a Brigadier or Brigadier-General), Royal Naval Air Service titles were used, although 'Squadron Commander' became 'Squadron Leader'. At first, the title 'Marshal of the Air' was proposed as the equivalent of Admiral of the Fleet or Field Marshal, but King George V, who had to bear this rank as well as the corresponding Army and Navy titles, rejected it, saying that it was far too grand, so the top rank became Marshal of the Royal Air Force. Uniforms were also a problem. The first attempt, purchased by many officers hoping to impress with their enthusiasm and so secure permanent commissions, in a pale blue with gold rings, was completely impractical, and was soon replaced with the uniform which survives to this day.

Far more serious were the disputes between the Army and the Royal Navy, both of which wanted to regain control of aviation – often, one suspects in order to abolish it altogether. After the war, the RAF contracted to just 12 squadrons, partly for financial reasons, but also because the new service's leader, Lord Trenchard, wanted to eliminate the old RNAS–RFC rivalries. There was another problem which kept the RAF weak in its early years: complacency. British defence was based for a period on the so-called Ten Year Rule, which postulated that the nation would have ten years in which to prepare for another major war.

Nevertheless, there were those who realized the dangers which lay ahead, including the strategist, Basil Liddell Hart, who wrote of the bomber and the need to be prepared in the early 1920s:

The seriousness of that threat can be gauged by comparison with the fact that during the whole of the last war only 74 tons of bombs were dropped on England by hostile aeroplanes. That quantity, dispersed in time and space, killed 857 people, wounded 2,058 and caused material damage which in monetary cost amounted to approximately £1,400,000. On such a basis of comparison, nearly a quarter of a million casualties, and over £100,000,000 worth of damage might be anticipated in the first week of a new war.'[2]

Liddell Hart's influence has sometimes been exaggerated. He was not the proponent of strategic air power, but instead he believed in the Blitzkrieg principle of air and land forces (the latter suitably mechanized and equipped with tanks) fighting together.

Meanwhile, the RAF soon found itself a new role, helping to keep the peace in territories ceded to the UK by the League of Nations.

AIR CONTROL IN MESOPOTAMIA, 1922–3

The RAF had shown that it could provide an effective role in what today would be described as 'peace-keeping' as early as 1919, during the Third Afghan War. Sqn Ldr Arthur Harris (later Marshal of the RAF Sir Arthur Harris), already a holder of the Air Force Cross at this time, commanded a DH9a bomber squadron, operating against dissident Afghan tribesmen, and he saw how a 20 lb bomb in the grounds of the palace of the Amir of Afghanistan deterred him from launching a war against India, then a British colony. Nevertheless, relationships with the Army were not happy. He recalled later:

> a bitter reminder of what happens when air forces, or any other forces with new weapons, are put under the command of another and older service and subordinated to the use of previously existing weapons. We lacked everything in the way of necessary accommodation and spares and materials for keeping our aircraft serviceable – the only thing there was never any shortage of were demands for our services when the trouble blew up on the frontier.' [3]

In fact, Harris seriously considered resigning his much-prized permanent commission, but he was posted to Iraq in 1922 to take command of 45 Sqn.

The Aircraft
At that time 45 Sqn was equipped with the Vickers Vernon, a development of the famous wartime Vimy, in which Alcock and Brown had made the

After the end of the First World War, the much-reduced RAF found that one role thrust upon it was air control, using bomber-transports such as the Vickers Vernon. This Vernon MkIII, seen on the ground in Iraq while serving with either 45 or 70 Sqns, was in service as an air ambulance. (IWM HU70792)

first direct transatlantic flight in 1919. This was a large biplane with twin Rolls-Royce 360 hp Eagle engines mounted on the wing struts. A biplane tailplane was another feature. The aircraft could manage slightly over 100 mph, and as a bomber, could carry up to 2,500 lb of bombs. The Vernons were later replaced by the more powerful Victoria.

Harris quickly realized that one Vernon had the bomb-carrying capability of a whole squadron of DH9as. He had the aircraft fitted with bomb racks, and had holes cut in the noses for sighting, converting them into 'bomber transports' for what might now be called counter-insurgency operations, but was then known simply as 'air control'.

The Action

The squadron had been employed in carrying supplies to the troops on the Kurdistan border, and bringing back casualties to Baghdad. 'We literally took beer up to the troops', said Flt Lt the Hon. R.A. Cochrane, one of Harris's flight commanders, 'and brought back casualties. But this wasn't at all in accord with Bert Harris's idea of what he wanted to do.'[4]

Air policing (or air control) seemed to work, and surprisingly, seemed to arouse little rancour among the rebels. RAF pilots who fell into rebel hands were treated with respect, and eventually returned alive, whereas ground troops were humiliated and punished, in one case being stripped naked and beaten, then left to walk back to their base, many dying along the way.

Harris took command of 45 Sqn at the time when Kemal Ataturk was forcing his way through Turkey, and having seized control of Eastern Thrace (European Turkey) and Istanbul (then still known as Constantinople), was trying to extend his share of Kurdistan by taking Mosul (now Al Mawsil) in Mesopotamia (now Iraq). Bomb racks were improvised and fitted, using designs worked on by Harris and his two flight commanders, and with the skilled assistance of the squadron's fitters. Harris had seen the primitive methods used on the DH9a, which had a fuselage-mounted bombsight, the hand-held bomb being dropped over the side. He had a hole cut in the noses of the Vernons so that the bomb-aimer could lie down and use a simple but reasonably effective bombsight, while the bomb release system combined a trigger and a length of rubber shock absorber cord attached to the bomb release cables on the under-wing racks. Cochrane recalls:

We realized that in the heat of Mespot the Vernon, when fully loaded, could only just get off the ground and wouldn't climb to much more than a hundred feet unless you got into an up-current. So the problem was to find the up-currents. Well, the engineering officer – a chap called Rope who was later killed in the R31 – an excellent fellow – and I developed an up-current indicator on the lines of ones we had used in airships – we had both been on airships. With a two-gallon petrol tin, some tubing and a disused turn-indicator on the instrument panel, we had what we needed. We used the petrol can with a pinhole bored in the cap as the pressure chamber and with this connected up to the instrument on the cockpit panel, up-currents were indicated by the needle. When you got into an up-current the needle went hard over. So when you took off and got to a hundred feet or thereabouts, there you stayed until the needle went hard over and indicated you were in an

Presumably there was a more offensive role for this Vernon MkII, again of either 45 or 70 Sqns, flying over the City of the Dead, near Baghdad, in 1925 or 1926. Contrast this with the aircraft used in the Gulf War more than sixty years later. (IWM HU70794)

up-current – then you proceeded to circle, to stay in the up-current, and to climb at the same time until you were at a thousand feet or more and out of the super-heated thin air.[5]

Harris's reaction was to suggest to his superiors that the Vernons should do the bombing and that the DH9a squadrons should deliver the beer! This was agreed, on condition that a bombing competition be held first. The Vernons of 45 Sqn won convincingly.

Turkey dropped its claim to Mosul, and this was ratified on 6 August 1923 under a treaty, but the unruly tribes in Mesopotamia meant a continued British presence was necessary, and it was felt that this could be exercised most economically and effectively, given the sometimes considerable distances involved, by the RAF. Harris decided that to do this effectively, the squadron would have to become experts at night operations, when the rebels might feel that they were free from attack, since even daylight operations had given the tribesmen a severe shock:

You could just imagine what they would think if they heard us over them in the darkness . . . 'By Allah they can ruddy see us in the dark too' . . . We made our own marker bombs by the simple process of screwing two pieces of bent tin on to the back of a 20 lb practice bomb, into which we clamped a white Very light. Between the clamp and the Very light we inserted a striker so that when the bomb hit the ground the

Very light was detonated and shot up into the air, illuminating the surroundings for a few moments and leaving a trail of smoke from the point where it had hit. Of course, the nights were very clear out there and visibility was excellent – and we flew at only one or two thousand feet – never more than three thousand – couldn't get higher. So . . . target finding was not too difficult . . . our crude marker bombs were very effective under those conditions.

Within a year . . . we were . . . doing active bombing by day and by night. Most of the bombing was done with baby incendiaries. We didn't want to hurt people if we could avoid it – except for the Turks who were invaders . . . after the Turkish war it was a matter of keeping the tribes in order by air control . . . we found that by burning down their reed-hutted village, after we'd warned them to get out, we put them to the maximum amount of inconvenience without physical hurt, and they soon stopped their raiding and looting of the quieter and better behaved areas.[6]

Comment

Using air power to maintain control of an area has never really worked successfully on its own – the presence of troops on the ground is important. The realization of the significance of air power was prophetic, but its degree was exaggerated, as subsequent experience has shown.

Nevertheless, air power does maximize the effect of ground forces, providing reconnaissance, suppressing enemy forces, and also, in the case of an aircraft such as the Vernon, providing greater mobility for ground forces so that fewer troops are needed. In its infancy, the RAF needed campaigns such as this to show its worth, both to commanders in the field and to politicians at home. Apart from anything else, these operations helped to maintain the combat-readiness of the new service during the peacetime years.

THE SPANISH CIVIL WAR, 18 JULY 1936–1 APRIL 1939

Apart from the RAF's operations in Afghanistan and Mesopotamia (in essence, what is now Iraq), the other three main applications of the bomber between the wars were by the Italians in Abyssinia (now Ethiopia), by the Japanese during the invasion of Manchuria, and during the Spanish Civil War. Of these campaigns, the last two were in many ways the most significant – instead of operating against tribesmen, the aircraft of both sides operated against cities and airfields as well as against ground forces. No less important, for the first time since the end of the First World War, bombers were often confronted by fighters. The Japanese operations in China were often one-sided, but in Spain both sides had the benefit of support from other European nations, with Italy and Germany sending forces to fight alongside the Nationalists, while the Republicans had support from volunteers from a number of other European nations, and the support of the Soviet Union.

The origins of the Spanish Civil War pre-dated the conflict by many years. The country had remained neutral during the First World War, but there were serious internal divisions between what might simply be described as the supporters of the status quo (the Nationalists) and anti-monarchist and anti-clerical factions, compounded by separatist movements and militant trade unionism, which found expression on the Republican side.

At the outset, both sides used a mixture of aircraft which had been in service with the nation's armed forces, but as the war progressed, the Nationalists had German and Italian aircraft, while the Republicans had aircraft from France and the Soviet Union.

Luftwaffe fighter pilots benefited from their experience with the Legion Condor during the Spanish Civil War. They had developed a defensive formation which started with the *Rotte*, a pair of aircraft operating together but widely spaced, at about 200 yd, with the pilots concentrating their search towards each other, so each covered the other's blind spots below and behind. Two *Rotten* created a *Schwarm* ('swarm') of four fighters, with the extremities 600 yd apart. In order to be able to maintain formation when turning, the cross-over turn was developed, which meant that the aircraft effectively reversed their positions during the turn. The next stage was the *Staffel* (echelon), consisting of three *Schwärme*, or 12 aircraft.

The Spanish Republican Government sought help from France, and although initially this was forthcoming, in due course opinions changed, and getting aircraft across the border proved difficult. Heavy deposits in French currency and then in gold were also part of the deal.

There were other problems as well, including a shortage of pilots, even though initially the balance of aircrew from the Spanish Air Force was in favour of the Government, in the ratio of 3:2. Pilots were offered a renewable monthly contract of 50,000 pesetas and life assurance of 500,000 pesetas. The problem in translating this into meaningful values is considerable, since the value of the gold peseta, used for international trade, varied wildly due to the difficult situation created by a civil war. Broadly speaking, the gold peseta was equivalent in the exchange rates of the time to 32 pesetas to the pound sterling in 1936 and 38 in 1939, or in US dollar terms (at the time the exchange rate was four US dollars to the pound sterling), the gold peseta varied from 5.18 to the dollar in 1933 to 8 in 1937 and 9.55 in 1939. The paper peseta used in everyday transactions within Spain was worth little more than half that of the gold peseta. Perhaps a better means of comparison would be with other wage rates in Spain at the time, when a Second Lieutenant in the Army earned 333 pesetas a month, while the average daily wage for a workman was just 5 pesetas. Government private soldiers received 10 pesetas per day, those of the Nationalists 3 pesetas, plus a 1.10 peseta daily supplement when engaged in combat. These figures are less slanted in favour of the Government soldier than his Nationalist counterpart than it might seem, because by 1937 the Nationalist peseta was worth twice as much as the Government peseta.

The Aircraft

At first, deliveries of fighters in particular favoured the Government, which received large numbers of Polikarpov I-15 and I-16 fighters (known respectively as the Chato and Rata) from Russia, and soon had six squadrons of each. The I-16 was the first low-wing retractable-undercarriage fighter to enter service. By contrast, the Nationalists initially had to make do with the Heinkel He51 fighter biplane, which was outclassed by the Russian aircraft and by the Hawker Fury biplane.

The Spanish Civil War provided an opportunity for the Luftwaffe to test its new aircraft and tactics – and marked the operational debut of the much-feared Junkers Ju87 Stuka dive-bomber. (IWM HU24780)

The arrival of the Condor Legion of volunteers from Germany only partly changed this imbalance, since its equipment included He51s as well as the new Messerschmitt Me109B. In mid-1937, the Legion had two squadrons of He51s and one of Me109Bs in Combat Group J-88, while Bomber Group K-88 had two squadrons of Junkers Ju52s, effectively 'bomber-transports', and one of the new Heinkel He111B. A reconnaissance squadron, A-88, had a number of Heinkel He70s and Dornier Do17Fs, while a small squadron, VB-88, used Henschel Hs123 dive-bombers. There were also a number of seaplanes, some Junkers Ju52 transports, and seven anti-aircraft batteries. Contrary to popular belief, few Ju87 Stukas served in Spain, with just five making a brief appearance and being repatriated by the Germans at the end of the conflict.

The Government had 13 fighter squadrons, 6 of these having Russian pilots flying Ratas and another 7 with Chatos, of which 3 were flown by Spanish pilots. Against them, the Nationalists had 11 squadrons, with 10 operating Fiat CR32s, and another operating Me109Bs. Both sides had obsolete types, such as the Government's Dewoitines, Letovs, Bristol Bulldogs and Nieuport Delage ND52s, and the Nationalists' He51s. The Nationalists later obtained a number of Heinkel He112Bs, which had been developed as a rival to the Me109 but were rejected by the Luftwaffe, leaving Heinkel to seek export customers.

For the most part, the bomber units operated obsolete aircraft. The Government had Potez 54s and Marcel Bloch MB210s, and its modern aircraft were what was regarded as a substantial force of 31 Tupolev SB-2s (sometimes designated ANT-40) Katiuskas, a light twin-engined bomber. The Nationalists had Junkers Ju52s and Savoia-Marchetti SM81s, both effectively obsolescent 'bomber-transports', while for modern aircraft they had a squadron with 12 He111Bs and another of SM79 trimotor bombers. Both sides had Fokker FVIIs and de Havilland Dragon Rapides pressed into service as bombers.

The statistics tell little of the real story, for it was the Nationalists who consistently used air power and who always managed to have air power over the front at any one time, much to the lamentations of many senior Government army officers. As the war progressed, many Government aircraft fell into Nationalist hands, and the better types were given fresh markings and designations.

The Action

The bomber played a significant role during the war, most notably – and notoriously – in the bombing of the Basque stronghold of Guernica. The Nationalists long maintained that Guernica was not destroyed by bombers, but by 'incendiarists', effectively maintaining a scorched-earth policy of destruction before retreating. Nevertheless, it does seem that the town was damaged by bombers, since there is no mention anywhere of a heavy artillery bombardment. No one has ever admitted to flying on the raid, and to this day there is no official record to show whether the bombing was by Spanish or Condor Legion aircraft, or a mixture of both. In fact, one oddity of the conflict is that the published accounts centre on the fighter pilots, with nothing from bomber aircrew, despite the fact that the role of the Ju52/3m bomber transport in particular was significant, including the movement of Spanish Foreign Legion troops from Spanish North Africa to Spain early in the war.

We have two accounts of aerial combat during the conflict. The first of these concerns the major Nationalist push in the north of Spain during summer and autumn 1937. During this campaign, Government forces mounted a major attack on the town of Belchite, to the south-east of the city of Zaragoza and close to the provincial border between Zaragoza and Teruel. On this occasion, the Government forces enjoyed overwhelming superiority, placing the Nationalists on the defensive, yet achieved little. As the Nationalists advanced, the situation of the Government forces became increasing desperate. Francisco Tarazona flew a Polikarpov I-16 Rata (known to the Government as 'Moscas') fighter during the campaign, commanding the remnants of a squadron, and recalled his experiences in his book, *Sangre en el Cielo* ('Blood in the Sky'). He remembers flying to the front in the remnants of two much-depleted squadrons with just eight I-16 Moscas between them instead of their offical establishment of eighteen aircraft each.

Their mission was described as doing 'a little bit of everything',[7] by which he meant that they must first escort the I-15 Chatos to the front line for a series of strafing machine-gun attacks, after which the Moscas themselves were to attack in support of a stranded army unit. While they were covering the Chatos, they were caught by a strong force of Condor Legion aircraft, which Tarazona managed to spot while they were about 6,000 ft above his unit, although at first he was not sure whether they were facing Messerschmitts or Heinkels. Realizing that they were about to be attacked, the Republicans formed a defensive position, flying in a large circle so that each aircraft was protecting the tail of the one in front, making it difficult for the Condor Legion aircraft to attack without falling into the Republican line of fire.

The Germans were too quick for them, however, as two Messerschmitts dived over to one side of the formation before it was completely formed, causing it to break up as three of the Republican aircraft chased after them, while three Heinkels chased after the third aircraft and shot it down:

The battle begins in earnest. The Messerschmitts attack Eloy and myself. Another is already behind Frutos. Looking ahead I can see two white trails which serve as a guide. Suddenly I feel my aircraft shudder violently, on turning my head I am nearly face to face with a yellow painted Messerschmitt about 200 feet from my tail. I flick into a sharp turn and push the stick right forward, diving as steeply as possible to avoid him. I manage to escape.

I look for my companions, to see a Mosca being chased by two Heinkels which are already breathing down his neck. I make for the nearest one and open fire. On seeing my first shots he abandons his attack . . .

I have very little fuel left, largely because of the full engine fire used in combat. I decide to make for home and look for someone to accompany me. I make contact finally with six other machines, a mixture of Chatos and Moscas . . . others are not to be seen anywhere.

[The nearest airfield had been bombed, so the surviving aircraft headed for their main base, but again, they found that this had also been bombed so badly that landing was impossible.] The fuel gauge tells me that we have barely enough fuel to fly for fifteen minutes . . . I have no option but to . . . go to Colunga. I turn my Mosca and the others follow. Huerta overtakes and points to where Sardina is trying to land on the road . . . Only Huerta and myself land at Colunga, together with a Chato . . .[8]

The second account is from the Nationalist side, and is by one of the great aces of the war, Joaquin Garcia Morato, who managed the rare achievement of flying no fewer than 30 aircraft types during the war, although out of his wartime total of 1,012 hours (he had already flown 1,860 hours by the outbreak of the conflict), he flew 784 hours in the Fiat CR32. He is credited with having made 511 wartime operational sorties, which involved 56 fighter combats, during which he is supposed to have shot down no fewer than 40 of his opponents. At the time of his account, mid-1938, he was in command of the second Fiat CR32 fighter group, 3-G-3, later becoming leader of the fighter squadron, holding this position until his death in battle on 4 April 1939, shortly before the end of the war.

On 25 June Morato flew his Fiat on a reconnaissance flight, alone, although it was usual for the CR32s to be flown in pairs. During his flight, he discovered a large force of some fifty enemy machines, which failed to see him. Unconcerned by the heavy odds against him, he took them by surprise, shooting two aircraft down in flames before they realized what was happening:

I was flying my faithful 3-51, completely alone, making a reconnaissance sortie over the front. Nothing in particular had happened when, suddenly, I saw the enemy air force appear; sweeping towards our lines was a mass of more than fifty aircraft, a mixture of fighters and bombers.

I quickly made up my mind. It was an unequal battle which I had every chance of losing, but I couldn't just sit back and let them attack our troops without trying to do something to stop it. Tactically speaking I should have avoided combat, since I was at a lower altitude than my adversaries, but this was impossible.

In fact, the speed with which I reacted allowed me to profit by the tactical disadvantage of lower altitude for, choosing a favourable moment, I attacked the bombers from below, so that they screened my aircraft from the higher flying fighters. Before they or the bomber pilots were aware of an enemy in their midst two aircraft were falling in flames. The remaining machines, thinking they were being attacked by a large number of aircraft, scattered all over the sky . . . The invisible enemy, of which they had seen neither the arrival or departure, had already gone.[9]

Comment

The Spanish Civil War was a modern, fluid war, with front lines changing and air power being deployed mainly tactically, but on occasion, strategically as well. Tactics developed during this conflict were to stand the Axis powers in good stead at the outset of the Second World War. On the other hand, many of the operations were conducted with relatively small numbers of aircraft, and more effective opposition could have resulted in many offensive operations failing.

BLITZKRIEG

In 1921 the Italian General Giulio Douhet published his book, *The Command of the Air*, which argued that air power would be the most significant use of arms in future wars, even to the extent that air forces would be able to bomb enemy forces into submission, with little assistance from surface forces: 'A people who are bombed today as they were bombed yesterday, and who know that they will be bombed again tomorrow and see no end to their martyrdom, are bound in the end to call for peace.'[1]

As the RAF grew stronger during the 1930s, it was organized into commands, including a Fighter Command and a Bomber Command, but such divisions were not unanimously accepted by senior officers. One doubter was Sir Edgar Ludlow-Hewitt, Air Officer Commanding Bomber Command in 1937, who argued against the official British doctrine that the 'bomber would get through': 'Experience in China and in Spain seems clearly to indicate that with the aircraft in use in these two theatres of war at present, Fighter Escorts are considered absolutely essential for the protection of Bomber aircraft. So far as I am aware this policy runs counter to the view long heard by the Air Staff.'[2]

PREPARING FOR WAR

During the late 1930s British planners made a number of predictions about the prospect of an all-out war, including just who would be allied to whom, and the way in which the war would develop, at least in its initial stages. The Air Ministry predicted massive use of air power, and although the fall of France was not actually predicted, it was seen as a possibility. By early 1937 the RAF was able to proceed with a rapid build-up, even the Army and the Royal Navy accepting that funds would have to be devoted to a strategic bomber force.

The one thing which the RAF, including Harris, could not predict was the appalling stupidity of the Luftwaffe's senior officers, and especially Kesselring, who had transferred to the Luftwaffe from the Army in 1933, when the air force was still a secret organization. It was Kesselring who decided that the role of the Luftwaffe was to support the rapid advance of ground forces, and who ruled out the development of true strategic bombers. *Generalfeldmarschall* Erhard Milch was State Secretary in the Germany Air Ministry and Armaments Chief of the German Air Force:

The RAF persisted with faith in the single-engined light bomber, notably the Fairey Battle. Supposedly able to outrun a fighter, once hostilities started, this aircraft proved to be a liability. (IWM HU59352)

They have already in the years 1936/37 considered the development of four-engined bombers. The Englander planned right from the beginning to use these bombers by night and not by day, because the speed and height of these planes were not suitable for daylight attacks in the face of our day-fighters' defence . . .

There are three main types. The best is the Lancaster, the worst the Stirling, and then there is the Halifax. These are the three types which are frequently mentioned in the German reports of planes shot down over German territory . . . Germany has certainly not observed this method of war well enough and has not been able to disturb the build-up of the forces of the Englander . . .

The attempt in our country to construct four-engined planes was started in 1934 and continued in 1935 and 1936, but on the basis of a tactical decision of the authorities in charge, this was given up in 1937 in favour of twin-engined planes . . . It is regrettable that this development [of four-engined bombers] which we started, and which seemed to be fruitful, was not continued and was abandoned in order to have available as great a number of planes as soon as possible. The two-engined planes were preferred because they could be constructed quicker and more easily.[3]

In December 1938 the Lord Chancellor attempted to justify the policy of appeasement with Hitler, telling an audience that: 'the Germans had it in

their power to let loose 3,000 tons of bombs in a single day'. Others took a less sensationalist view, with Liddell Hart, the great inter-war commentator on military matters, declaring that the Germans could only drop some 600 tons of bombs on the UK in a single day.

INVASION OF POLAND, 1–27 SEPTEMBER 1939

Germany invaded Poland on 1 September 1939, provoking an ultimatum from the British and French governments which was to result in a declaration of war on 3 September. Many German military planners were planning for war with the UK and its Empire to start in 1945, suggesting that Hitler was counting on an Anglo-French acceptance of the situation, as had happened the previous year, when Germany had invaded Czechoslovakia. One other difference on this occasion is that the Soviet Union invaded and occupied the eastern provinces of Poland on 17 September.

While the Poles fought valiantly, their armed forces were outnumbered and outclassed. At the time Poland was among the poorest nations in Europe, and the equipment of its armed forces reflected this situation. The Polish Air Force had achieved autonomy from army control the previous year, and had ambitious re-equipment plans, but for the most part the Poles had too few aircraft, and too many of these were obsolete. Even so, the Luftwaffe did not have everything its own way, and 2nd Lt Wladyslaw

Gnys of 122 Fighter Sqn, Polish Air Force, was the first man to shoot down a Luftwaffe aircraft.

The Aircraft

A number of aircraft types were used in the bombing operations which accompanied the Polish campaign, including the Junkers Ju87 Stuka dive-bomber, the Dornier Do17 and Heinkel He111 medium bombers. We will consider the Ju87 and He111 later on p. 32, and look at the Do17 in detail here.

Originally developed as an airliner for the German airline, Deutsches Luft Hansa (predecessor of the present-day Lufthansa), the Dornier Do17 had an extremely thin fuselage, which gave rise to the nickname 'the flying pencil'. It was completely unsuitable for commercial passenger airline operations, although it found limited use as a mail plane, and no doubt the DLH order was set to mislead the intelligence sources of Germany's many uneasy neighbours. As a medium bomber, the aircraft performed well, joining the Luftwaffe in 1937, when all attempts to disguise German military aspirations had been discarded. A twin-engined medium bomber, the Do17 had two 1,000 hp Bramo radial engines. In accordance with Luftwaffe custom at the time, the so-called 'rear gunner' was positioned a short distance behind the cockpit in a position more akin to that of the British and American 'mid-upper gunner' location. Some commentators believe that the German practice of having the crew all working relatively close together was supposed to be good for morale, and it was certainly more comfortable than the cold and isolated position of the tail gunner on a British or US heavy bomber.

The Action

German troops moved swiftly across the border with Poland early in the morning of Friday 1 September, the first bombing raids following at daylight, designed to cripple Polish airfields and destroy the Polish Air Force, giving Germany early aerial superiority so that the Luftwaffe could then provide support for the German ground forces. A few days after the invasion started, a Nazi newspaper, the *Völkischer Beobachter*, carried this report from a German airman in a Do17 bomber squadron who was involved in the campaign against the Polish Air Force on that first day:

> . . . the telephone rings shrilly. We all read the announcement from the adjutant's face: 'Be ready to take off tomorrow morning at 4.20 am.' Rapidly the needed instructions are passed to the squadrons: 'Wake up time 2.00 am. Breakfast 2.30 am, flight briefing at 3.15, crews man their planes at 4.00. Machines warmed up at 4.10. Now everyone go to sleep at once!'
>
> A cool morning greets us as we go to our flight briefing . . . The group is going to make a ground attack on Krakow Airfield. Attack time 5.45 am.
>
> We are on course. At first it is hard to keep our bearings in the thick morning haze. We know that at this same moment our comrades on the ground are tearing down the boundary posts and beginning the attack

. . . Slowly it gets light, visibility is good now. We are flying over enemy land . . . Another squadron is flying to our left: we see that it is being fired on. Then a cloud of black smoke on the horizon shows us our target. We are alongside, we see fire, smoke, more fire and explosion after explosion. We nose our aircraft to 150 feet so that the bombs will bite on impact . . . a short distance ahead at the edge of the airfield, we see a neatly-arranged string of Polish fighter planes. The bomb trail is launched . . . Red explosions are bursting all over the ground, the threads of enemy anti-aircraft shells pull around us. Our machine-gun barrels are hot; probably the turrets have never rotated so fast. Then, pressed close to the ground, we race off on the course for home.[4]

Comment

The German aim of eliminating all aerial opposition was obviously the right one, both strategically and tactically, while the Polish Air Force was caught unprepared, so many of its aircraft were destroyed on the ground. A lack of combat experience on the Polish side was also apparent, with fighter aircraft parked in lines, so that a bomber or even a strafing fighter would have to make just one run over the airfield. Obviously, the newspaper account was tinged with propaganda, but there is no reason to doubt that, despite some losses, the Luftwaffe was continuing to have things very much its own way.

RAID ON THE FIRTH OF FORTH, 16 OCTOBER 1939

At the outset of war Bomber Command seems almost to have been at a loss over what to do. Many of the pre-war plans had been made in anticipation of aerial combat, or threatened heavy German civilian casualties, for which there was no stomach – and in truth, little reason – at such an early stage in the war, when its future course was unclear and the massive Blitz of 1940–1 was yet to come. The early operations consisted mainly of leaflet-dropping, eventually known as the 'Nickel' operations, and the laying of mines in the Schillig Roads, an important part of the war effort known as the 'Gardening' sorties.

At first, even Hitler insisted that only military and naval targets be attacked, and that no action should proceed if there was a danger of death or injury to British civilians. The use of precision dive-bombers was favoured over high-altitude bombing.

The Aircraft

The aircraft usually associated with dive-bombing is the Junkers Ju87 Stuka, but the Germans also had a more modern aircraft that could be used either as a light bomber or as a dive-bomber, as well as serving as a night-fighter: the Junkers Ju88. A mid-wing, twin-engined aircraft, the Ju88 used two 1,200 hp Junkers Jumo engines to provide a maximum speed of as much as 300 mph when empty. On the early versions, a bombload of 3,960 lb could be carried in the large bomb bay and on four large racks on the inner wing. On later versions with more powerful engines, such as the 1,700 hp BMW 801G radial, the bombload was increased to more than 6,600 lb.

The Action

The need to avoid civilian casualties was also very much in mind when, on 16 October 1939, nine Junkers Ju88 bombers of I. *Gruppe* of *Kampfgeschwader 30* were sent to attack the giant battlecruiser HMS *Hood*, believed to be at anchor in the Firth of Forth on the east coast of Scotland. The information was not quite right, for they found the ship in Rosyth Dockyard, on the north shore of the Firth, where there was a risk of civilian casualties, placing it effectively 'out of bounds' for the Luftwaffe.

Another German medium bomber was the Junkers Ju88, shown here about to take off from a base in Italy for a raid on the island of Malta. (IWM HU55065)

Hauptmann Helmut Pohl, leading the attack, ordered his crews to turn their attention to other warships anchored in the Firth of Forth, which included the two cruisers *Edinburgh* and *Southampton*. Pohl attacked *Southampton*, sending a 1,100 lb armour-piercing bomb into the ship through its port side, through three decks and out through the starboard side, before it exploded below the waterline and caused further structural damage. *Edinburgh* also came under attack, suffering minor damage from bomb splinters, as did a destroyer. At this stage, Spitfires from 602 and 603 Sqns caught the bombers, forcing them to break off their attack, and then chasing them out to sea, shooting down two aircraft, including that of Pohl.

Lt Horst von Riesen, the pilot of one of the bombers, recalls being under attack by the Spitfires:

> Now I thought I was finished. Guns were firing at me from all sides, and the Spitfires behind seemed to be taking turns at attacking. But I think my speed gave them all a bit of surprise – I was doing more than 400 kilometres per hour [250 mph], which must have been somewhat faster than any other bomber they had trained against at low level – and of course I jinked from side to side to make their aim as difficult as possible. At one stage in the pursuit I remember looking down and seeing what looked like rain drops hitting the water. It was all very strange. Then I realized what it was: those splashes marked the impact of bullets being aimed at me from above.[5]

Fortunately for von Reisen, the Spitfires soon had to break off their attack because of their limited range, but not before one of them had managed to damage the Ju88's starboard engine cooling system, leaving the aircraft with just one engine labouring to keep it airborne. This gave von Reisen a problem, since during training he had been told that a Ju88 would not maintain height on one engine, and his damaged aircraft was now struggling. He rejected the idea of ditching as it was getting dark, and it was unlikely that they would be picked up, leaving them to drown or die of exposure. A crew member suggested turning back to Scotland, and crash-landing there, but one of the others shouted over the intercom, 'No, no, never!',[6] adding forcefully that Spitfires would be waiting for them.

The crew struggled to keep their aircraft airborne, even hand-pumping fuel from the starboard wing tank to the port wing tank, to keep the good engine running, while the navigator wrapped his belt around the left rudder pedal and pulled hard, in an attempt to take the pressure off von Reisen. As fuel burnt off and the aircraft became lighter, it was possible to regain some altitude, but even so, it was still only at 2,000 ft when, after three hours' flying, it managed to struggle home to its base on Westerland.

Comment

Both sides were attacking the other's fleets at this time, and this was typical of many attacks mounted by both the RAF and the Luftwaffe, although at this stage of the war the Germans were the more successful. It could also be said that they had more targets to choose from, since the Royal Navy had far more surface ships, and especially cruisers and destroyers which were highly vulnerable to bombing, in contrast to battleships, on which there was always the chance of a bomb bouncing off the heavily armoured decks or gun turrets, and of a bomber suffering severe damage, or worse, from the very heavy AA fire which such a large warship could muster.

The massed air attacks which were so much a part of the concept of Blitzkrieg were strangely lacking here, suggesting that the Luftwaffe's commanders failed to appreciate the impact that crippling the Royal Navy could have had on the outcome of the war. Certainly, by the standards of the day, the RAF would have been reasonably happy if it had enjoyed as much success against the German fleet, although nothing was sunk or damaged beyond repair.

In the years which followed, many bomber aircrew on both sides would make similar valiant efforts to get their aircraft home, with a surprising number succeeding against the odds.

GERMANY STRIKES WEST, 10 MAY–6 JUNE 1940

After the invasion of Poland, nothing seemed to happen, at least in the recollection of most of the populations of the supposedly warring nations. In fact, a great deal had been happening on certain fronts, especially at sea, and the RAF and the Luftwaffe had both expended energy and lives on attacking each others' fleets. To the British, this period from September 1939 to May 1940 was known popularly as the 'phoney war', while to the Germans it was known as the 'sitting war', which was probably more accurate, with the opposing Anglo-French and German Armies sitting on either side of the Franco–German border.

At the outbreak of war on 3 September 1939 RAF Bomber Command had 33 squadrons. Ten of these, equipped with the Fairey Battle light bomber, had been sent to France on 2 September as the Advanced Air Striking Force, intended to provide air support for both the British Expeditionary Force (BEF) and their French comrades.

All this suddenly came to an end on 10 May 1940 when, at 05.35, the German forces began their advance westwards, ignoring the neutrality of Luxembourg, Belgium and the Netherlands. The Luftwaffe had 3,834 aircraft, including 1,482 bombers and dive-bombers, 42 ground attack aircraft, 248 Zerstörer ('fighter-bombers'), and 1,016 fighters. Against this force, the French could raise 1,604 aircraft, of which 260 were bombers, 764 fighters, 180 reconnaissance aircraft and another 400 or so aircraft in Army support duties. The UK had a substantial proportion of its combat aircraft in France with the so-called Advance Air Striking Force (AASF) which had accompanied the BEF, some elements arriving before the declaration of war. The British had 456 aircraft, of which 261 were fighters, 135 bombers, and 60 reconnaissance aircraft. Belgium had just 180 aircraft, of which 81 were fighters, while the Netherlands had 132 aircraft, of which 35 were fighters and 23 fighter-destroyers. Luxemburg then, as now, had no air force of its own.

The AASF was largely equipped with aircraft which were little match for the Germans, who scored in both quality and quantity, and through having combat-hardened aircrew. The French Armée de l'Air was no better. Nationalization of the French aircraft industry had induced chaos, with many

Fairey Battles provided the bomber backbone of the Advanced Air Striking Force (AASF) in France – here a flight is seen on patrol over France near the front line in 1940. (IWM C454)

promising designs, but too few modern aircraft coming off the production lines. The lack of quality as well as the limited number of aircraft available was to prove an unbearable and disastrous combination. In addition, the French in particular were concerned that neither of the two Allied air forces should press heavy bombing raids against German industry for fear of German reprisals against French targets. The British soon started to husband scarce resources and trained aircrew for the defence of the British Isles.

The Aircraft

The British AASF included a number of obsolescent types, the most modern aircraft being a few Hawker Hurricane fighters – a type which was later to prove an effective anti-tank aircraft and fighter-bomber during the North African campaign, but which at this stage was operated purely on fighter duties. Many of the fighters were Gloster Gladiators, the RAF's last biplane, completely outclassed by the Messerschmitt Me109s of the Luftwaffe.

The British bombers included the Fairey Battle light day-bomber, the Handley Page Hampden medium bomber and a few of the new Vickers Wellingtons, the RAF's heaviest bomber at the time.

The Fairey Battle provided the mainstay of the AASF's bomber force. It was the result of an Air Ministry requirement in 1933 for a light bomber, but did not enter service until 1937, the same year as the Do17. The aircraft embodied Sir Richard Fairey's belief that a light single-engined bomber could match the performance of fighter aircraft, making it invulnerable. Whether or not this was true in 1933, by 1937 fighters had improved in performance, and the Battle was pitifully inadequate, unable to carry a decent warload, lacking effective means for self-defence other than a couple of machine-guns in its wings, and certainly unable to outrun a fighter.

Although powered by the famous Rolls-Royce Merlin engine, this was only of 990 hp, giving a maximum speed of 240 mph without a bombload. Despite these shortcomings, the aircraft remained in production until 1941. After the British evacuation from Dunkirk, the Fairey Battle was relegated to target towing and training duties.

The Action

The response from the defending air forces was inadequate from the start. On 11 May the Belgians sent nine bombers to attack the bridges over the Albert Canal, seized by the Germans in a surprise attack. They did no damage, and seven of the aircraft were lost. Later that same day, at 18.00, the Armée de l'Air sent 12 LeO-45 night-bombers, a modern aircraft, against three bridges west of Maastricht in the Netherlands, and against German tanks moving towards Tongres, but they inflicted no damage, and one of the aircraft was lost, along with four of the fighter escort.

The following day, 12 May, six AASF Fairey Battles, with an escort of two Hurricane fighters, were sent against the Vroenhoven and Veldwezelt bridges, across which the German forces were streaming, and four of the aircraft were shot down as they approached the targets, which were left undamaged. One of the Battles was burning 'like a torch' as it dropped its bombs, but its pilot, Flying Officer McIntosh, managed to land it safely behind enemy lines, and the crew spent the rest of the war as prisoners. McIntosh was told by one German officer: 'You British must be mad. We took the bridges early Friday morning. You gave us the whole of Friday and Saturday to build up our flak entrenchments, and then on Sunday, when everything was ready, you came here with three planes and tried to blow the thing up.'[7]

One of the two remaining Battles crashed on its return flight.

Comment

Taking three days to attack a significant target in a fast-moving and fluid war showed that the RAF had much to learn about the support of ground forces at this stage, whereas the Luftwaffe had learnt much about this from the experience of the Condor Legion during the Spanish Civil War. Action against targets of strategic value has to be prompt as well as accurate. In addition, the Battle was inadequate for the task, lacking the performance, defensive measures or warload to be effective, while sending such a small force of just six aircraft against a heavily defended target meant simply that the German AA gunners were able to concentrate their fire.

THE BATTLE OF BRITAIN, 10 JUNE–31 OCTOBER 1940

Having consolidated their position in France and the Low Countries, as well as in Denmark and Norway, German ambitions turned next to the possibility of an invasion of Britain. Some historians now doubt whether the Germans seriously intended to invade Britain at all, arguing that the positioning of invasion barges and large numbers of troops were intended to distract the RAF from operations against Germany itself, and that the Germans probably did not have the capacity to mount a full-scale invasion against the south coast of England across the Channel in the way that the Allies managed on D-Day four years later. These arguments must be taken seriously, but whether

For many, the rapid German advances across Poland, through France and the Low Countries, and then into Russia, were typified by the heavy air attack by Ju87 Stuka dive-bombers, seen (above left) in formation . . .
. . . and (above) banking, ready to begin their diving attack. (IWM HU54422)

they are right is a matter for research and debate – Hitler's style of leadership was such that much effort was wasted in anticipating what those around him thought might be his wishes. Others have suggested that the build-up of forces in France was to deter any British attempt to land back in Europe, which seems unlikely, and to reduce pressure on the Soviet Union until Hitler was ready to launch an invasion, OPERATION BARBAROSSA. Both of these theories appear unlikely, since Germany was later to excuse its massive concentration of troops in Poland before the invasion of Russia by declaring that they were being kept away from RAF air attacks.

If the invasion barges assembled in French ports late in 1940 were intended to distract RAF Bomber Command from other targets, the ploy worked. In fact, an invasion of Britain *was* in Hitler's mind. The Luftwaffe set out to destroy the RAF after the fall of France, seeking to eliminate it as a fighting force, and started with the classic manoeuvre of attempting to destroy the RAF on the ground. The RAF considers the Battle of Britain as having started on 10 July 1940 and continued until 31 October, but the Luftwaffe considered the main attack as having started on 5 August. On 1 August Hitler ordered the Luftwaffe to destroy the RAF as a prelude to an invasion of Britain. That same day, copies of the translation of a speech delivered by Hitler to the Reichstag (German Parliament), entitled 'Last Appeal to Reason', were dropped from aircraft flying over Hampshire, Dorset and Somerset.

After Britain's defeat in the Battle of France came the Battle of Britain, intended to destroy the RAF and its bases. This was the sergeants' mess at RAF Sealand after a raid on 14 August 1940. (RAFM P021824)

Opposite: Both sides used leaflets for propaganda purposes, hoping to convince the civilian populations of the futility of continuing the conflict. Here is an English translation of a speech by Adolf Hitler, dropped by air in August 1940.

The Aircraft

For the operation on 18 August the aircraft used included the Dornier Do17 (see p. 24), the Junkers Ju87 and the Heinkel He111.

The Junkers Ju87 Stuka dive-bomber was one of the most feared aircraft of the early years of the Second World War, even though it was supposedly obsolescent. The cranked wing aircraft could carry a 1,000 lb bomb under the fuselage, or more usually, a 500 lb bomb and four 110 lb bombs on strongpoints under the wing. The under-fuselage bombs were thrown clear of the aircraft and the propeller by a launching mechanism. For defence, the radio operator in the cockpit behind the pilot had a single machine-gun, while there were two machine-guns in the wings, largely for strafing, since the aircraft's performance was such that it had little hope of tackling a fighter in a dogfight. Although early versions used in the Spanish Civil War had a 610 hp Junkers Jumo 210 engine, later versions used a single 1,100 hp Junkers Jumo, and before the war ended, the streamlined Ju87D with a 1,400 hp engine could carry a bombload of 3,960 lb. The effect on those on the ground of being dive-bombed by a Stuka was heightened by the addition of a siren which provided a 'trumpets of Jericho' effect.

The Heinkel He111 was another medium bomber, and again this had been developed under the guise of an airliner for Deutsches Luft Hansa. A twin-engined low-wing monoplane, the aircraft was attractive in appearance, but poorly armed, so it was vulnerable to fighter attack. Despite its cigar-shaped fuselage, an improvement on the Do17's, the low wing meant that really heavy bombs could not be carried, and usually the load consisted of up to eight 550 lb bombs. He111s usually had a crew of three, including a bomb-aimer/observer and a mid-upper gunner, whose position was exposed to the elements in early versions. Various power ratings were available from the twin engines, depending on the variant, but typically a He111H, in production for most of the war, used two 1,350 hp Junkers Jumo 211F engines, providing a maximum speed of 220 mph when fully loaded.

Dropped at North [illegible]
Somerset.
Sunday August 11. 19[?]

A LAST APPEAL TO REASON

BY

ADOLF HITLER

Speech before the Reichstag, 19ᵗʰ July, 1940

I have summoned you to this meeting in the midst of our tremendous struggle for the freedom and the future of the German nation. I have done so, firstly, because I considered it imperative to give our own people an insight into the events, unique in history, that lie behind us; secondly, because I wished to express my gratitude to our magnificent soldiers; and thirdly, with the intention of appealing, once more and for the last time, to common sense in general.

If we compare the causes which prompted this historic struggle with the magnitude and the far-reaching effects of military events, we are forced to the conclusion that its general course and the sacrifices it has entailed are out of all proportion to the alleged reasons for its outbreak — unless they were nothing but a pretext for underlying intentions.

The programme of the National-Socialist Movement, in so far as it affected the future development of the Reich's relations with the rest of the world, was simply an attempt to bring about a definite revision of the Treaty of Versailles, though as far as at all possible, this was to be accomplished by peaceful means.

This revision was absolutely essential. The conditions imposed at Versailles were intolerable, not only because of their humiliating discrimination and because the disarmament which they ensured deprived the German nation of all its rights, but far more so because of the consequent destruction of the material existence of one of the great civilized nations in the world, and the proposed annihilation of its future. [...]

All attempts made by democratic Germany to obtain equality for the German people by a revision of the Treaty proved unavailing.

World War Enemies Unscrupulous Victors

It is always in the interests of a conqueror to represent stipulations that are to his advantage as sacrosanct, while the inheritor of self-preservation in the vanquished leads him to reacquire the common human rights that he has lost. [...]

[...]

Britain and France Considered Understanding a Crime

On October 6, 1939, I addressed the German nation for the second time during this war at this very place. I was able to inform them of our glorious military victory over the Polish State. At the same time I appealed to the insight of the responsible men in the enemy States and to the nations themselves. I warned them not to continue this war, the consequences of which could only be devastating. I particularly warned the French of embarking on a war which would horribly eat its way across the frontier and which, irrespective of its outcome, would have appalling consequences. [...]

One of the most attractive German bombers of the war years, the Heinkel He111 was limited by range and bombload – here an He111 nose is seen in silhouette while waiting for its next mission. (IWM HU54424)

The Action

On 18 August 1940 the Luftwaffe opened the day's activities with a series of reconnaissance flights, to report on weather conditions over target zones and to look for any convoys. It was also important to assess which fighter airfields would be fully operational. The RAF's fighters maintained patrols over coastal convoys, but it was not until midday that the Chain Home radar stations reported that enemy aircraft formations were developing over northern France. Within half an hour, more than 80 aircraft were noted near St Omer and Abbéville. Soon, fighters were being scrambled so that they could reach the necessary height for a sound defence: the fighters took 4 minutes to become airborne, and it then took another 17 minutes for a Spitfire and 20 minutes for a Hurricane to reach 20,000 ft.

As the raids developed that day, the Luftwaffe's tactics soon became clear. A first wave of bombers was soon engaged by the RAF, and while this was going on, a second wave of *Luftflotte 2* raced across the Channel at low level to raid the important fighter base at Kenley. Among these were nine Dornier Do17s of 9 *Stafel*, of *KG76*, whose crews were specially trained for low-level attacks. The *Staffelkapitän*, *Hauptmann* Roth, was in the leading aircraft. As they crossed the coast, fighters from 111 Sqn at Croydon were scrambled. The Do17s, flying in three Vics of three aircraft each, swept over the airfield at Kenley, as yet untouched by the fighters, but then the airfield's AA defences opened up. *Oberleutnant* Ahrends' aircraft, leading the port Vic, was immediately struck by heavy AA fire, and slowly rolled to starboard, out of control. On the starboard Vic, *Oberleutnant* Magin, its leader, was also hit by light machine-gun fire and fatally wounded, although his observer, *Oberfeldwebel* Illg, managed to lean over him and grab the controls. The aircraft pressed onward, climbing to 45 ft, the minimum release altitude for the 20 110 lb bombs carried by each of them.

As the attack was pressed home, the defenders used another technique available to them – rockets which lifted cables into the air – one of them

finishing off Ahrends' aircraft, while another hit Roth's aircraft. After attacks by defending Hurricanes which had now caught up with the Do17s, Roth eventually crashed near Biggin Hill. Feldwebel Wilhelm Raab, who was flying in Roth's leading Vic on his leader's starboard, saw the rockets rising in front him without at first realizing what was happening, and immediately banked steeply to starboard, feeling his port wing strike something, then break free. It was only then that he realized that he had struck a 'rocket-driven cable'. Raab struggled to get his aircraft back to France, where his story was not believed by his superiors until it was confirmed by a detailed technical examination of the aircraft's port wing.

By this time the Hurricanes were extracting their full revenge from the Do17s, including that of *Unteroffizier* Günther Unger, who had been flying on the port side of Ahrends. His aircraft had lost its starboard engine to ground-based Lewis gun fire as he was about to release his bombs, but he pressed home his attack, and then started to take evasive action, flying low past trees and buildings in an attempt to reach safety while the avenging Hurricanes gave chase. Inevitably, the fighters looked for stragglers such as Unger:

At first they tried attacking from the sides, where my armament was weakest. But by sticking very low, and dodging behind trees and buildings, I was able to make things very difficult for them. Then one of the fighters came in from behind and I felt the impact of his bullets against my wings and fuselage. I struggled to keep the Dornier as low as I could and make the most of the available cover, while my engineer and wireless operator returned the fire. Suddenly he came roaring past us; streaming black smoke the fighter pulled up and the pilot baled out.[8]

Unger managed to shake off his pursuers, but his other engine failed over the Channel, forcing him to ditch. Escaping from the aircraft with his crew, they were in the sea for some hours before being rescued by a German minesweeper, suffering from exposure. Another aircraft of their unit also ditched, and its crew were rescued. Four more were so badly damaged that although they managed to cross the French coast, they had to crash land, so that just one aircraft returned safely to its base at Cormeilles-en-Vexin.

Nevertheless, the Germans had destroyed all but one of the four hangars at Kenley, as well as 6 Hurricanes, a Blenheim and 4 training aircraft; another 3 Spitfires and a training aircraft were damaged, while 30 vehicles were destroyed and a number of buildings were also damaged, including the station commander's offices, the sickbay and the officers' and sergeants' messes. Severe damage to the landlines of the sector operations building meant that fighter direction was impossible, and a standby operations room nearby had to be activated.

Meanwhile, further intruders were moving in, aiming to attack the RAF's airfields, as more than a hundred aircraft entered formation over Cherbourg and Le Havre; they were the dreaded Junkers Ju87 Stuka dive-bombers, escorted by Messerschmitt Me109s. They came from the three *Gruppen* of *Sturzkampfgeschwader 77* as well as the first *Gruppe* of *Sturzkampfgeschwader 3*. Their targets covered a substantial section of the coast of Hampshire and Sussex, ranging from Gosport in the west – with its two Fleet Air Arm bases, aircraft maintenance yards, and the submarine base and training centre at HMS *Dolphin* – and the airfields at Thorney Island and Ford in Sussex. In all, 109 Ju87s were escorted by 157 Me109s of *JG2*, *JG27* and *JG53*. The raid on Gosport went well for the Luftwaffe, but a heavier defence was mounted over the Sussex airfields, where *Oberleutnant* Otto Schmidt of *StG77*'s *1 Gruppe* managed to drop his bombs on Thorney Island, and then after pulling out of his dive, looked for the rest of his unit. He could see the scattered wreckage of an aircraft in the calm waters of the English Channel, and distracted for a moment suddenly realized that a Spitfire was racing up behind him trying to get into a firing position. Turning would not have saved him: 'So I side-slipped, a tricky manoeuvre for a Junkers. She came out of the slip and the attacking fighter was foiled. I looked around at my radio operator. He was hanging forward in his straps and his machine-gun was pointing aimlessly into the sky. I didn't realize that either he or the aircraft had been hit.'[9]

In the mean time, the Spitfire had turned again and was coming in for another attack, determined to finish the job. Schmidt realized that the Spitfire pilot must have seen his helpless gunner, so he side-slipped again, and the Spitfire went screaming past. While this was happening, one of his comrades, flying low, suddenly plunged into the sea and disappeared, and he saw another Ju87 shot down, bouncing on the surface of the sea before disappearing.

After this, he managed to shake off his pursuers and make his way back to his base at Caen, near Le Havre. His Ju87 had more than 80 holes from the Spitfire's machine-guns, and his radio operator/gunner was seriously wounded, dying from his wounds in hospital some weeks later. *StG77* had paid a heavy price, with 14 aircraft shot down, 4 damaged beyond repair and another 4 with repairable damage, and of these, 10 of the losses and

One of the He111's features was the good visibility forwards, at the expense of a good rearward view – here an He111 in flight is seen through the nose of another of these aircraft. (IWM HU 58516)

2 of those damaged beyond repair had come from the first *Gruppe*. Defending the Ju87s, eight Me109s had been lost for the loss of four Spitfires and two Hurricanes. In return, two hangars had been destroyed at Thorney Island, with one aircraft destroyed and another damaged on the ground. At Ford, a hangar and a number of workshops were destroyed, and the fuel storage was set alight. At nearby Poling, the radar station was knocked out of action for a week, and a mobile unit put in its place.

The German losses could not be sustained at this rate, and the immediate conclusion drawn by the Luftwaffe was that the Ju87 was outclassed over Britain, and could not be used over British targets again.

The Luftwaffe's losses were mounting, and the fighters were ordered to escort the bombers more closely, using the twin-engined Me110 with its longer range whenever possible, with Me109s escorting these aircraft because of the latter's superior manoeuvrability, although like the opposing Spitfires and Hurricanes, the Me109's Achilles heel was its limited range.

Otto von Ballasko was a Heinkel He111 bomber pilot with *III/KG1* engaged in attacking British airfields during the Battle of Britain. He was sceptical about the motives of the Luftwaffe's fighter escorts. At first, the fighters had accompanied the bombers all the way from the French coast to the target, but this proved to be impractical even when the targets were close to the coast, as the escorts began to run short of fuel just when they most needed it – on the return flight, when the British fighters often engaged in greatest force. A different tactic was then tried, sending the fighters on *Freijagd* ('freelance hunting') patrols, to clear the route to the target for the bombers. The RAF soon became wise to this, and would send in a few fighters from one side: 'When our fighters saw them they thought "Ah, victories" and dived after them; no fighter pilot gets a *Ritterkreuz* for preventing bombers being shot down. That was usually the last we saw of our fighters; and since their radios did not work on the same frequencies as ours, we had no way of calling them back.'[10]

With the fighters preoccupied by the RAF, shortly afterwards a second RAF fighter formation would appear to tackle the now unescorted bombers.

The Luftwaffe commanded the fighter units to provide close escort for the bombers, with a high cover of fighters in addition, to break up British counter-attacks, but it proved impossible to provide this intensity of cover as the battle developed. RAF Fighter Command had its own problems, not least that many squadrons were using the Boulton Paul Defiant, a fighter with a rear-gunner, which proved too slow and cumbersome for fighter-to-fighter combat, and was hard pushed in combat with the newest of the Luftwaffe's bombers. To cut the losses of experienced pilots, the order was given that the Defiants had to be assigned to attacking bombers.

One He111 pilot was Leutnant Roderich Cescotti of 2 *Staffel* of *KG26*:

When we came under attack by British fighters we always closed our formation right up, to concentrate our defensive fire. As a young pilot my position was right at the end of the formation; usually all I ever saw of the air battle was the tail of the aircraft in front and the bomber to the side of me. But on Sunday 15th a Spitfire came diving down on our formation from in front; it was one of the rare occasions when I saw an enemy. He was already on fire and a Messerschmitt was hard on his heels and firing at him. Nevertheless the Spitfire pilot pulled up and loosed off an accurate burst at my Heinkel, scoring several hits on one of my engines. He pressed home his attack to close range, then banked over and spun away. The pilot must have known that his aircraft was doomed, yet he pressed on without regard for his own life. I never saw whether he was able to bale out; I hope he did – he was a very gallant gentleman.[11]

Comment

The tactics of the Luftwaffe during the Battle of Britain are hard to fault, and might have prevailed had the campaign lasted longer, although there were two other prerequisites to success which were lacking. The first of these was a truly heavy bomber with good defences of its own. The second was the lack of a highly manoeuvrable long-range fighter escort, perhaps a German equivalent to the North American P-51 Mustang.

To some extent, technology inhibited the operation of the ideal fighter aircraft at this stage in the war, but the lack of a heavy bomber with sufficient range was to be the Luftwaffe's undoing as an offensive force. At no stage of the war could they have attacked every British airfield in strength. The RAF also made the best of its resources, saving the faster Spitfires for fighter-to-fighter combat whenever possible, and leaving slower aircraft to tackle the bombers.

'BLITZ': THE NIGHT-BOMBER CAMPAIGN, AUGUST 1940–MAY 1941

Even while the Battle of Britain was at its height, the Luftwaffe was starting to attack British cities, and this campaign, usually known as the 'Blitz', short for *Blitzkrieg*, or 'lightning war', continued through the winter and into May 1941, by which time German attentions were turning to the invasion of the Soviet Union. In mounting a major strategic bombing campaign, the Luftwaffe was faced, as was the RAF, with the need to ensure both accurate navigation and then bombing accuracy over the target – not easy at night or in dense cloud. Night operations were preferred for high-level bombing, since the risk of fighter interception during the early months of the war was minimal.

The first technique used by the Luftwaffe was called *Knickebein* – radio beams transmitted by ground-based stations in occupied Europe, from northern France to the south of Norway, capable of covering the whole of the British Isles. By the end of August 1940 there were 12 of these stations, but by this time too, 80 Wing of the RAF had started jamming the *Knickebein* beams. Otto von Ballasko recalls:

> At first we were very excited about *Knickebein* . . . But after we had used it on operations once or twice, we realized that the British were interfering with it . . . the fact that our enemy obviously knew that the beams existed and that they were pointing towards the target for the night was very disconcerting. For all we knew, the night-fighters might be concentrating all the way along the beam to the target; more and more crews began to use the *Knickebein* beams only for range and kept out of them on the run up to the target.[12]

Eventually, the RAF's countermeasures became more sophisticated and effective, with 'Meacons' bending the beams. The Luftwaffe then introduced more sophisticated radio beams, *X-Gerät* and *Y-Gerät*. *X-Gerät* used four beams, the first being pointed at the target for navigation, while the other three crossed the main beam at pre-set points in advance of the bomb release point, assisting accurate bomb-aiming. The first beam was 50 km (31 miles) from the bomb release point; the second was at 20 km (12.5 miles) from the bomb release point, at which the observer started a special clock which effectively acted as a stop watch, although with two hands; the third beam

Two Dornier Do17Zs of 2/KG77 being serviced at Freux auxiliary airfield in Belgium, 1940. (IWM HU22376)

was at 5 km (3 miles) from the bomb release point. At the third beam, the observer pressed the button on the clock which stopped the first hand, and when the second hand caught up with it, electrical contacts were closed and the bombs were released automatically. The clock was essential to accurate bombing, complementing the beams by providing accurate information about the aircraft's ground speed, which could otherwise put accuracy at the mercy of the prevailing winds.

Y-Gerät used a single ground station which produced a complicated beam of 180 directional signals per minute, which had to be interpreted by a special device aboard the aircraft, whose functions included re-radiating the signal back to the ground station, ensuring that the operators on the ground knew the aircraft's position exactly. This meant that they could then signal the aircraft at the bomb release point. The sophistication of the equipment, with both *Gerät* systems using higher frequencies and more accurate radio signals than the original *Knickebein*, meant that specially trained crews had to be used, effectively the German equivalent of the RAF's Pathfinders, and working within a special unit, *Kampfgruppe 100*, flying Heinkel He111s.

Kampfgruppe 100 was moved forward from Germany to a base at Vannes, in Brittany, on 11 August 1940. The unit's first operation was two days later, on the night of 13/14 August, against Castle Bromwich in the English Midlands, where a 'shadow' factory was preparing to start production of Spitfires. There were another eight operations before the end of the month.

A defensive measure used by both sides during the war was to operate aircraft with their engines desynchronized (that is, one running faster than the other), so that the resultant throbbing note made the use of sound locators to detect the position of aircraft about to fly overhead extremely difficult.

The Aircraft

The aircraft used on the night attacks on British cities were mainly Dornier Do17, and Heinkel He111s (see pp. 24 and 32).

The Action

The impact of the bombing on those on the ground was considerable. The first heavy daylight attack on London was on 7 September 1940. That night saw the first heavy German night raid on London, with 318 German bombers sent against the city, with no risk of interception by night-fighters. In contrast to raids later in the war, no effort was made to concentrate the attack, which lasted from 20.10 on 7 September until 04.30 the following morning. Finding the target was not a problem, since the fires from the daylight attack were still burning. Of nine fires defined by the London Fire Brigade as a 'conflagration' (a fire that is spreading and requires more than 100 pumps), the one in the Surrey Docks, at the Quebec Yard, was the fiercest recorded in Britain. Elsewhere, there were other hazards:

At Woolwich Arsenal men fought the flames amongst boxes of live ammunition and crates of nitro-glycerine under a hail of bombs directed at London's No. 1 military target. But in the docks themselves strange things were going on. There were pepper fires, loading the surrounding air

heavily with stinging particles, so that when the firemen took a deep breath it felt like burning fire itself. There were rum fires, with torrents of blazing liquid pouring from the warehouse doors and barrels exploding like bombs themselves. There was a paint fire, another cascade of white hot flame, coating the pumps with varnish that could not be cleaned for weeks. A rubber fire gave forth black clouds of smoke so asphyxiating that it could only be fought from a distance, and was always threatening to choke the attackers. Sugar, it seems, burns well in liquid form as it floats on the water in dockyard basins. Tea makes a blaze that is 'sweet, sickly and very intense'. One man found it odd to be pouring cold water on hot tea leaves. A grain warehouse when burning produced great clouds of black flies that settled in banks upon the walls, whence the firemen washed them off with their jets. There were rats in their hundreds. And the residue of burned wheat was 'a sticky mess that pulls your boots off'.[13]

There were also 19 major fires (defined as those requiring 30 or more pumps), 40 serious fires and 1,000 smaller fires. Set against this, it seems almost miraculous that the death toll was no higher than 430 killed and 1,600 injured.

AA defences consisted of largely wild and uncontrolled shooting, as the control systems broke down. Londoners would afterwards claim that they could tell German bombers from British because of the distinctive engine note, but all that happened was that the German pilots put their engines on different power settings while over the target area, to confuse sound direction-seeking equipment.

The Luftwaffe sent another 207 aircraft over the following night, aiming for the fires which had defeated the fire brigade's efforts, so that by the morning of 9 September, there were no fewer than 12 major conflagrations. Another 412 people had been killed and 747 seriously

Sufficient air raid shelters could not be provided in time for all of London's large population, so improvisation was essential, using the deep level underground 'tube' railway stations. (IWM HU44272)

injured. The four main railway termini serving the south of England were so badly damaged that railway services could not be operated for a short period. Interestingly, many of these lines had been electrified by the Southern Railway between the wars, and electric trains proved as reliable among wartime damage as the hardier steam locomotives.

This was the result of two nights' bombing by medium bombers. The Luftwaffe was back for 64 of the following 65 nights, the exception being due to bad weather.

The Luftwaffe had a massive, indeed overwhelming, strength, but this did not mean that the bomber crews had an easy time with ample rest between sorties. *Unteroffizier* Horst Goetz flew with *KG100* during the Blitz on London, and in one three-week period he flew against London on 23 September, twice on 24 September (once in the morning and again in the evening), and then again on the evenings of 27, 28, 29, 30 September, and 2 and 4 October, before flying against Manchester on 7 and 9 October, and then against Coventry on 12 October. Coventry, in the Midlands, and Manchester, in the north-west, were more distant targets than London, hence the less intensive nature of these operations.

An experienced pilot, Goetz had flown 1,800 hours before he even started operations against Britain. He recalls: 'I have no particular memories of individual operations. They were all quite routine, like running a bus service. The London flak defences put on a great show – at night the exploding shells gave the place the appearance of bubbling pea soup; but very few of our aircraft were hit – I myself never collected so much as a shell fragment.'[14]

Goetz maintains that it was a rare occasion for one of his crew to catch sight of a British night-fighter, and they never attacked. On the return flights the radio operator would often tune his receiver to a music programme to provide some relief from the monotony.

One of the heaviest attacks during the London Blitz was that of the night of 15/16 October, starting at 20.40 and continuing at 04.40 the following morning. A force of 400 bombers was sent against the city, approaching it at between 16,000 and 20,000 ft. The aircraft came from bases in the Netherlands, Belgium and northern France, crossing the coast at many points between West Sussex and Essex. One pilot, *Feldwebel* Günther Unger, flew two sorties, one in the evening and another early the following morning, with a two-hour break on the ground between them. In an interesting contrast to bomber operations later in the war, he had to remain over the London Docks, circling for as long as possible to cause the maximum confusion for the defences, and dropping a bomb every five minutes or so, so that on each sortie he spent some 25 minutes over the target area. The AA fire ranged from between 13,000 and 20,000 ft. Some 41 night-fighters, including some Blenheims equipped with radar, were sent to intercept the bombers, but in desperation, the obsolete Boulton Paul Defiants were put into the air as night-fighters, although they lacked radar, and on the night of 15/16 October, one of these from 264 Sqn managed to shoot down a German bomber – believed to have been the only RAF success that night.

London's Blitz lasted from 7 September until the morning of 14 November, a total of 67 nights, with just one night without attack from the air. The major raid on Coventry took place on the night of 14 November. No fewer than 449 bombers approached the target, which was marked by 13 He111s of *Kampfgruppe 100* using incendiary bombs. The bomber streams converged on the target, with one approaching over the Wash on Britain's East Coast, another over Brighton and a third over the Isle of Wight, both on the South Coast. *Feldwebel* Günther Unger flew on the Coventry raid: 'While we were still over the Channel on the way in we caught sight of a small pinprick of white light in front of us, looking rather like a hand torch seen from two hundred yards. My crew and I speculated as to what it might be – some form of beacon to guide British night-fighters, perhaps? As we drew closer to our target the light gradually became larger until it suddenly dawned on us: we were looking at the burning city of Coventry.'[15]

The city of Coventry, in the English Midlands, was, as it still is, a major centre for manufacturing industry, including the motor industry, which had stopped producing cars and was producing military vehicles and aircraft under the 'shadow' factory programme which had converted civilian manufacturing to the British war effort. The Luftwaffe had decided to attack British industrial centres in addition to London, which had relatively little heavy industry although it was important from the point of view of communications, especially its massive dock system.

The night of 14/15 November 1940 saw 499 Luftwaffe bombers raid Coventry, devastating the city centre and causing civilian casualties. A much smaller city than London, Coventry was so seriously hit that production in its factories (it had been a centre of motor vehicle production before the war, and now, in addition to producing military vehicles, also contained many 'shadow' aircraft factories) ground to a halt. Much of the city was flattened. A total of 506 people were killed, and another 432 seriously injured. Out of 119 night-fighter sorties, just seven sighted bombers, and none was shot down, but two bombers were shot down by AA fire.

The Blitz continued throughout the winter and into the spring. On the night of 12/13 March the major port of Liverpool was the target. By this time

Targets marked on a German aerial reconnaissance photograph taken before the raid on Coventry, with the prefix 73 assigned to factories and 52 to energy targets such as transformers and gas works. (IWM HU66030)

the British night-fighter operations were becoming much more effective, with 178 aircraft put into the air to counter 339 Luftwaffe bombers converging on the target from their bases in France and the Low Countries, and in this case from Norway as well. Once again, 15 He111s from *KG100* operated as pathfinders, dropping their incendiaries visually from around 12,000 ft, assisted by 14 He111s from *III/KG26*, which used *X-Gerät* and dropped their incendiaries from upwards of 16,000 ft. The bombers attacked from between 7,000 and 12,000 ft on a clear moonlit night.

As a defensive measure Fighter Command despatched the Bristol Blenheims of 23 Sqn to patrol over airfields in northern France, and it is believed that one He111 from the 'pathfinder' unit *III/KG26* was shot down, despite the absence of any claims by the RAF. Closer to the target, 93 Sqn had an elderly Harrow bomber on patrol off the south coast of England ready to drop aerial mines in front of the bombers, but the slow aircraft, faced with relatively fast-moving bombers coming from a number of different bases, was unable to get into position, despite remaining on station for three hours. The next line of defence was the night-fighters, including the GCI (ground-controlled interception) Bristol Beaufighters of 604 Sqn, whose seven aircraft that night reported one bomber shot down, another probable and two damaged. At least two more were then shot down by Defiants over southern England, and another was shot down by a Hurricane as it approached Liverpool. The bombers flew too low to be caught by Defiants and Hurricanes on patrol high over the target, although

The centre of Coventry after the air raid on the night of 14 November 1940. (IWM H5599)

barrage balloons ensured that the bombers had to keep above 5,000 ft, but the improved accuracy of British AA fire by this time accounted for a number of aircraft, including a new Junkers Ju88 being flown by *Feldwebel* Günther Unger, who was just releasing his bombload of four 550 lb and ten 110 lb bombs: 'I looked round and saw a small but very bright glow on the cowling immediately behind the starboard engine. The metal was actually burning, which meant that there must have been intense heat, probably from a fire inside the nacelle. At first the visible spot of fire was very small; but it grew rapidly and flames began to trail behind the aircraft. I could see there was no hope of our getting home so I ordered the crew to bale out.'[16]

His flight engineer opened the escape hatch at the rear of the cabin and jumped, followed by the radio operator. After they had gone, Unger turned the bomber until it was pointing out to sea, so that when it crashed there would be nothing for the British to find. He left his seat as the observer dropped out of the hatch. The Junkers was properly trimmed, flying straight and level perfectly well on both engines. Unger recalls that, for a moment he considered trying to get home alone, but a further glance at the blaze made it clear that this would have been impossible. He moved to the rear of the aircraft and followed his crew out of the hatch.

Unger was flying with *II Gruppe* on this occasion, rather than his own *III/KG76*, having volunteered while the rest of his unit was converting to the new type. He had attacked from 10,000 ft, aiming at shipping. On a typical bombing run such as this, his observer, *Feldwebel* 'Ast' Meier, sat next to the pilot, crouching over his *Lotfe* bombsight, with his left hand resting on Unger's right foot on the rudder pedal, finely adjusting the course of the bomber during the crucial seconds before bomb release.

Unger and his crew all landed safely, Unger himself having the most difficult escape, landing in shallow water and then spending an hour wading ashore as he tried to avoid the deeper water channels cutting across the coastal mud banks. He gave himself up to a Home Guard member on reaching Wallasey.

While the toll of some seven bombers – four to fighters and three to gunners – was the heaviest Luftwaffe loss rate at that time of the war, such losses were affordable, and far less in percentage terms than on many of the early RAF raids. Another two aircraft crashed on occupied territory, probably as a result of damage inflicted, although the less experienced pilots found landing very difficult on the many makeshift airfields in occupied France and Belgium. The bombs fell on Birkenhead and Wallasey, Liverpool and Bootle, starting more than 500 fires. The Luftwaffe force had carried 270 tons of high explosives and dropped almost 2,000 incendiaries.

This photograph gives an idea of how complete was the devastation wrought by the heavy bombers. (IWM FX14907)

A second attack on Liverpool took place the following night, although with just 65 aircraft, while another force attacked Hull, and the main force of 236 aircraft attacked Glasgow. It was on this evening that a Harrow of 93 Squadron, flown by Flt Lt Hayley-Bell, managed to strike a German bomber with one of its aerial mines. Having taken half an hour to climb to 17,000 ft, flying off Swanage, he was directed by ground radar to intercept a stream of bombers, being positioned four miles ahead of them and 3,000 ft above. The mines were dropped at 200 ft intervals in front of the bombers, and soon afterwards, Hayley-Bell heard an explosion, and then heard and felt a second one. One of his mines had hit an aircraft, which had then blown up. The irony was that his minefield had missed the bomber formation for which it had been intended by ground control, and struck an aircraft in another formation of four aircraft.

Comment

The Luftwaffe campaign against British cities caused considerable disruption and loss of life in return for relatively light German losses at this stage in the war. As war progressed and improved equipment became available, the RAF's night-fighters became a more formidable threat. Nevertheless, once again the Germans were paying the price of not having a heavy bomber fleet and lacking the bombloads, bomb sizes and range to make effective strikes against British cities, despite having the benefit of advance bases in France and Belgium. The constant raids on London

Coventry had effectively ceased to function. Here, two days after the raid, people walk past the burnt-out wreckage of a double-decker bus. (IWM KY1063C)

showed that even a persistent campaign could not break such a large target without large enough aircraft. It also overlooked the fact that much of Britain's industry had been widely dispersed, with relatively little heavy industry based in the capital itself.

The Germans did not maintain their Blitz on Coventry, or any other British city other than London, in the way that the RAF and USAAF were to persist with their German targets later in the war. Some believe that had the Germans persisted in their raids on Coventry, or had they not relieved the pressure on London by switching to provincial centres, civilian casualties and morale would have been so shaken that peace terms would have had to be sought. Whether or not this would have been the case can only be guessed at.

German casualties during the onset of the bombing campaign were relatively light, and the reason for such lack of persistence, first in the Battle of Britain against British airfields, then in the Blitz on London, and then again in the campaign against Britain's industry, seems due simply to poor strategic planning and direction. On the other hand, would the Luftwaffe, lacking a true heavy bomber force, have been capable of causing the damage which the heavy bombers, sometimes attacking in twice the strength of the Coventry raid, inflicted upon German cities. Did the Germans seek surrender after these heavy and often-repeated raids? They did not. It can be argued that even the RAF and USAAF probably moved on to their next target prematurely, since many, including Goebbels, Hitler's propaganda chief, doubted their country's ability to take much more punishment at times. In defence of the commanders of the bomber forces, they were always under massive military and, most of all, political pressure to attack many more targets than resources permitted, so too often, targets were allowed time for reconstruction.

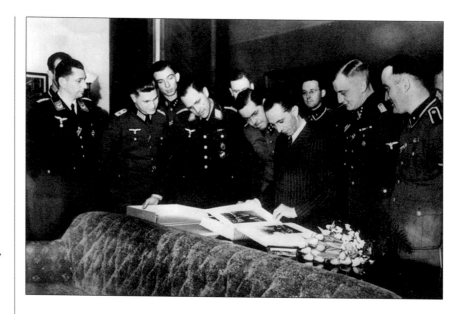

Meanwhile, back in Germany, the Propaganda Minister, Dr Goebbels, received a collection of war photographs from German war correspondents. (IWM HU39423)

BARBAROSSA: THE INVASION OF THE SOVIET UNION, 22 JUNE 1941

Germany invaded the Soviet Union on 22 June 1941, starting at 03.15, attacking along a line drawn from the Baltic in the north to the Carpathian mountains in the south. The attack was not unexpected, and Stalin had ordered that all units were to be decentralized and camouflaged, but this message was received too late for the various headquarters to pass the message on to all units in time.

The USSR had some 18,000 aircraft, although only a fifth of these could be regarded as modern, and many of the pilots were still undergoing training. Half of the aircraft were deployed in the West. Against this figure of around 9,000 Soviet aircraft, the Luftwaffe had 1,945 aircraft, with 1,400 immediately ready for combat, including 510 bombers, 290 dive-bombers, 440 fighters, 40 fighter-destroyers (fighter-bombers) and 120 long-range reconnaissance aircraft. This force was in three air fleets: *Luftflotte 1* under Gen Keller was assigned to Army Group North, *Luftflotte 2* under Field Marshal Kesselring was assigned to Army Group Central, and *Luftflotte 4* under Gen Lohr was assigned to Army Group South. The total Luftwaffe strength was augmented by that of Germany's allies, giving another 1,000 aircraft. Romania sent 423 aircraft, while Finland, still recovering from its war with the Soviet Union, sent 317, although only 41 of these were bombers. The Italian Regia Aeronautica sent 100 aircraft to operate in the southern zone, operating as the *Comando Aviazione* (the air command of the Italian Expeditionary Force), but these didn't arrive until late July. *Luftflotte 4* also had the Hungarian 'Express Corps' with a fighter and a bomber squadron, as well as some reconnaissance units, and the Croatian Air Legion, with a fighter group and a bomber group, another 50 or 60 aircraft.

The Aircraft

The aircraft used included the Junkers Ju87 Stuka dive-bomber, as well as the Heinkel He111 and Dornier Do17 (see pp. 24 and 32).

The Action

The Luftwaffe caught most of the Soviet airfields by surprise, and a second wave was launched as the main attack, with 637 bombers and 231 fighters attacking 31 Soviet airfields. Later in the morning 400 bombers attacked 35 Soviet airfields. Altogether, these 66 airfields accounted for 70 per cent of the Red Air Force's strength in the West. One Red Air Force officer, Lt Gen Kopets, lost 600 aircraft without making any impact on the Germans, and committed suicide on 23 June. Almost half the Red Air Force aircraft were believed to have been non-operational on the first day of the invasion.

The Russian tactics as the German advance got under way showed considerable desperation. When 2nd Lt S.Y. Sdorovzev found that despite scoring hits on a He111 bomber, the aircraft continued to fly, he approached the bomber from the rear, and inserted his propeller into the He111's elevator. He tried again, and this time managed to get the He111 to crash, before flying back to his base, a distance of almost fifty miles, with a damaged propeller.

In the first few months of the air campaign in support of BARBAROSSA, the Luftwaffe came across large marching columns of Russian troops and substantial troop concentrations. The ground on either side of the roads had been baked hard in the summer heat, and was also being used as a roadway, so that the roads were often as much as 100 yd wide. Yet, because of a shortage of bombs of the right types, the Luftwaffe was unable to press home all of the advantages which aerial supremacy had granted it. There is little doubt that the inability to disrupt these troop concentrations was a contributory factor at Moscow and Stalingrad.

As an aside, the battles of envelopment which arose where strong Russian forces were trapped in large pockets by rapidly advancing German Panzer units supported by small contingents of motorized infantry might have been overcome had the Luftwaffe had the aircraft and the paratroops to act quickly, but too many of these had been lost in the Battle of Crete. This meant that the more energetic and confident Russian commanders could often break out. There were at least seven major pockets of Russian ground forces. The Germans captured 2,256,000 Russian soldiers, 9,336 tanks and 16,179 artillery pieces, but again, these figures could have been much higher, especially in the case of the soldiers.

A good idea of the extent to which the Luftwaffe was facing serious operational difficulties during the Russian winter comes in extracts from a report written by Lt Gen H.J. Rieckoff. This refers to the Luftwaffe's experience during the winter of 1941–2, when the temperatures in the theatre stayed between –30° and –50°C for periods of several weeks, relieved only by those occasions when temperatures plunged to –70°! The General commented that, for the most part, the problems were at their most serious when aircraft were on the ground, being prepared for operations:

extensive icing of wings and tail assemblies . . . cannot be removed manually . . . Canvas covers are used to protect smaller aircraft . . . a completely inadequate measure because the covers themselves freeze stiff and are then almost impossible to handle, especially when . . . there is a violent wind. Closed . . . hangars are rarely available. The attempt to prevent ice forming . . . with water-repellent oils has failed due to the shortage of lubricant supplies . . . Snow-skid landing gear has proved ineffective except for the Fieseler Storch . . . which can be kept ready under any snow conditions by this method.[17]

The report also noted that the cold affected engines when they were started up, requiring precise observation of the instructions for a successful cold start, which was carried out by feeding a lubricant diluted with gasoline to the engine while starting. It took some 20 minutes of flying time for the gasoline additive to evaporate and for the engine to run at normal oil temperature. Often, the main problems involved the equipment used to start the engines, as oil froze in its pipes, rather than with the engines themselves. To improve matters, fires were sometimes started under aircraft and start-up equipment. Great care was needed, as the starters' shafts sometimes broke if engaged abruptly. Propellers sometimes iced up during flight, and on occasion damage occurred to aircraft and their crews were injured by flying chunks of dislodged ice.

The report was comprehensive. The aircraft instruments seemed to cope very well with the cold, as did the communications equipment, although this did suffer badly from the effects of moisture. Aircraft guns, on the other hand, didn't like the cold, usually because the oil was unsuitable for the low temperatures, while electrically guided weapons suffered from the effects of condensation. Given a depth of snow of 3 ft or more, short-fused bombs, whether high-explosive or fragmentation, were much less effective, as the snow muffled the effects of the explosion. It was also noted that up to 75 per cent of the detonators on fragmentation bombs failed to work in deep snow, although they remained active and acted as land mines. Frozen ground shattered high-explosive bombs without them exploding.

The Germans used one- or two-piece sheepskin flying suits, which proved to be cumbersome if the wearer had to walk any distance, such as after an emergency landing. Apparently, thermal suits were worse, requiring attention to regulate the temperature, and they were so fragile that they could be damaged in an emergency landing, after which they could provide the wearer with little protection against the cold. The suggestion was made that lightweight fur or camel hair clothing with waterproof linings should be provided, but nothing of leather (a material which the Germans loved to wear normally). Russian felt boots were regarded as more suitable, especially on a long walk, than German fur boots, which did not fit tightly enough, and good anti-skid soles were also required.

Between the start of OPERATION BARBAROSSA and mid-May 1942 the Luftwaffe lost almost 3,000 aircraft, and another 2,000 were badly damaged. Of the losses, 1,026 were bombers and another 762 were fighters. Meanwhile, the Russians had gathered 3,164 aircraft on the Soviet Western Front, of which more than 2,100 were of modern design. A new commanding officer, Gen A.A. Novikov, took command of Red Air Force units on the front. A further indication of the way the tide was turning came from the battles around Kharkov in mid-May, when the Germans had just 1,500 aircraft, and the Soviets twice as many.

On 28 June 1942 the Germans started their second summer offensive on the Eastern Front, supported by the Luftwaffe's 8th Air Corps under Gen Fiebig. Gen von Weichs moved his troops out from Kursk against Soviet troops at Bryansk under Gen Golikov.

By June 1943 the Luftwaffe units on the Eastern Front were confined for the most part, to tactical operations in support of the increasingly beleagured ground forces. The intensity of the Allied bombing campaign had forced the Luftwaffe to deploy its best fighter aircraft to protect German cities, so on the Eastern Front, the mainstay of the German defences was the Me109, while the Russians were receiving new equipment, much of it from the USA and the UK, which sent the Russians 18,000 aircraft during the period from June 1941 onwards.

One of the few Luftwaffe strategic bombing raids on the Eastern Front was by the bomber wings of the 4th *Luftflotte*, under *Generalfeldmarschall* von Richthofen. On 3 June 1943 they raided the Molotov Collective Combine in Gorki, one of the few major armaments plants left west of the Urals after the massive evacuation of Soviet war industry to the east of the Urals. This was a major tank factory, about 2½ miles square, and reputedly producing 800 T-34 tanks per week. At 20.00, 168 bombers, mainly He111s of the 3rd, 4th, 27th, 55th and 100th Bomber Wings, took off from their base at Bryansk, just within reach of the target. Most of the aircraft were carrying 1.7 to 2.4 ton mine bombs, but there were also large quantities of fragmentation, high-explosive and incendiary bombs.

This was intended to be a precision bombing attack using the new *Lofte 7D* homing device, which was newly operational, although they also navigated using the Moscow transmitter, avoiding the city by flying in a wide arc to keep clear of its AA defences. At midnight 149 aircraft reached the target, and began dropping 224 tons of bombs from altitudes between 13,000 and 20,000 ft. Five aircraft were shot down. This was the first in a series of raids, designed to help prepare the way for the summer offensive. The second raid was on the night of 4/5 June, sending 128 aircraft to the target, where they dropped 179 tons of bombs for the loss of just two aircraft. A third raid followed on the night of 5/6 June, with 154 bombers dropping 242 tons of bombs for the loss of one aircraft. Finally, on the night of 7/8 June, 20 bombers dropped 39 tons of bombs.

The result, according to German intelligence, was that production was suspended for six weeks, but others claimed that little disruption occurred. The following night, 9/10 June, 109 bombers were sent on another long-range operation, to bomb the synthetic rubber plant at Yaroslavl. They dropped 109 tons of bombs.

It was to no avail. On 12 July Soviet forces mounted a massive counter-offensive. From this time onwards, the Germans were on the defensive. Hitler had other priorities following the Allied invasion of Sicily two days earlier, and he transferred important elements of the Luftwaffe from the Eastern Front to Italy, doubtless to the immense pleasure and relief of those involved.

As the Germans advanced into the Soviet Union, the Red Air Force was quickly overwhelmed, and those aircraft which did get into the air were outclassed by the Luftwaffe's equipment. In desperation, some Russian pilots tried ramming, although without the suicidal consequences of the Japanese later in the war. This Heinkel He111 survived a ramming attack by a Russian Rata fighter early in November 1941. (IWM HU39684)

Comment

OPERATION BARBAROSSA was delayed because of the German armed forces' heavy commitments in Yugoslavia and Greece, where they had to take over after the Italians failed to occupy these two countries. Some commentators also believe that the operation could not have started much earlier because of the time needed for the ground to harden, having been too soft for tanks and other heavy vehicles after the winter snow had thawed. Nevertheless, the late start meant that the Germans were overtaken by the harsh winter before they had met their objectives. That such a supposedly efficient nation should have allowed their armed forces to advance so far into Russia without adequate precautions for the winter months almost beggars belief.

The failure to allow the Panzer units to advance well ahead of the infantry has been mentioned by some as one reason for the slow progress across Russia, but even if this had been allowed, infantry would have been required to deal with prisoners, and this could only have been overcome by using paratroops. Both the Luftwaffe and the Red Air Force practised a strategy of operating in close support of ground forces, which would have been ideal had greater progress been made.

Most of Russia's heavy industry had been moved east of the Urals before the outbreak of war, and so once again the Germans reaped the bitter harvest of not being able to mount a truly strategic heavy bombing offensive.

The many omissions in the planning and execution of BARBAROSSA are all the more difficult to understand because one of the compelling reasons for mounting the campaign was to secure vital strategic supplies which had been provided by the Russians.

'HIT AND RUN' RAIDS, 1942

As the war progressed, the scale of the German raids against British targets was reduced, partly because of the demands of the Eastern Front, and partly because of the improved defences. Never short of imagination, the summer of 1942 saw an innovation from the Luftwaffe. A new high-altitude bomber was developed from the Junkers Ju86, the Ju86R, creating a new very high-altitude bomber for a series of 'hit and run' raids in daylight.

The Aircraft

The aircraft chosen for these raids was the Junkers Ju86R, capable of operating at heights in excess of 40,000 ft, although at such altitudes the warload was limited to a single 550 lb bomb. Modifications to the original aircraft included stretching the wingspan by 30 ft to 104 ft, putting the two crew members into a fully pressurized cockpit (the first instance of this being incorporated in any bomber), and adding exhaust-driven turbo-superchargers and nitrous oxide injection equipment to the twin diesel engines. In this way, an aircraft which had been at best obsolescent at the outbreak of war gained a new lease of life, relying on altitude for its success rather than speed, which remained a stately 180 mph.

Two of these aircraft were delivered in July to the Luftwaffe's special high-altititude trials unit, *Höhenkampfkommando der Versuchsstelle für Höhenflüge* at Oranienburg, and then, after trials had shown that the high-altitude bombing concept was sound, both aircraft were moved to Beauvais in northern France for a programme of raids against targets in Britain.

The Action

One of the pilots was *Feldwebel* Horst Goetz, who took part in a series of raids over England, all of which were conducted in daylight since little interference was expected from the RAF or ground-based defences. Goetz's first operational flight in a Ju86R was on 24 August, when the aircraft climbed to 39,000 ft over France (this took an hour), and then flew across the Channel, crossing the coast near Selsey Bill, and then flying on to Camberley, near Aldershot, where it dropped its bomb and then returned to base, this time crossing the coast further east, over Brighton. The aircraft had spent more than half an hour over England without any reaction from the defences. The second aircraft attacked Southampton that day, and although 15 fighters were scrambled to intercept, none could approach it.

The following day, Goetz undertook a second daylight mission, cheekily tempting the defences by flying a circuitous course after crossing the coast at Southampton, flying via Swindon, well to the west of London, to Stansted, to the north-east of the capital, where they dropped their bomb, then returning to base via Shoreham, near Brighton. The idea behind this was not simple foolhardiness, but a deliberate plan to set off as many air raid sirens as possible, but while nine Spitfires were despatched to intercept the bomber, and all were unsuccessful, the air raid sirens were not activated because it was considered to be a reconnaissance aircraft, because of its high altitude.

The RAF had difficulty in identifying the 'new' aircraft, possibly because nothing seemed to be able to get within 2,000 ft of it. Reports described it as a Dornier Do217 or a Heinkel He177. Over the next two weeks, a further nine raids were made by the two Ju86Rs.

In conflict, every new measure gives birth to an effective counter-measure. Recognizing the danger, RAF Fighter Command created a 'Special Service Flight' as part of 11 Group at Northolt, to intercept the new threat. Two Spitfire MkIXs were modified, with lightweight wooden propellers, just two 20 mm cannon instead of the mix of cannon and four machine-guns, and with all armour and unnecessary equipment removed. Even so, it took these aircraft half an hour to reach the necessary altitude. A special ground control was established for them, recognizing the need to be able to cover a far wider area than with conventional fighter and bomber interceptions.

The first attempt at interception, on 11 September, failed because a radio breakdown in the Spitfire, which had managed to reach 45,000 ft, meant that the controllers could not direct it towards the Ju86R.

The following day, Goetz took off with his observer, *Leutnant* Erich Sommer, to attack Bristol, the largest city and major seaport in the west of England. The high altitude of the Ju86R flights proved on this occasion to be a weakness, being picked up by a Chain Home radar station at 08.53, when the aircraft was at a range of 120 miles and had been climbing for twenty-eight minutes. At 09.15, the aircraft was noted to be on a northerly course, confirming suspicions that this was to be another high-altitude 'hit and run' raid. A Spitfire MkIX flown by a White Russian émigré, Plt Off Prince Emanuel Galitzine, was scrambled. Meanwhile, the Ju86R crossed the coast near Southampton at 09.50, cruising at 42,000 ft, heading north on a course which would take it over Salisbury, when Goetz recalls:

Suddenly Erich, sitting to my right, said that there was a fighter closing on us from his side. I thought that there was nothing remarkable about that: almost every time we had been over England in the Ju86, fighters had tried to intercept us. Then, he said, the fighter was climbing very fast and was nearly at our altitude; the next thing it was above us. I thought Erich's eyes must have been playing him tricks, so I leaned over to his side of the cabin to see for myself. To my horror I saw the Spitfire, a little above us and still climbing.[18]

The danger of being attacked in a pressurized aircraft was that it could explode if just one cannon shell penetrated the cabin. Goetz dumped his bomb, depressurized the cabin, he and his observer putting on their oxygen masks, boosted engine power with extra nitrous oxide, and started to climb the aircraft. The Spitfire, by this time sitting behind the Ju86R, followed. It closed to a position 600 ft behind the aircraft, and then fired, with at least one cannon shell passing right through the port wing of the Ju86R without causing any damage, before the Spitfire's port cannon jammed and the recoil from the starboard cannon sent the aircraft out of control. Passing through the Ju86R's slipstream, the Spitfire's canopy misted up.

By the time the Spitfire pilot had regained control and his canopy had cleared, the Ju86R was diving and some distance away. Giving chase, the Spitfire caught up with the Ju86R three times, but each time the jammed port cannon meant that the aircraft spun out of control whenever it fired, and the cockpit canopy misted up again, while Goetz demonstrated his considerable skill at evasive manoeuvres, even in such a slow and unwieldy aircraft.

With the evidence of the damaged wing, the Luftwaffe realized that high-altitude bombing held few prospects for the longer term. The possibility of an aircraft being lost for the sake of dropping a mere 550 lb bomb meant that it just wasn't worth the risk.

There was an alternative: low-level attacks in an attempt to keep below the radar coverage of the Chain Home network. By contrast, such raids were mainly concentrated on coastal cities, many requiring the Luftwaffe aircraft to be over Britain for no more than six minutes. Often, fast fighter-bombers were used on these raids.

Comment

The main benefit of these operations was to alert the air raid defences and add to the strain felt by those operating them – there was no military advantage in expending such resources to drop a single small bomb, very inaccurately, on British cities.

C H A P T E R   F O U R

STRIKING AT THE ENEMY

At the outset of the Second World War, there was a marked reluctance to attack enemy civilian targets, as was shown earlier by the Luftwaffe's decision to attack warships lying at anchor in the Firth of Forth, but not to press home an attack on the British battlecruiser, HMS *Hood*, at Rosyth Dockyard on the shores of the Forth. At the declaration of war, the President of the United States, Franklin Roosevelt, asked the combatant nations to desist from bombing civilian targets; the UK agreed immediately, and the French within 24 hours, but Germany took several days.

The decision came under considerable strain once Germany moved westwards. The RAF was all for mounting bomber raids against German targets as the Battle of France got under way, but the French objected, for fear that it would invite retaliatory raids on French towns and cities. The RAF's aircraft and bombing techniques at this early stage of the war meant that such raids would have been of marginal value, and would doubtless have resulted in heavy losses of aircraft and, far more important, men. On the other hand, the great restraint exercised by the British and French during the first winter of the war may have increased the bloodshed by giving the Germans the impression that the British and French had no stomach for another major war.

The time taken to train aircrew, and especially pilots, was to be a major problem for all the combatants during the war. The British and Americans coped, with the RAF and the Fleet Air Arm both benefiting from training programmes in the friendlier skies of Rhodesia and Canada and, after the USA entered the war, the USA itself. The Japanese failed miserably, and the Germans managed with difficulty. Part of the problem for the Germans was their failure to create a permanent transport force, so whenever a major airborne operation was required, the instructors from the bomber training schools were pressed into service, and the losses incurred had a knock-on effect on the German bomber units. The British tried a short cut to relieve the pressure on the limited pool of pilots, eventually operating their heavy

Known as the 'flying pan handle', the Handley Page Hampden was nevertheless one of the more effective British medium bombers at the outset of the war. Here three aircraft of 44 Sqn fly in formation. (RAFM P013519)

bombers with just one pilot. This may have halved the numbers required, but it undoubtedly increased the losses among newly qualified pilots. AVM Donald Bennett, who created the RAF's élite Pathfinder Force, was one of those who believed that experience as a second pilot would have cut the loss rate, giving the RAF fewer bomber pilots, but with a much greater chance of survival. We shall never know. Certainly, staying at the controls of a heavy aircraft for eight, ten or even twelve hours at a time, often on a cold dark night with poor visibility (the longer missions were always flown during the winter when the northern nights were longer) was exhausting no matter how experienced the pilot, and a great burden for one man on his own.

More modern in appearance, the Bristol Blenheim did not have a distinguished career as a bomber – this was a Mk1 of 18 Sqn, based at Upper Heyford, ready to take off from Debden during the summer of 1939. (IWM HU55030)

In the beginning the British concentrated on attacking the German fleet and its anchorages, dropping mines as well as bombs on the 'Gardening' operations, and on leaflet raids known as the 'Nickel' operations.

Even these tasks showed the deficiencies in equipment and, sometimes, training. The RAF lost no time in mounting its first operations against Germany, with a Bristol Blenheim MkIV of 139 Sqn ready to take off as soon as the Prime Minister finished his broadcast to the nation. Its task was to reconnoitre the German fleet at Wilhelmshaven, radioing the position back to its base, where a flight of three Blenheims waited, bombed-up and ready for take-off. The Blenheim took off at 11.48, but flew at 24,000 ft, some 2,000 ft in excess of its official service ceiling, and when it did spot the fleet leaving Wilhelmshaven and passing into Schillig Roads, its radio had frozen and the reconnaissance report had to wait until the aircraft landed back at its base at 16.50. The crews of the waiting Blenheims then had to be briefed, and when they eventually took off, they flew into heavy thunderstorms and, in the failing light, wisely decided to return to base. Later that night, ten Wellingtons, the RAF's latest and heaviest bomber, were sent on a leaflet-dropping raid, but poor navigation left most of their load preaching to the converted in Denmark and the Low Countries.

Bristol Blenheims of 139 Sqn on the ground at RAF Wyton . . . (RAFM P019243)

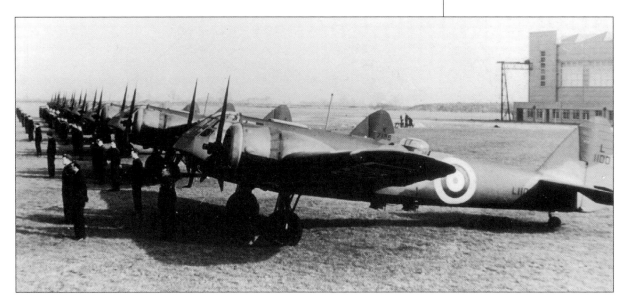

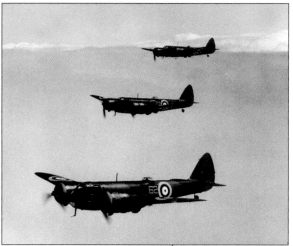

. . . and in the air. These aircraft looked fast and purposeful, but were too slow and too lightly armed. (RAFM P019244)

The next day was scarcely a success. A force of 29 Blenheims and Wellingtons was sent to attack the German fleet, which was led by the battleship *Admiral von Scheer*. Visibility was poor, and many aircraft did not find the target. In order to see the target, those that had found it had to make their bombing run so low that the 11-second fuses on their 500 lb bombs failed to detonate, and bounced off the armour plating of the larger warships. One Blenheim crashed onto the cruiser *Emden*, causing the only real damage of the raid, but even this failed to put the ship out of action. In all, the raid cost the RAF two Wellingtons and five Blenheims – almost a third of the aircraft involved.

Heavy losses were to be common in the early stages of the war. Later in September a force of 11 Handley Page Hampdens attacking two German destroyers was countered by a formation of Messerschmitt Me109Es, with the loss of five of the bombers.

It is easy to be critical of the RAF during these early years. The problem was that aircraft navigation techniques were inadequate. Navigation was by sextant, dead reckoning or eyeball, with the former suited to a ship travelling at 15 kts or so, but unsuitable for an aircraft flying at more than ten times that speed. Dead reckoning worked if wind and other conditions were constant and the pilot and navigator had a feel for these matters, but over longer distances, there were unlimited possibilities for serious error. Eyeball was fine in daylight and good visibility, both of which put the bomber at risk, but useless in the changeable weather and poor visibility of northern Europe. Worse still, meteorological science was relatively primitive, and often the weather conditions predicted over a major target were largely guesswork, although aided later in the war by meteorological reconnaissance.

AIRCREW TRAINING: PILOTS

At first the system couldn't cope. A typical volunteer for training as a pilot waited from September 1939 until the following June or July before being called up, not for training, but for interview and assessment. Later, things moved much more quickly for the aspiring pilot. Training itself was rapid, and the new entrant of June or July could expect to be a sergeant pilot by Christmas. Interview for a possible commission usually followed, but it often depended on whether or not the presiding squadron leader approved of the school attended by the candidate.

At first, the newly qualified pilots would, after attending an Operational Training Unit (OTU), fly as a second pilot, but this practice was soon discontinued as the RAF's bombers moved to single-pilot operation.

Learning at the OTU had its own difficulties. The Handley Page Hampden medium bomber was generally regarded as being nice to fly, although a full 2,000 lb bombload worried even the best of pilots, and it was soon reduced to 1,500 lb. However, this was a single-pilot aeroplane of exceedingly narrow fuselage dimensions, and the trainee pilot learned to fly it by standing behind

A line-up of Hampdens at sunset, ready to take off for the night's work. (IWM HU42423)

the instructor, leaning over his shoulder. One pilot who crashed his Hampden at OTU received a mild rebuke from his CO, since the wartime RAF realized that allowances had to be made for inexperience, and no one had been injured, which was what counted. Yet because the same pilot and his crew were seen walking away from the wreckage without their uniform caps, they were punished by having to march around inside a hangar for an hour!

Losses at OTUs could be heavy, and given the standards of aviation safety of the day, could also be distressing. One pilot, Leslie Biddlecombe, saw a Whitley crash in flames. He and the others watching saw the crew scramble clear, except for the tail gunner, trapped in his turret as the flames spread, and then they witnessed the agony as he caught fire. An officer put an end to his suffering, 'his face set, raised his pistol, took careful aim and fired. The boy's agony was over.'[1]

Biddlecombe was eventually posted to a Hampden squadron, 61 Sqn, initially as second pilot, navigator, bomb-aimer and front gunner. Given the cramped conditions inside the Hampden, it would have been extremely difficult for the second pilot to take over if anything happened to the pilot.

AIRCREW TRAINING: AIR GUNNERS

Initially during the Second World War RAF air gunners often ranked no higher than LAC (Leading Aircraftmen), although before long the lowest rank for aircrew became sergeant. It took just six weeks to become an air gunner. There were three gunnery positions at most on RAF aircraft – the nose, mid-upper and rear – although not all aircraft had all three positions, which were effectively the preserve of the four-engined heavies,

Designed for single pilot operation, the Hampden was known for its narrow fuselage and narrow cockpit. Even when a newly qualified pilot was flying as second pilot, all he could do was watch over the shoulder of the pilot, and if the pilot should be seriously wounded or killed, there was little chance of getting to the controls. (RAFM P018590)

the Lancaster, Stirling and Halifax. The mid-upper gunner had the best view, but the rear gunner had the most dangerous position, isolated from the rest of the crew, often cold, and often the first part of the aircraft to be hit by a Luftwaffe fighter. It was difficult to get out from the rear turret in a hurry, after which it was a scramble to put on one's parachute and find the way to the hatch, providing you weren't trapped in the tail by a fierce fire. Many rear gunners removed the doors from the back of their turrets to reduce the chance of being trapped in an emergency, and to expedite a speedy escape.

At the outset of the Second World War RAF aircraft had the advantage of powered turrets, which in the Wellington, initially described as a 'heavy' bomber, had two .303 Browning machine-guns in the nose turret, and four in the tail turret. One rear gunner, Sgt (later Sqn Ldr) Reg Scarth, found that there were advantages in being in the rear turret, however. Scarth had joined the RAF in 1938, and, bored with a posting to Rhodesia, he had volunteered, and been accepted, for training as a pilot, until he switched to the intermediate trainer, a North American Harvard, when he discovered that he was too short to see over the instruments!

Eventually reaching the UK after training as an air gunner, Reg Scarth was posted to 15 OTU at Harwell, where he became part of a Wellington crew. During one night-flying exercise the aircraft encountered technical difficulties, forcing it to divert to a blacked-out air base where, unknown to the Wellington's crew, the Army was training glider pilots. In the blackout, seeing a green landing light flashing and believing that this was intended for them, the Wellington crashed on top of a Horsa glider, killing the instructor and his pupil. Reg felt the impact of the crash in his rear turret. Unaware of what was happening, he thought that his aircraft had landed, and relaxed, facing backwards. Almost immediately the Wellington crashed heavily on to the runway, swerving off the concrete and hitting a jeep, injuring its driver, and also injuring all the rest of the crew except Scarth.

Joining another crew, mainly Canadians, Reg found himself on more cross-country training flights. Bomber aircrew had been warned to keep an eye open for enemy night intruders – the all-too-potent twin-engine Junkers Ju88. On this particular night they were flying over the Bristol/Taunton area when a twin-engine fighter suddenly dived at them. It did not fire, but as it broke away, Reg raked its belly with his four Brownings:

On landing back at base all hell was let loose. The attacking aircraft had not been a Ju88, but a 'friendly' night-fighter – a Bristol Beaufighter. The shaken pilot landed at his squadron and filed his report immediately. Angry messages were exchanged between Fighter Command and Bomber Command. Each blamed the other for the incident. In the end, Reg was exonerated. It was established that the fighter pilot was guilty of an error of judgement in swooping in at night on an RAF bomber – especially the easily identifiable 'Wimpey', with its characteristic 'Wellington boot' silhouette.[2]

'NICKEL' OPERATIONS: DROPPING LEAFLETS

Both sides dropped leaflets during the war, although the British were far more persistent – one might say optimistic – about this than the Germans. Many bomber formations attacking real targets with real explosive bombs were given leaflets to drop as they made their way home from the target. The RAF's bomber crews were unimpressed, and their feelings were echoed by the commander later in the war, ACM Sir Arthur 'Bomber' Harris, who famously claimed that all they were doing was 'providing the Germans with enough toilet paper to last the war'.

As the war developed, the responsibility for leaflet raids would often fall to the inexperienced crews of the OTUs, as a means of introducing them to flying over enemy territory. These raids were known in the RAF as 'Nickel' sorties.

The Aircraft

For these two operations described here, two different aircraft were used. In the first operation, the aircraft was an Armstrong Whitworth Whitley III, which when it had first appeared in 1936 had been one of the RAF's first monoplane bombers. Officially classified as a medium bomber, it was obsolescent by the outbreak of war. Two 918 hp Bristol radial engines provided a maximum speed of 220 mph and a range of 1,000 miles, while up to 3,500 lb of bombs could be carried. The aircraft had tail and nose turrets, but no mid-upper turret. Operationally, the maximum speed would often be considerably less than the stated maximum.

The second operation involved leaflet-dropping as the aircraft prepared to return home after a bombing operation, and used the Avro Manchester. As the British struggled to create a heavy bomber fleet, one of the failures was the Avro Manchester, a large twin-engined bomber which suffered from chronic unreliability from its engines, two 1,760 hp Rolls-Royce Vultures. With an extended wingspan and four Merlin engines, it became the superb Lancaster,

The early war years soon showed many of the aircraft then in service to be inadequate for the tasks ahead, especially the strategic heavy bombing campaign. Many were transferred to training units, but fifteen Armstrong Whitworth Whitley MkVs were transferred to the newly formed British Overseas Airways Corporation, BOAC, initially to fly supplies between Gibraltar and Malta, and later for the ball-bearing run between Sweden and Scotland, before they were replaced by Mosquitos. (IWM HU64722)

The aircraft transferred to BOAC were the lucky ones. This is another Whitley V, of 102 Sqn, which crashed on its return to RAF Topcliffe in December 1940. (RAF Museum P016006)

Another view of the same aircraft. (RAF Museum P016008)

but it took time for the Manchester's failings to be fully appreciated, until those in authority recognized that these were more than just teething troubles.

The Action

The operation set for the night of 8/9 September 1939 was destined to drop leaflets on the towns of the Ruhr, Germany's industrial heartland. This required the leaflet-dropping bombers to fly some ten miles north of the river and parallel to it at 5,000 ft, so that the leaflets would be blown into the centres of the towns, at least in theory. Edgar Hall was a flight-sergeant pilot on a Whitley III, one of two pilots for each aircraft at this stage of the war. He recalls:

> in those days all our navigation was dead reckoning. On a blacked-out Europe there was very, very little chance of a fix, your last chance of a fix was as you crossed the coast – the European coast – unless you were lucky enough to see the Rhine or one of the things where you could pick up a fix . . . You did see the lights of Holland but once you were over Germany it was only moonlight and rivers that you had a chance . . . no wireless bearings at all, we had a wireless silence – not that our wireless was frightfully good anyway – and you relied more or less entirely on the met wind. Whilst you were crossing the sea you could drop a float and you could take a drift.[3]

Navigation was to become more difficult once the neutral Netherlands had been overrun by Germany the following spring: 'Nobody knew what

STRIKING AT THE ENEMY

really to expect . . . we rather expected to be blown out of the sky, and the ground crew had certainly given my crew, and all the others, quite a number of farewell drinks. I had a second pilot, a sergeant observer, an LAC wireless operator, an AC air gunner . . .[4]

In many ways, there was a sense of innocence during the early stages of the war. On the way out, Hall recalls encouraging his crew to have a singsong to pass the time while they crossed the North Sea, then having difficulty stopping them once over enemy territory when they had to be alert. Many of the aircrew, and especially the pilots, were exhausted from intensive flying during the previous few days – the first week of war – dispersing aircraft to their wartime locations to minimize the risk of their being destroyed on the ground by a surprise Luftwaffe raid. He asked one member of his crew to drop the leaflets:

I remember saying to him 'Isn't it time you started dropping the leaflets?' And he said 'I've done it.' I said 'How long did it take you?' He said 'Twenty-five minutes.' I said 'Well, I don't remember you going, don't remember you coming back.' He said 'I thought you were asleep.' And I must have been asleep for twenty-five minutes and we hadn't lost height . . . and we hadn't had George (the automatic pilot) in because George wasn't all that reliable in those days. And then we turned for home.[5]

The journey home was uneventful, picking up a course from a beacon in France.

On bombing operations, the pressure to drop leaflets meant that, while still over enemy territory, a member of the crew had to be taken from some other task which was possibly more vital, to drop the leaflets through the aircraft's flare tube. John Bushby was an air gunner aboard an Avro Manchester, a year or two later in the war, when the task fell to him:

The cartons of leaflets were stowed amidships near the triple flare chute from which illuminating flares and the photo flash were launched. I had never done this job before and in the light of my torch groped at the large package. I saw that it was composed of smaller bundles each with an elastic band to hold the bundle together. I gathered up three or four bundles and unthinkingly slipped off the elastic and pushed them down the flare tube. No one had told me that the idea was to push them out elastic-bound end first, and that the slipstream would then scatter them to the four winds to flutter slowly down on to an unsuspecting enemy. What I had forgotten was the half gale which, induced by our motion through the air, continually roared up the flare tubes whenever the protective cover at the bottom was slid back. I filled the chute with bundles and then slid back the cover. In an instant I was the centre of a fiercely whirling mass of paper, spiralling and twisting madly inside the fuselage. I had leaflets clinging to me from head to toe and could see nothing for the flapping and snapping of the paper as it was whirled round my head. I slid the chute closed and the storm subsided. I gave it up and crawled back to my turret.

We landed just before dawn and in the light of several torches examined the interior of the Manchester. By then, most of the hydraulic oil, which seems to settle on everything inside an aircraft in flight, had soaked into the thick carpet of leaflets and we were ankle deep in oil-soaked paper.

'It looks like a bombed lavatory' . . . and I must agree that the description was not inaccurate.[6]

Comment

The leaflet raids were a waste of time, fuel, flying hours and, sometimes, aircrew. Judging by the fact that one of the pilots fell asleep from exhaustion (and possibly the effects of drink), this operation was also unnecessarily hazardous – and for what? By the time John Bushby became involved, aircrew discipline was much tighter, leaflet-dropping was an incidental to the main operation rather than an operation in itself, and people knew that they had to be alert, especially when over enemy territory, for by this time the German night-fighters were becoming a menace to any bomber crew which failed to maintain a state of readiness, and even then the bombers' machine-guns were at a severe disadvantage compared to the fighters' cannon. The air gunners had far more important things to do while over Germany or German-occupied territory than struggle to drop leaflets.

'GARDENING' OPERATIONS: SKAGERRAK AND KATTEGAT, 11/12 AND 14/15 APRIL 1940

Mine-laying operations were known to the RAF as 'Gardening' operations, no doubt because a minefield is 'sown'. During the first winter of the war, the British placed great store on mine-laying operations. These were usually conducted from the air, because the stretches of water which could be mined to best effect were generally those which had extensive naval defences, and even fast mine-layers such as *Manxman* and her sisters would have been placed at great risk. There were other advantages of mine-laying. It posed relatively little risk to the bomber crews, even given the poor defences of the British bombers in service at the start of the war, because the mine-laying took place away from military targets, with their extensive AA defences. It also avoided having to make hard decisions about bombing major naval bases, with the attendant risk of civilian casualties. Finally, it gave the bomber crews much-needed additional experience of night flying and navigation.

The object of using mines was twofold. It helped enforce the naval blockade of Germany, forcing the Germans back on whatever supplies of strategic materials they could get overland, usually from Eastern Europe. It also made it more difficult for the German Navy (or Kriegsmarine), to send ships to sea, where they were less likely to look for a major battle with the Royal Navy, as at Jutland during the First World War, than to harass the vital convoys bringing much-needed supplies to the UK. Of course, after the fall of France, the Germans had access to French ports with much easier access to the open sea.

The Aircraft

The Handley Page Hampden was the one British medium bomber in service at the beginning of the war which bore some resemblance to the principles on which the German medium bombers had been designed, with the entire crew accommodated well forward. Even its long, thin tail was vaguely reminiscent of

One of the duties which fell to the Hampden was mine-laying, known to the RAF as 'Gardening' sorties. Here is a magnetic mine being loaded into the bomb bay. (RAFM P021820)

the Do17, and combined with the deep but narrow forward fuselage, it earned the aircraft the nickname 'The Flying Pan Handle'. In contrast to many of the other RAF bombers in service at the time, there was no room for a second pilot, and although inexperienced second pilots sometimes went on operations to gain experience and act as backup for the first pilot, as more than one has said, given the tight fit of the cockpit, there wasn't much they could have done. There was a rear gunner's position underneath the fuselage, and what amounted to a mid-upper position a short distance behind the cockpit.

In service with the RAF from 1938 to 1942, the mid-wing twin-engined Hampden was powered by two 1,025 hp Bristol radial engines. In theory, the aircraft could carry a 4,000 lb bombload at speeds of up to 255 mph, but it was more usual for it to carry a 2,000 lb bombload. This usually meant four 500 lb bombs, but even experienced pilots were unhappy with the handling characteristics when so heavily loaded, so the load was normally reduced to 1,500 lb.

Life in a Hampden squadron had its difficulties, not least of which was the ease with which the aircraft could be mistaken for a Messerschmitt Me 110 or a Dornier Do17, which kept the crews on alert even over friendly territory.

The Action

By spring 1940 the RAF's 83 Sqn had spent much time practising, but its only overt operations were leaflet-dropping and some basic reconnaissance. Nevertheless, these operations gave the squadron, with 49 Sqn, more night-flying experience than others, so the unit was assigned to a number of special operations. A more aggressive role awaited them, dropping the new British magnetic mine, weighing 1,700 lb, which was virtually sweep-proof in the Skagerrak and Kattegat, the two strips of water separating Denmark from Norway and Sweden, and Germany's outlet to the world's oceans. Bombing

Kiel, which would have been regarded as an even better measure later in the war, was not permitted at this time because of the risk of damage to civilian property and the near-certainty of civilian casualties – known today as 'collateral damage'. No one seems to have considered the fate of neutral shipping.

With any new weapon, or any new aid to navigation or bomb-aiming, the rule was that nothing should fall into enemy hands. This meant that the mines had to be dropped over open water, and under no circumstances were they to be dropped over land or in very shallow coastal waters. If anything happened to the aircraft over land, the crew, in baling out, were to leave the aircraft ('the ship'), in such a position that it would crash, blowing itself and its load to pieces.

Guy Gibson was flying Handley Page Hampden medium bombers in 1940 with 83 Sqn in RAF Bomber Command when Germany invaded Denmark and Norway. The squadron's first mine-laying operation, on the night of 11/12 April, was relatively uneventful. Guy Gibson's recollection of the first operation was of the cold and the tedium of a long flight: 'Now in a Hampden the pilot can't move out of his seat, so after eight hours I was feeling pretty cramped. Eight hours on your bottom is a long time, but worse was to come, nine, ten, even eleven hours at a stretch – an awful long time.' [7]

Not the least of the problems facing a solitary bomber pilot was how to answer calls of nature. Gibson recalled that pilots usually restrained themselves, except in an emergency, when beer bottles or empty Very light cases were used. The Hampden had a long rubber tube which trailed through a hole in the aircraft, but this was prone to sabotage by ground crews, who showed their dislike of a pilot by tying a knot in it, with disastrous results, so most pilots avoided using it.

The 'Gardening' operation for the night of 14/15 April was aimed for Middlefart, a bottle-neck channel to the west of the Great Belt of Danish islands, on the west coast of the island of Funen:

It was instrument flying all the way there, then came a patch of clear and we saw Denmark ahead. It did not take Jackie Withers long to pin-point the southern point of Sylt. Then we set course for the Bottle. As we buzzed along about two thousand feet above Denmark we ran into more low cloud. Although we were skimming the tops its base must have been pretty well on the deck . . . .A little later Jack told me to start easing down. Gradually at about three hundred feet a minute the old Hampden slid into the murk. All the time came Jack's voice reading the altimeter.

'900 feet; 500 feet.'

There was silence for a while, still we were going down; outside the swirling cloud, inside the soft glow of the instruments. It was getting darker and darker. I saw my altimeter and it was reading nearly zero. 'Come on Jack, what's the height?' I said, pressing the emergency intercom button. With a click his voice burst in, 'Sorry, my intercom plug came out. Christ, if my altimeter's reading right we're a ruddy submarine!'

Quickly we levelled out. Then I saw the bridge. It was Middlefart Bridge all right, straight in front of us. There was nothing for it, no question of recklessness. If we went up we would be back in the clouds and completely lost, we could only stay low down. And so Mac, in the mid-upper position, was very surprised when he saw the bridge whistle over him.

Then –

'Bomb doors open. We're here.'

'OK. Hold it.'

'Steady, steady, not too soon.'

'OK Mines . . . Gone.'[8]

As the mines shot out with a slap and a clonk, a flak ship opened up on the aircraft, which was only at 100 ft, but quickly pulled up into the cloud with the bottom rear gunner firing his guns even after the flak ship was lost to sight in the clouds. Gibson recalls that the man in question had only come along as a passenger. At that early stage of the war, there were few NCO aircrew. The wireless operators (or 'jeeps' in RAF slang) were AC1s, and the gunners were AC2s. Both received the grand sum of 6*d* (10 US cents, at the exchange rate at the time) extra flying pay a day. Many of the gunners had never even been to gunnery school, but had picked up what they could in the squadron in their spare time.

Comment

Relatively unglamorous, the mine-laying operations did cause damage to enemy shipping, and at this stage of the war, when the Germans had yet to acquire bases in France, the benefits were even greater than later. Mine-laying also tied up minesweepers.

While it is tempting to suggest that mine-laying might not have been as effective as attacking ships in port or at sea, 4 surface warships, a submarine and 21 other vessels are supposed to have been destroyed at sea in this way, and probably a number of the 152 surface warships, 21 submarines and 127 other vessels sunk in port would have been accounted for by mines – not bad for a relatively low-risk activity.

THE NIGHT RAID ON ESSEN

Essen, in the Ruhr Valley, was at the heart of German industry. The towns of the Ruhr were relatively easy to find, given the navigational standards of the day, because of their position on the river, but they were also heavily defended, both by intense AA artillery (or 'triple A' in modern parlance), and with night-fighters.

During the Battle of France the RAF was still reluctant to attack any target which might incur civilian casualties, and there was also pressure from the French, concerned about reprisal raids on French cities. Edgar Hall's squadron had mounted a raid on Sylt, on the island of Hornum, attacking a German seaplane station, and during the Battle of France had attacked communications targets, many of which appear to have been crossroads – difficult to hit, especially at night, and relatively easily repaired compared to railway junctions, tunnels or bridges.

The Aircraft

Hall still had his faithful Whitley (see p. 61).

The Action

The raid seems to have been prepared at extremely short notice. By this time, Bomber Command's losses were mounting, and the decision to do without experienced second pilots had just been taken, although they were still allocated at this stage, albeit inexperienced ones. Experienced second pilots quickly became aircraft captains themselves. Hall had lost his experienced second pilot and also his observer, an Irishman who had deserted back to the neutral Irish Republic. On 19 May Hall's new second pilot and observer had arrived, and he had been told that he would have three weeks to train his new crew. With nothing to do that day, he had gone home to his wife, who lived close to the base. Within an hour of arriving home, a messenger arrived asking him to report to the squadron office. On arrival, he was told that he was flying that night with his new crew, whom he hadn't even met, let alone trained with.

The target was Essen, but this was not an area bombing raid. The bomber pilots were given a specific factory as their target.

Despite having an almost completely new crew, retaining only his radio operator, Hall was fairly confident. He believed that if he jinked his aircraft, changing course or height every ten seconds at around 15,000 ft:

a good gunner couldn't hit you, the only ones that hit you were bad gunners that shot them off and happened to place their shell where you happened to be . . . you know by that time we'd got fairly nonchalant about flying.

So when we got to Essen, which was more my navigation . . . because they'd done practically no navigation and certainly no night navigation, and when it came to Essen and I could see the factory . . . it was a lovely moonlight night. But Dick [Sgt Dick, his observer/bomb-aimer] had no idea at all. So I remember going on a southerly course and telling Glover [Plt Off Glover, the second pilot] . . . it was the first time he'd been at the controls of a Whitley . . . 'Just keep her going down there and jink' while I showed Dick the target . . . I tried three or four runs and put the 'plane on the target but he'd not picked it up. So I nipped down bottom and showed him the target; I said 'Look, there it is, there's the river, there's the target, now do you recognise it?' 'Yes'. So I nipped back to find Glover flying us straight and level, we were combed in the searchlights and box barrage all round us. We did the run and dropped the bombs but we lost an engine, we got hit, it was on fire, we got the fire out, we got the box barrage and turned for home. And we kept going for a considerable time. The engine caught fire again and we were getting shot at all the time and we did get hit again. Eventually we were

The best British bomber during the early years of the war was undoubtedly the Vickers Wellington. This aircraft shows battle damage after one of the first RAF raids of the war, on Heligoland on 4 September 1939. (RAFM P017453)

This Wellington is surrounded by some of the crews who flew their Wellingtons on an early Berlin raid on the night of 25/26 August 1940, in retaliation for the previous night's raid on London. (IWM HU44271)

losing height, [and] we'd only started at about six thousand feet over Essen; by the time we got down to one thousand eight hundred I told them to prepare to abandon aircraft. And when I realized I couldn't keep up much longer, the fire was going again, I told them to bale out.

. . . One thing that I didn't know at the time . . . my observer had gone back to South [sic] Ireland and had deserted, he'd left his parachute in our aircraft just behind my seat in stowage. When I told them to bale out I hung on as long as I could. I seen the observer Dick and Glover go down through the forward hatch, I seen McCutchan go to the rear and Murray had acknowledged the bale out and pulled out his intercom so from that moment I had no idea of what happened behind. And I just kept on as long as I could till it got pretty hot and I went out . . .[9]

Hall left the aircraft, and could see two parachutes, which he took to be those of Dick and Glover, so he assumed that he had left the other two behind in the aircraft. On landing, he buried his parachute, and believing that he was over the Dutch border, set off to seek assistance. In fact, he was still in Germany, and when he went into a farmyard to get a drink from the trough, he was arrested by the farmer wielding a shotgun. Within a quarter of an hour, a small party of German soldiers arrived to take him away. He was fed, by the German soldiers, who believed that the British were on the verge of starvation, before being handed over to the Luftwaffe for interrogation. He finished the war as a PoW.

Comment

Given the shortage of experienced aircrew, mounting a raid with complete novices was nothing short of folly. There was no way a novice pilot could fly the aircraft through a defensive course, yet Hall felt that he couldn't waste the opportunity of hitting such an obvious target because of the inexperience of his observer/bomb-aimer. The irony is that once he had had the target shown to him, there was still no guarantee that the bombs were dropped at precisely the right moment.

Running over the target four times was a practice which was eventually discouraged, just one pass being regarded as prudent, since most aircraft were shot down on a second or third pass – as we will see later, there were times, such as the famous 'Dam Busters' raid, when several passes were necessary, but the risk was tremendous. Far better to return to base without dropping the bombs. Clearly, at this early stage of the war, the RAF's training was sadly lacking in many of the basics, and the losses which resulted delayed the accumulation of experience.

APRES DUNKIRK, JUNE 1940

After the British Expeditionary Force's retreat towards Dunkirk and the subsequent evacuation, the RAF attempted to disrupt enemy communications. Many officers believed that this would allow the French sufficient time to regroup and for the British Army to send a fresh force to the front. 'Bomber' Harris, at this stage commanding a group within Bomber Command as an Air Vice-Marshal, saw one remedy as being an attack on the German Army's lines of communications. One idea was that RAF bombers could drop their bombs in front of railway tunnels, with the bombs fused so that they could roll into the tunnels before exploding.

Ironically, later, as C-in-C of Bomber Command, Harris was to dismiss attacks on communications and the oil industry as 'panacea targets'. Indeed, by this time the world had seen the German bombing of Rotterdam, a city completely devoid of air raid defences, and the days of attempting to avoid, or at least minimize civilian casualties, were coming to an end. Even after British forces had been evacuated from the Channel Islands with a substantial proportion of the civilian population, leaving the islands completely undefended, German bombers attacked the two main islands, Jersey and Guernsey, killing a number of the civilians who had been left behind. From this time onwards, the mood changed, and civilian casualties were at first no longer regarded as sufficient justification to avoid attacking a particular target, and before long they were regarded as legitimate targets.

The Aircraft
The aircraft used on this raid was still the venerable Hampden (see p. 64).

The Action
This was another raid by Guy Gibson's 83 Sqn. He recalled that after they took off and flew over the North Sea, passing Rotterdam, the city was still smouldering. They then flew across Belgium, finding Brussels to be badly blacked-out, and on into Germany:

In fact, everywhere we noticed that the black-out was fairly bad and people were waving to us with torches. Away on the left an aircraft was being coned by searchlights at about thirteen thousand feet and being shot to hell by heavy flak. For some reason it had its bottom identification light on, and later we heard that this was some fellow in A Flight who had forgotten to turn it out after taking off. No wonder he told the boys, 'You'd think I was the only aircraft in the sky . . .'

By map-reading carefully from canal to canal we at last came to our tunnel near Aachen. By now the moon had gone down so I released a flare. Like striking a match in the dark to see the way so suddenly we saw our tunnel clear and sharp in the yellow light. There was no time to waste, as these flares only burn for about three minutes, and so we dived into the attack. Down the railway lines we went like a high-speed train, and I noticed almost subconsciously that the signals were up. Then, when the cliff face seemed to be towering high above us we pulled right up and at the same time let go a couple of 500-pounders. A few seconds later, during which we saw trees miss our wing-tip by inches, there came a welcome roar and turning round we saw the entrance to the tunnel had collapsed. This was fine and we still had two bombs on board. When we came to our next tunnel, about ten miles further on, we encountered a snag. The other reconnaissance flare would not fall off. This was terrible. It was too dark to see without one. If the armourers had heard even a quarter of what we said in that aircraft in the next few minutes, even they would have been embarrassed.

In the end Watty and I hit upon a plan. We flew down on to the railway line as low as possible and then I turned on my landing light, which lit up the permanent way enough for me to see the sleepers rush by. At the same time, Watty held the Aldis light straight forward, acting as a spotlight waiting for the tunnel to loom up in its light. All the while the cliff face drew nearer and nearer at 200 miles an hour. For a few minutes we flew like this, watching the shiny surface of the railway lines, while I prayed there would be no night fighters about. While we were flying along like a Brock's Benefit, some lonely soul opened up with a machine-gun nearby, but must have been squinting because it went about half a mile behind.

Then – 'Here comes the tunnel. Bombs . . . Bombs gone.'

On the word 'Gone' I slammed the throttles forward and remembered seeing the tunnel spotlighted in our Aldis lamp before I yanked back the stick. The old Hampden, relieved of her bombs, went up like an elevator, and we just cleared a 400-foot [120 m] cliff by a few feet. I remember this well because it was a white cliff with a chalk face, and we could see it quite clearly; eleven seconds later came that pleasant muffled crump, showing that we had reached our mark.

When we landed Pit had a better story to tell. He had been back an hour before and had had an even easier time, and in my opinion had done a much better job. When he found his tunnel he had noticed a train steaming into it. Full of cunning he had quickly flown round the other end and by careful aiming had sealed it up: then he dashed back to the end the train had entered and had sealed down that entrance too. What a chap! Especially for the son of a Scottish Presbyterian Minister![10]

Comment

Precision bombing such as this was a rare achievement throughout the war, and extremely rare at the outset, especially at night. More of this would undoubtedly have had a disastrous effect on the German war effort, although deep-penetration precision raids inside Germany itself had to await the arrival of the de Havilland Mosquito. It took outstanding airmanship and great courage to fly low along a railway line at night with a cliff face approaching at high speed.

TARGETING GERMANY

After the fall of France, the British were free to pursue the war in their own way – in theory at least. One target which was attractive from the outset was the oil industry, which was essential to the German war effort and had the advantage of generally being located well away from areas of population. Yet striking against the oil industry was easier said than done. Portal and Peirse remained in favour of precision bombing, but accurate navigation, the first essential, was all too rare, while bomb-aiming was also an imprecise art at this time.

During the early days of the war, the bombloads on British aircraft were also pitifully low. A report at the end of December 1940 showed that the bombing raid on the two oil plants at Gelsenkirchen, in which 296 aircraft

A flight of Wellingtons from 9 Sqn flying in formation. (RAFM P03358)

Wellingtons in formation on their way to attack a Luftwaffe base, early in the war. (IWM CH4)

dropped 262 tons of bombs, had inflicted little damage. As 1941 dawned, the first of the heavy bombers, the Short Stirling, was ready for service. The Stirling was to mark a massive step forward in bombloads, although its relatively low wing meant that the load had to be divided into two, and as 4,000 lb 'cookie' bombs became more commonplace, the aircraft could not carry them. The operational debut of this aircraft was against the oil storage tanks at Rotterdam on 10/11 February 1941.

AREA BOMBING

The concept of area bombing would have been frowned upon at the outset of the war, when so much effort was devoted to leaflet-dropping, and the most likely targets were seen as the oil industry and naval and air bases. Nevertheless, a growing acceptance of the inevitability of civilian casualties meant a change in attitudes. One reason was the difficulty of striking at many targets because of their location amid residential areas, and the other was that they should feel the 'weight of the war'.[1] In many industrial areas, including those connected with the war effort, workers lived close to their workplace. Some air power theorists maintained that wars could be won from the air by terrorizing the civilian population, while others, with much justification and more logic, argued that the people producing tanks, aircraft or ships were just as much a part of the war effort as any soldier, airman or sailor.

As early as July 1940 Churchill wrote to the Minister of Aircraft Production, Lord Beaverbrook, drawing attention to the failure of any attempt to blockade Germany, and demanding raids on a number of German cities, although ACM Sir Richard Peirse, Vice-Chief of the Air Staff, preferred persistent attacks against selected military targets until these were destroyed. Eventually, the instruction was given that priority was to be accorded to oil targets, followed by communications, with war industry as secondary targets. Berlin was to be the exception, to cause disruption to industry and disturbance to the civilian population. As the city was the seat of government, this can be readily understood. Later, strategists were to argue for the need to copy the German policy of 'fire-raising' attacks, with follow-up attacks targeted onto the fires to make fire-fighting more difficult. In urban areas, gas works and power stations were added to the list of targets so that life would be disrupted as much as possible.

The raid on Coventry, on 14/15 November 1940, when 499 Luftwaffe bombers devastated the city centre, led to demands for retaliation, but Bomber Command's losses had risen sharply that month, to more than 4 per cent, having dropped from 3.8 per cent in July to 2.4 per cent in October. There had been an attack on Hamburg the following night, but this had been planned beforehand. Revenge for Coventry came in mid-December. The target was the city of Mannheim, and for the first time, British bombers were ordered to aim for the centre. In another first, the raid was led by a force of Wellingtons manned by some of Bomber

The first British four-engined heavy bomber, the Short Stirling suffered from the division in the bomb bay caused by the mid-wing layout, but it was regarded as a nice aircraft to fly. (IWM CH6365)

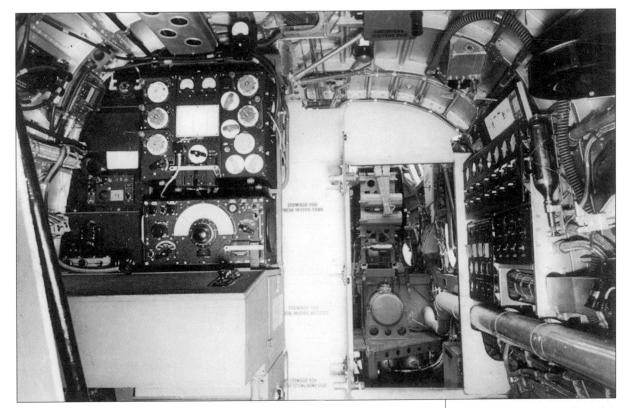

This interior shot of a Stirling Mk I shows the radio operator's position on the left, and the flight engineer's control panel on the right. The open door leads to the cockpit. (IWM HU64728)

Command's most skilled crews, dropping incendiaries to ensure that the target was clearly marked for the aircraft following. A force of 134 aircraft was deployed, of which 102 claimed to have dropped their bombs on the target. Subsequent photographic reconnaissance showed that little damage had been done – which was borne out by intelligence reports received by British diplomats in neutral capitals. The RAF became seriously concerned about the accuracy of its bombing.

The early poor results of the bombing campaign against Germany even raised doubts among members of the British War Cabinet, although the evidence of the potential damage of the bomber was there for all to see: the Luftwaffe killed or caused serious injury to 93,000 British civilians during 1941, and this was without one heavy bomber being used. Bomber Command felt the need to prove itself, and the night of 7/8 November 1941 saw raids on Berlin, Boulogne, Cologne, Ostend and Mannheim, as well as mining the Ruhr. The cost in aircraft and in human terms was immense. On the Berlin raid 169 aircraft were deployed and of these 21 failed to return. The Ruhr mine-laying raid suffered even higher casualties proportionately, with 9 out of the 43 aircraft failing to return, and another 7 were lost from the 55 targeting Mannheim. Another 133 aircraft had been divided between the other three raids, and these managed to escape unscathed.

One conclusion which can be drawn from this is that the air defences around the target were just part of the problem, with aircraft on the deep-penetration raids having to fight their way to and from the target, leaving one to suppose that the absence of casualties on the Cologne raid was either a fluke, or the result of German attentions being distracted elsewhere

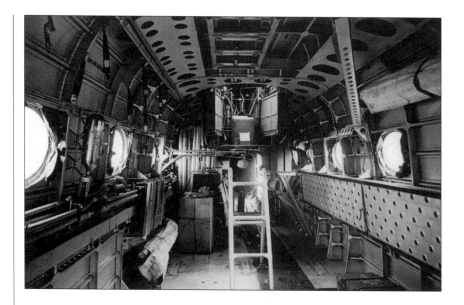

Another interior shot of a Stirling Mk I, again looking forward, and showing the mid-upper gunner's position. (IWM HU64732)

The Short Stirling was capable of taking heavy damage and still getting back to base – this Stirling of 15 Sqn at RAF Wyton shows both flak and fighter cannon damage. (RAFM P04508)

by the other raids. It is also true that an aircraft badly damaged or suffering mechanical problems over Boulogne or Ostend might just make it home, while this would be well beyond an aircraft returning from Berlin.

The impact of such heavy losses cannot be underestimated. It took eighteen months from joining before a bomber pilot was ready for his first operational sortie, provided he survived training, since 5,327 Bomber Command pilots were killed during training, and another 3,113 injured.

GEE

One of the first steps forward in ensuring accuracy was the introduction of 'Gee' (named after 'G' for grid) which provided signals from ground-based stations to guide the bomber to its target, while the navigator had a chart with the Gee grid overprinted. The signals were picked up by the bomber and displayed on a cathode ray tube. Using signals from three stations to fix the aircraft's position, the system was able to provide an accuracy of between half a mile and 5 miles over distances of 300–400 miles, sufficient to reach the Ruhr. Bomber Command were far from complacent, appreciating that they probably had six months of operating Gee from its introduction early in 1942 before German jamming or bending of the radio beams.

Not all early results were impressive, and not all the crews used the system properly or had full confidence in it – training so many in a short time was an insurmountable problem. On one raid against Essen, 20 aircraft using Gee were instructed to drop their flares 'blind' if need be,

WILHELMSHAVEN DOCKS.

Barrage

Prime targets for the RAF and the USAAF during the war were the enemy's ports and naval bases. This reconnaissance photograph shows Wilhelmshaven in 1944, with the major warships Tirpitz, Scheer *and* Hippers Hafens, *as well as the Ems–Jade Canal. (IWM HU71210)*

since this target was notorious for being obscured by industrial haze, but only 11 did so. Even before they could interfere with the signals, the Germans used dummy flares and fires to divert the following bombers into dropping their bombs out of harm's way.

Inevitably, one of the bombers lost on a later raid against Lübeck enabled the Germans to gain possession of a set of Gee receiving equipment.

Of course, in the round of retaliation which the bomber campaigns of both sides generated, Hitler launched a series of raids against British towns known as the 'Baedeker Raids', after the tourist guide books. Lord Cherwell minuted Churchill on the evidence collected so far of the impact of the German bombing campaign, which was that 1 ton of bombs destroyed '20–40 dwellings and turns 100–200 people homeless', which he felt had a greater impact on civilian morale than casualties. Cherwell wanted a campaign against homes in the top 58 German cities. Portal was among those taken with the force of this argument.

OVER THE ALPS, SEPTEMBER 1940

As the war progressed the RAF sought to ease the pressure on Malta and British forces in Greece and North Africa by taking the war to Italy. This was no mean achievement. Aircraft of 57 Sqn, by this time flying Vickers Wellingtons as part of 3 Group, RAF Bomber Command, were fitted with

The fuselage of a damaged Avro Manchester of 61 Sqn following a raid on the German battlecruisers Scharnhorst *and* Gneisenau. *Warships were always a difficult target, with bombs likely to bounce off their armour plating, while the concentration of defensive anti-aircraft fire was far heavier than on most targets ashore. (RAFM 19788)*

overload tanks and took off from their base at Feltwell in Norfolk, with each aircraft able to carry just three bombs: a mixture consisting of a single 1,000 lb bomb and one each of 500 lb and 250 lb. The return flight took more than ten hours, and altogether the squadron made three such raids on Genoa in September 1941.

For much of the time, however, the targets lay in Germany. A more worthwhile load could be carried on such sorties, including the large 4,000 lb Cookie, but the drawback was that the Germans were ready and waiting. As the German night-fighter defences developed, there were some interesting moments, as when one of the squadron's bombers, 'A-Apple', reported being caught over Düsseldorf on the morning of 28 December by a German fighter with a blue searchlight fitted in the nose.

The following year saw the start of the famous 'Thousand Bomber Raids' which were to prove so effective in both hindering the German war effort and reducing Bomber Command's heavy losses. Nevertheless, there were many incidents at home, and during that severe winter of 1941/2, Germany's best defence against air attack lay in the weather. In the spring, as a portent of things to come, an advance party of senior NCOs from the US Air Force came to the squadron, now at Methwold, for night-flying experience. They were soon assuring their hosts that their squadron could not operate under such primitive conditions, since the base lacked a control tower or perimeter lighting, and managed with a caravan at the end of the runway and goose-neck flares. The RAF had managed to cope, however, and a member of the squadron, Cpl John Holmes, recalled:

We did it there for two years and I only recall one crash. An undercarriage leg collapsed and the aircraft ended up on the road, sitting on a 4,000-pounder like a pregnant duck. An army officer arrived to take charge of the situation but left quickly when told that the bomb was very much alive. We had no crane available, so resorted to a set of shear legs. These collapsed with the extra weight, giving the cookie another shaking.[2]

Barrage balloons were a menace to bombers over the target, and many aircraft were fitted with explosive cable-cutters on their wing leading edges. Ted Vaisey was an airframe fitter, and he recalls with amusement an engine fitter explaining the dangers of these devices to a newcomer, as he stood on a maintenance platform and tapped the wing with a screwdriver to emphasize his words: 'Suddenly, there was a deafening bang – Yorky had inadvertently done the very thing that he had been warning against! The pair were ashen faced but unhurt, Yorky still clutching the useless stump that remained of his pride and joy. "Eh," he grumbled, "that were me best bluddy cowling screwdriver an' all!"'[3]

THE BOMBER
AT SEA

While the main bombing effort in Europe was carried out by land-based bombers, the bomber was also deployed at sea by the Royal Navy, the Imperial Japanese Navy and the US Navy. The Japanese had already gathered experience in using the bomber in their campaign in China during the late 1930s, although the naval involvement had tended more towards ferrying aircraft than operations. As always, the use of carrier-borne aircraft only made sense in operations which were either outside the reach of land-based aircraft, or where secure land bases could not be guaranteed. Land-based aircraft would always have the advantage of range and warload compared to carrier-borne ones. Nevertheless, the Second World War proved beyond all doubt that a substantial role existed for naval air power, which could be relied upon to tip the balance of any major campaign.

Yet the outbreak of war in 1939 found the Royal Navy's Fleet Air Arm in a poor state. The pioneers of carrier-borne aviation had lost control of their aircraft in 1918 with the formation of the RAF, with the exception of seaplanes operated from cruisers and battleships. While between the two world wars the Royal Navy developed aircraft carrier design until, in the *Illustrious* class, on order at the outbreak of war, it had the finest aircraft carriers of the war, the situation over aircraft procurement was far different. The RAF, short of money during the recession, had concentrated on developing a strategic air role for itself, and the development and procurement of naval aircraft had been neglected. The fault was not so much that of the RAF as of the original decision to place all the nation's air power with a single service. The RAF's founding fathers showed great wisdom in seeing the strategic role as a priority, and would reap the benefit in the conflict to come. The Royal Navy only regained control of its own aviation in 1937, and denial of control over its own air power meant that the Royal Navy lost the chance to develop a generation of senior officers aware of the potential of air power, men who would not simply know how to 'fight the ship', but how to take a different and altogether wider perspective, given the speed and range of the aeroplane.

Perhaps one indication of the Royal Navy's attitude to aviation was the fact that aircraft carriers were treated as second-rate ships, and those aboard were made to feel it. These ships were among the last to have radar fitted.

This was to change. The Fleet Air Arm's brilliant and gallant attack on the Italian fleet at Taranto settled the role of naval aviation, although it also had the unfortunate effect of impressing upon the Japanese a means, as they saw it, of eliminating the imbalance between their own fleet and that of the USA in the Pacific. Later, as the US forces fought their way back across the Pacific to Japan, the world was to see how naval air power could be used to good effect when targets were either out of reach of land-based aircraft, or before land bases could be made secure or even constructed in the first place.

OPERATION JUDGEMENT: THE ATTACK ON THE ITALIAN FLEET AT TARANTO, 11/12 NOVEMBER 1940

No one, least of all the British, had been surprised when Italy entered the Second World War on the side of the Germans on 10 June 1940. The late 1930s had shown Italy to have strong territorial ambitions in North Africa, while Hitler and the Italian dictator Benito Mussolini shared a political ideology. Both the RAF and the British Army were pessimistic about the fate of the island of Malta, then a British colony, following Italy's entry into the war, although the Royal Navy persisted in the view that Malta could continue as a base for submarines and for fast light surface forces. This did not mean that the Royal Navy was complacent. The threat posed in the Mediterranean by the powerful, modern Italian fleet was clear at a time when the Royal Navy was heavily over-stretched in the North Atlantic and in home waters, and although Japan had yet to enter the war, it also had to keep a substantial part of its resources in the Far East.

Malta was to struggle to survive heavy aerial attack by the Italian Regia Aeronautica, which was later joined by Luftwaffe units.

HMS *Illustrious* entered service in 1940, and joined one of the Royal Navy's early carriers, *Eagle*, in the Mediterranean. Her CO, Capt (later Rear Adm) Denis Boyd, was apprehensive when the Commander of the Mediterranean Fleet, Adm (later Admiral of the Fleet) Sir Andrew Cunningham, called his COs to a conference. Boyd's fears that Cunningham might want the carriers to leave the Mediterranean were to prove groundless as he opened the conference by asking for their ideas on how best to strike at the enemy.

It is widely believed that the inspiration for the operation at Taranto came from the Fleet Air Arm's success during the Norwegian campaign earlier in 1940, when land-based aircraft operating from Hatston in Orkney successfully attacked and sank the German cruiser *Königsberg*. The truth was, the idea had been conceived by Capt Lister, who commanded the aircraft carrier *Glorious*, which was with the Mediterranean Fleet in 1935 when the Abyssinian crisis had erupted and the League of Nations had toyed with the idea of intervening to curb Italy's ambitions in North Africa. With a rare awareness for the time of the potential of naval aviation, Lister had ensured that his crews were proficient in night-flying, and also had them train for an attack on Taranto, the Italian Navy's most southerly base, but the call for action

never came. By late 1940, Lister was Cunningham's Rear-Admiral Carriers.

The idea was to use aircraft from both ships, but *Eagle* was forced to remain at Alexandria for repairs after being damaged in an Italian aerial attack, which had disabled her aviation fuel system. *Illustrious* had also had problems after a serious hangar fire, so the original planned date for the attack, 21 October, the anniversary of Nelson's great victory at the Battle of Trafalgar, could not be kept. The fire had damaged the ship, and although it had only destroyed two aircraft, the remainder had been doused with water and had to be stripped down before they could be returned to service. Failure to meet the original date meant that the operation had to be delayed until the next moonlit night, 11/12 November.

Ships and Aircraft

The aircraft carrier *Illustrious* was the first of a fleet of six fast armoured aircraft carriers of 23,000 tons each. In these ships, the armoured box which protected the hangars was regarded as more important than the total aircraft capacity, so the ships were not simply an improved version of the pre-war *Ark Royal*. For the time, they also had good AA gunnery, although it did not compare with that aboard US carriers at the height of the Pacific War.

The aircraft to be used were the veteran Fairey Swordfish biplanes, first flown in 1934, and known to the Fleet Air Arm as 'Stringbags'. Usually a three-seat aircraft, with a pilot, an observer (as the Fleet Air Arm called the navigator) and a telegraphist-air-gunner (TAG), for the raid on

Capt Denis Boyd, commanding officer of Illustrious *at the time of the operation. (FAAM PERS/314)*

Taranto an extra fuel tank was installed and the aircraft operated with just the pilot and observer. A versatile aircraft, capable of operating as a dive-bomber or torpedo aircraft, the Swordfish was slow, rarely achieving its official top speed of 140 mph, and usually flew at around 100 kt, powered by a 690 hp Bristol Pegasus radial engine.

The Action

Surprise was difficult to achieve in the Mediterranean, the Mediterranean Fleet's main base at Alexandria being home to a network of Italian spies, but the departure of *Illustrious* with her cruiser and destroyer escort on 6 November coincided with a convoy of reinforcements for Greece and another convoy to Malta – one advantage of the delay. The original plan would have involved 30 aircraft from the two carriers, and to compensate to some extent for the absence of *Eagle*, some of her aircraft were transferred to *Illustrious* to give her 815 Naval Air Sqn a total of 24 aircraft.

The omens for the operation were bad, with one aircraft ditching in the sea the day before, and on the day of the operation this was repeated by a second aircraft. Investigation showed that one of the carrier's aviation fuel tanks had been contaminated by sea water, so all the aircraft had to have their fuel systems drained and then refuelled. Nevertheless, all was ready when, at 20.00, *Illustrious* was just 170 miles from Taranto.

Leader of the raid was Lt Cdr Kenneth Williamson, with the then Lt Norman 'Blood' Scarlett-Streatfield as his observer. The aircraft were divided into two waves, 12 in the first and 9 in the second, with some aircraft carrying bombs and others torpedoes, as well as two dropping flares in the first wave. Climbing through thick cloud, the first wave broke up, losing 3 out of the 4 dive-bombers and 1 torpedo-bomber, although the two flare-droppers managed to maintain formation. Final navigation to the target was helped by the port's AA guns firing on an RAF Short Sunderland flying boat.

The flare-droppers went in first, followed by the torpedo-bombers, which were to attack while the Italian warships were silhouetted against the flares. Their job over, the flare-droppers were able to watch the action. Hugh Janvrin was an observer in one:

We dropped our flares at about 8,000 ft. And in fact, we were fired at considerably. We had a fair amount of ack-ack fire and most extraordinary things which looked like flaming onions . . . one just sort of went through it and it made no great impression. One didn't think they would ever hit you.

. . . the torpedo aircraft went down and they attacked in two sub flights. The leader took his sub flight down and attacked . . . attacked a Cavour-class battleship, launched his torpedo, which hit, and was shot down immediately afterwards.

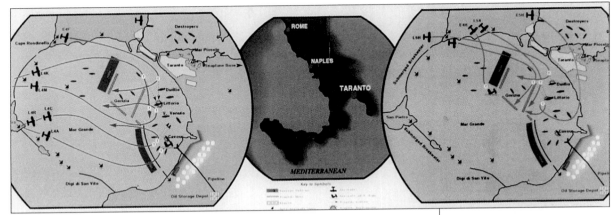

The location of Taranto, and the routes of the first and second waves of aircraft against the target. (FAAM TARANTO/42)

. . . we had bombs as well, and we dive-bombed some more fuel tanks . . . and then we returned to the carrier.[1]

Janvrin had seen Williamson sink the battleship *Conte di Cavour* in shallow water, but as he turned in the middle of the harbour, his aircraft crashed into the sea, although whether because of Italian AA fire or an accident even those on board could not be sure. Scarlett-Streatfield recalls:

We put a wing tip in the water. I couldn't tell. I just fell out of the back into the sea. We were only about twenty feet up. It wasn't very far to drop. I never tie myself in on these occasions.

Then old Williamson came up a bit later on and we hung by the aircraft which still had its tail sticking out of the water. Chaps ashore were shooting at it.

The water was boiling, so I swam off to a floating dock and climbed on board that. We didn't know we'd done any good with our torpedo. Thought we might have because they all looked a bit long in the face, the Wops.[2]

The first strike had a diversionary bombing element, with each aircraft carrying six bombs which they were to drop on cruisers or destroyers, both normally lightly armoured, or on oil storage tanks. Sub Lt Bill Sarra and his observer, Midshipman Jack Bowker, were in one of the dive-

A Fairey Swordfish, minus undercarriage, showing the extra fuel tank fitted in the observer's position for the raid. (FAAM TARANTO/31)

Even Illustrious *was not completely invincible – this is some of the heavy damage sustained in an attack by the Luftwaffe off Malta in January 1941. The ship's heavily armoured flight deck saved her, but she had to be sent to the United States for repairs. (FAAM CARRIER I/37)*

bombers: 'Diving to 1,500 ft, Sarra was unable to pick out his targets. He had passed over the dockyard when he spotted the hangars of the seaplane base ahead – an excellent alternative. He dropped his bombs from 500 ft and saw one explode in a hangar and the others on the slipways. Despite anti-aircraft fire Sarra landed back on *Illustrious* without a scratch.'[3]

Three battleships had been sunk, *Littorio*, *Caio Duilio* and *Conte di Cavour*, although the last of these was refloated and repaired at the end of the war. The cruiser *Trento* was damaged, but had a lucky escape because the bomb had passed right through her decks and through the bottom of the hull without exploding. Important fuel tanks had been destroyed in addition to the damage to the seaplane base. The Italians did not use Taranto for the rest of the war.

After their return, the aircrew were keen to mount a repeat raid the following night, but the weather was worsening, and Cunningham vetoed any further action. Just two aircraft were lost on the operation, and the crew of one of these, Williamson and Scarlett-Streatfield, survived to be taken prisoner.

Comment

No warship ever lived up to her name as well as *Illustrious* that night. Thanks to air power, no single warship ever inflicted so much damage on an enemy fleet. Sadly, neither Cunningham nor Churchill appreciated just how successful the Fleet Air Arm had been, and the ship's sailors were infuriated when the meagre awards for the operation were posted, tearing the first list of awards from the ship's noticeboards. The awards included a DSC for Scarlett-Streatfield. No one received Britain's highest award, the Victoria Cross.

The raid itself had far fewer aircraft than one would have expected for such success, and it seems little short of miraculous that the losses were so few. Given the weather and the fierce AA fire, as well as the primitive nature of the aircraft used, the degree of accuracy was astounding. By any standard this was a precision bombing and torpedo-dropping operation, which was rare, especially so early in the war.

JAPAN'S SURPRISE ATTACK: PEARL HARBOR, 7 DECEMBER 1941

For a number of years war between Japan and the USA had seemed inevitable to many Japanese, who were jealous of US influence in the Pacific, and also had their eyes on the colonies of the UK, France and the Netherlands. The US was also determined to curtail Japan's ambitions in China and Indo-China, especially after the signing of a non-aggression pact between Japan and the Soviet Union. Embargoes on vital materials were followed by a freeze on Japan's assets in the USA in July 1941, and the UK followed the US lead. The impact of these moves on Japan was severe, leaving the country with just a strategic reserve of 55 billion barrels of oil, enough for just eighteen months of war, unless supplies could be secured by invading the Dutch East Indies.

While the country's leadership was prepared for war with the USA, the C-in-C of the Imperial Japanese Navy's First Fleet, Adm Isoroku Yamamoto, was opposed to war with the USA. He recognized his country's limitations, knowing that it could not match the US militarily or industrially. His view was that Japan could win major victories during the first year of war, but that the United States would have recovered by the second year, and would move to the offensive. While the US Navy's strength in the Pacific was less than that of Japan, the balance of power would change once ships were transferred from the Atlantic. This led Yamamoto to consider a major blow to the USA in the Pacific, in effect to provide Japan with at least six months, and ideally longer, to establish its planned empire, the Greater Asia Co-Prosperity Sphere, which would secure the oil and vital strategic materials which Japan desperately needed.

The plan was to destroy most of the Pacific Fleet with a surprise attack on its main base, Pearl Harbor, on the Hawaiian island of Oahu. The Royal Navy's success at Taranto showed that this plan could work. More than that, the Imperial Japanese Navy could send a far more powerful force to Pearl Harbor than the British had managed to muster for Taranto.

Ships and Aircraft

Six aircraft carriers were assigned to the raid on Pearl Harbor. The First Carrier Division had the converted battlecruiser *Akagi* and the converted battleship *Kaga*, while the Second Carrier Division had the smaller carriers, *Hiryu* and *Soryu*, and the newly formed Fifth Carrier Division had two new purpose-built carriers, the sister ships *Shokaku* and *Zuikaku*. In some ways, the two new ships were the equivalent to the *Illustrious* class, as large, fast carriers, but they lacked the heavy defensive armour of the British ships, even though their speed was faster, at 35 kt, and they could carry more than 70 aircraft, with three lifts rather than two to expedite movement between flight deck and hangars. These six ships were to carry no fewer than 423 aircraft belonging to the First Air Fleet, including fighters, torpedo-bombers, dive-bombers and level-bombers.

For the Japanese raid on Pearl Harbor Akagi *was Vice Adm Nagumo's flagship. (IWM MH5933)*

Kaga, *another of Japan's early aircraft carriers, was also part of the attack fleet. Japanese carrier design had many eccentricities, including downward-pointing funnels, shown here. (IWM MH6489)*

Japan's leading naval bomber aircraft at the time was the Nakajima B5N, known to the Allies as 'Kate'. First flown in 1937, this was a single-engined monoplane with all-metal stressed-skin construction, power-folding wings, retractable landing gear, integral wing tanks and a variable-pitch propeller. Powered by a 1,000 hp Nakajima Sakae 12 radial engine, it had a top speed of 230 mph. There were forty torpedo versions and 103 level-bomber versions of this aircraft in the force which attacked Pearl Harbor.

The other major bomber was the Aichi D3A1 dive-bomber, known to the Allies as 'Val'. A single-engined monoplane with a fixed spatted undercarriage, this aircraft was powered by a 1,075 hp Mitsubishi Kinsei 44 radial engine, and could carry a single 550 lb bomb.

The Action

The attack was led by Cdr Mitsuo Fuchida, who had been so convinced from his days as an officer cadet that the USA was Japan's future enemy that he had learnt English. Fuchida was the First Air Fleet's senior flight commander. Against his own judgement, he was ordered to use aerial torpedoes, despite his protests that the shallow waters of Pearl Harbor, just 40 ft deep, and the likelihood of the Americans using torpedo nets would mean that the torpedoes would be wasted. The force was still to include level- and dive-bombers, both to attack ships double berthed and for the air bases ashore. Apart from this, Fuchida was given a relatively free hand, not least because his commanding officer, Vice Adm Nagumo, knew little about air power.

As at Taranto, the decision was taken to mount the attack in two waves. Although an element of surprise was expected because Japan never declared war in advance of an attack, Nagumo expected to have to fight his way to the launching point, and expected to lose between a third and half of his ships. Approaching through a tropical storm, the fleet remained undetected.

On the day of the attack – 8 December to the Japanese, on the other side of the International Date Line from the Americans – the weather was so bad that Fuchida would have cancelled flying if the fleet had merely been exercising. The aircrew were awake at 05.00. Despite the bad weather and the heavy pitching and rolling of the ships, there were few accidents as the aircraft took off in the dark, and at 06.15 Fuchida signalled to the circling aircraft of the first wave to follow him as he led the way to Pearl Harbor. Although generally cast as the lead pilot, Fuchida was actually flown on this operation by Lt Mutsuzaki. The first wave had 183 aircraft, and the second 170 aircraft, a total of 353 aircraft out of the 423 embarked aboard the ships.

Sunrise came while the aircraft were flying towards their target, and a local radio station in Hawaii inadvertently provided both a weather briefing and a homing signal.

Fuchida's aircraft passed over the northernmost point of Oahu at 07.30, and shortly afterwards Fuchida called out '*Tenkai*', the order for aircraft to move into their attack positions. Once this was done, Fuchida fired a rocket signalling Murata, the leader of the torpedo-bombers, to begin the attack. Fuchida fired a second rocket, believing that one of the fighter formation leaders had missed the first, and Takashi, the dive-bomber leader, took this as a signal to attack. While the first formations swooped down on Pearl Harbor, Fuchida remained at 10,000 ft, watching the attack through binoculars. The Japanese had expected nine battleships, but one, the *Pennsylvania*, was in dry dock, while they had also counted the *Utah*, a target ship, in the battleship total. Intelligence reports had indicated that there would not be any aircraft carriers in port, and this proved to be correct.

In a tightly controlled operation, the actual attack was held back until 07.49, when Fuchida broadcast the attack signal, '*To! To! To!*' All this happened without arousing any AA fire or fighter defences.

Architect of the operation was Adm Isoroko Yamamoto. (IWM HU36485)

As fighters strafed the dockyard and the airfields, dive-bombers dropped onto Ford Island, their bombs exploding and causing fires. On Battleship Row, the torpedo-bombers raced across the harbour so low that it seemed that they would never clear the towering superstructures. The torpedo-bomber pilots knew that they had to inflict heavy losses.

As the initial attack cleared, Fuchida ordered the level-bombers to begin their attack, again over Battleship Row. AA fire had started, and Fuchida's aircraft was hit – almost severing the control wires leading to the tailplane – and then shaken by a near miss. Fuchida made three runs over the battleship *California* before dropping his bomb. He recalled seeing an

A captured Aichi D3A1 'Val' dive-bomber of the type used at Pearl Harbor. (FAAM For.Mil/90)

A Japanese pilot's view of Pearl Harbor under attack. (IWM HU55848)

explosion during the second run: 'The flame and smoke erupted skyward together, it was a hateful, mean-looking red flame, the kind that powder produces, and I knew at once that a big magazine had exploded.'[4] He had seen the death throes of the battleship *Arizona*, which had been fitted with radar and additional AA defences the previous year.

While the AA fire was intense, the strikes against the airfields kept all but a few US aircraft out of the air. Fuchida, after completing his bombing run, had to remain for the second wave. He could see the *Arizona* 'blazing like a forest fire', while the *Oklahoma* and *Utah* had capsized, and the *California* and *West Virginia* were slowly settling. The light cruiser *Helena* had been crippled. The Americans had not used torpedo nets, and the torpedo attack had been devastating.

Fifty minutes after the attack had started, Shimazaki arrived leading the second wave. This consisted entirely of bombers, both dive- and level-bombers, since the torpedo-bombers were seen as vulnerable once the element of surprise had been lost – US experience at the Battle of Midway was to prove this view accurate. As it was, most of the 29 aircraft lost on the operation belonged to the second wave, with heavy AA fire from gunners

Taken at the height of the attack, this picture shows shipping on fire and heavy anti-aircraft fire attempting to repel the Japanese strike aircraft. (IWM MH6014)

who 'had got their eye in', and in between the two waves some American fighters which had escaped destruction in the raids on the airfields had managed to get airborne. The second wave was also less successful, as smoke from the many fires obscured the targets. Nevertheless, the dive-bombers successfully attacked the battleship *Nevada*, which was attempting to escape to sea, but failed to sink her and block the harbour mouth before her CO managed to beach her where she would not become an obstacle. Two destroyers and the *Pennsylvania* in dry dock were damaged.

On their return to the carriers, another 15 aircraft were so badly damaged that they had to be pushed over the side.

Fuchida was anxious to mount a second attack after lunch, but Nagumo decided against it, despite Fuchida's protests. He was told abruptly by Nagumo's chief-of-staff, Kusaka, that the objectives of the raid had been met.

Comment

The raid on Pearl Harbor was in many ways a classic bomber operation, with a large number of aircraft first surprising and then overwhelming the defences. Strategically, it was a serious mistake, bringing the USA into the war and ensuring defeat for the Axis powers. Tactically, it was successful up to a point, with accurate bombing and devastating results to the US Pacific Fleet, but it failed to inflict such damage on the shore installations that Pearl Harbor was rendered unusable.

When he heard that a further attack had not been made, Yamamoto knew that Nagumo had bungled the operation. To this day, it remains a mystery why this decision was taken, because Nagumo had expected heavy losses, and the risks of sending a further major raid would have been outweighed by the advantages. The only possible explanation is that he feared being caught by the US carriers, but even so, his forces outnumbered them three to one.

The other mystery is why the Japanese, such accomplished navy men, failed to mine the approaches to Pearl Harbor. Sowing mines in shallow water would have hindered the attempts to clear up the mess and sealed ships in port. Even more important, while they still had the resources, why did the Japanese leave the Panama Canal untouched? A planned operation to attack the canal later in the war using aircraft-carrying submarines never took place, but by then it was too late anyway. At the very least, the approaches to the Panama Canal could have been mined.

JAPAN TASTES DEFEAT: THE BATTLE OF MIDWAY, 3–7 JUNE 1942

At the Battle of the Coral Sea on 7–8 May 1942 the Japanese were still able to claim a victory. The Americans had sunk the light carrier *Shoho* and caused severe damage to the larger modern carrier *Shokaku*, but had lost the *Lexington*, while the *Yorktown* had suffered severe damage. In terms of tonnage lost, the Japanese were the victors. Yet *Shokaku* was to be sorely missed at the Battle of Midway, while the Japanese advance had been stopped and their planned invasion of Port Moresby foiled.

The next step for the Japanese was to occupy Midway Island, a controversial plan among the planners at the Japanese Imperial Headquarters in Tokyo, where many favoured moves which would isolate Australia from the USA. The attraction of Midway was that it would help to provide a defensive ring, a move forced upon the Japanese by the 'Doolittle' raid, OPERATION SHANGRI-LA, in which 16 North American B-25 Mitchell twin-engined bombers had been launched from the aircraft carrier *Hornet* on 18 April to bomb several Japanese cities, including Tokyo. Little damage had been done, but the impact on Japanese confidence had been great. Concern over the protection of the Emperor lay behind many operational planning decisions from this time onwards.

At the time of Pearl Harbor, Shokaku was one of Japan's most modern aircraft carriers. (IWM MH5931)

Midway was also a belated attempt to destroy the US Pacific Fleet, which the Japanese planned to lure beyond the atoll, where it could be destroyed. Once again, Nagumo was to be in command of the First Air Fleet, which would cover the landings, while the assault fleet also had a carrier of its own, the *Zuiho*. Adm Yamamoto was to be in overall command, aboard the battleship *Yamato*, although this was to be 300 miles behind the carrier force with the main force of battleships, cruisers and destroyers, and the light carrier *Hosho*. Apart from the need for the operation, there were other areas of disagreement among the Japanese. Nagumo felt that his ships needed to be refitted, while too many experienced aircrew had been taken away for other operations, despite losses having been incurred during operations in the Indian Ocean and in the Battle of the Coral Sea. Fuchida, leader of the attack on Pearl Harbor, also wanted the aircraft carriers to operate as a single force, with the battleships and cruisers, rather than have the available forces divided.

Unknown to the Japanese, the Americans had already broken their codes and were well aware of Japanese plans.

Ships and Aircraft

A force of six aircraft carriers was assembled for the operation, the last time the Japanese would be able to assemble such a powerful force. Four of the ships had taken part in the attack on Pearl Harbor, *Akagi*, *Kaga*, *Hiryu* and *Soryu*. These formed the main striking force under Nagumo. The battle fleet was supported by the small *Hosho*, Japan's first aircraft carrier, just 7,470 tons, converted from an oil tanker while still on the slipway. The *Zuiho*, supporting the assault force, was a converted submarine tender, displacing 11,262 tons, with a narrow beam and a maximum speed of no more than 28 kt.

The Japanese were using the same attack aircraft types as at Pearl Harbor (see p. 86).

US aircraft for attack duties consisted of two main types, the Douglas SBD Dauntless series of dive-bombers and reconnaissance aircraft, and the Douglas TBD Devastator, which could operate as a bomber or as a torpedo-plane.

The Dauntless was in US Navy and US Marine Corps service from 1940 until the end of the war in 1945. The standard US Navy production machine on the outbreak of war was the SBD-3, with a 1,000 hp Wright R-1820 radial engine powering the low-wing monoplane. The Dauntless had a retractable undercarriage and self-sealing fuel tanks, as well as armour protection. Armament consisted of two .5 in forward firing guns instead of the .3 in weapons used on the USMC SBD-1 and the US Navy's original SBD-2s.

The Devastator had first seen service in 1937, and by the time of the Battle of Midway was already obsolete, even though far more modern than the Royal Navy's Fairey Swordfish. Aptly described as a 'good aircraft kept in service for far too long', the Devastator was a three-seat monoplane powered by a single 850 hp Pratt & Witney R-1830 radial engine, which enabled it to carry either a 1,000 lb bomb or a torpedo of similar weight. Its continued presence in US Navy service was due to the prevailing philosophy that dive-bombing should be augmented by torpedo-bombing, and this combination had already proved effective at both Taranto and Pearl Harbor.

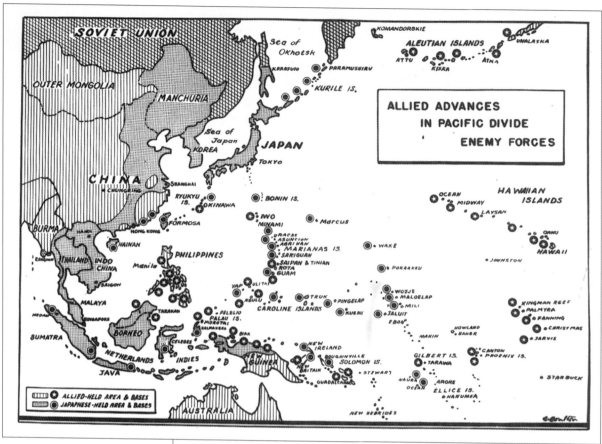

The Japanese advanced rapidly across the Pacific and through South-East Asia, but before long the Allies were fighting back. This map shows the vast distances which had to be covered during the war in the Pacific. ((IWM NYF73462)

The Action

The C-in-C of the US Navy's Pacific Fleet, Adm Chester Nimitz, was aware that the Japanese intended to invade Midway Island in early June, and had time to concentrate the available naval forces to defend the island. The Japanese were expecting a strong defence, and indeed hoped for an all-out decisive battle with the Americans. In an attempt to distract the Americans, the Japanese sent a diversionary force with the carriers *Ryujo* and *Junyo* to attack Dutch Harbor in the Aleutians, close to Alaska, on 3 June. Indeed, that day the main Japanese fleet was located by the Americans, and during the afternoon, USAAF Boeing B-17 Flying Fortresses were sent to bomb the assault fleet, but without success.

Fuchida could not lead the air attacks on Midway because he was in *Akagi*'s sickbay recovering from appendicitis. On 4 June, determined to see his pilots off on their mission even though he was still weak from the operation, Fuchida decided to go to the flight deck. Because the ship was closed up for battle stations, this meant that he had to make his way through ten watertight bulkheads between the sickbay, which was below the waterline, and his cabin, each time unlocking the manhole in the bulkhead by means of a wheel, and then closing it again after he had climbed through. He rested briefly on reaching his cabin, before shaving and putting on his uniform. He then climbed to the control centre before the dive-bombers were ready to take off. Due to his persistence, we have an eye-witness account of life aboard the Japanese carriers that day.

For the Battle of Midway, four Japanese carriers were involved in the main striking force, including the Soryu. *(IWM MH6490)*

Lt Tomonaga took Fuchida's place as leader of the attack. Reconnaissance aircraft had already taken off, and when he saw their search patterns, Fuchida was alarmed to find that large areas of sea would be left uncovered.

The first wave of attack aircraft left the carriers at dawn, with more than a hundred aircraft sent to destroy Midway's defences. While this operation was in progress, a mixed force of US Navy and USAAF shore-based aircraft from Midway found and attacked the Japanese carriers, disrupting the formation of the fleet and strafing and killing a number of crewmen working on the decks. The raid was a costly exercise for the Americans, losing 17 aircraft to AA fire and Japanese Zero fighters scrambled from the carriers.

One USAAF Martin B-26 Marauder missed the *Akagi*'s bridge by some 30 ft, and plunged into the sea. Fuchida, on the flight deck propped up against the island taking notes, exclaimed that this was fun – a view not shared by those around him, who had taken heed of the outcome of the Battle of the Coral Sea.

Meanwhile, Tomonaga's aircraft were inflicting heavy damage on Midway's shore installations, although the airfield and AA installations remained fully operational. Tomonaga radioed a report to this effect to the striking force, and Nagumo decided to send a second wave to maintain the pressure on the defences. This could not be done immediately because the

Another carrier at Midway was the Hiryu, *one of two Japanese carriers with the novel port-side island. (IWM MH5928)*

aircraft left aboard the carriers had been armed with torpedoes for an attack against US warships, and these had to be changed for bombs. While this task was still being completed, a reconnaissance aircraft radioed that it had discovered ten American warships, prompting Nagumo to change his mind, reversing the order. The torpedoes were taken off and the bombs put back on again, while there was a further delay to allow the first wave of aircraft, by now short of fuel, to be recovered.

While they were still waiting for the first wave to return, at 09.00 a reconnaissance aircraft radioed that it had spotted a US aircraft carrier, probably the *Yorktown*. This came as a surprise to the Japanese, who had assumed that there were no US carriers nearby because of the absence of fighters for the earlier attack on the Japanese striking force.

None of the Japanese ships had radar of any kind. The first wave had landed, and the second wave with their torpedoes were ranged on the flight decks ready for take-off when the first wave of US carrier-borne aircraft attacked. Rear Adm (later Vice Adm) Raymond Spruance, in command of the US carriers *Enterprise* and *Hornet*, had put his entire force into the air, while Rear Adm (later Vice Adm) Fletcher sent half of *Yorktown*'s aircraft, making a total of 156 American carrier-borne aircraft on their way to the Japanese striking force.

The first wave consisted of 41 Douglas Devastator torpedo-bombers, of which 35 were quickly shot down by Japanese AA fire and by those

The Douglas Dauntless dive-bomber was the great success of the Battle of Midway.

fighters which managed to get airborne. Whole squadrons virtually disappeared, with all but one aircraft from *Yorktown*'s VT-3 Devastator squadron shot down: many of their crews had neither the time nor the altitude to escape from their low-flying aircraft before they crashed into the sea. The mood aboard the Japanese carriers was one of jubilation, with the confidence lost at the Battle of the Coral Sea suddenly fully restored.

Radar might not have given much warning of the low-flying Devastators, but had it been available, the second wave of Douglas Dauntless dive-bombers would have been detected. While the striking force was still preoccupied with the torpedo-bombers and its fighters were still at sea level, the Dauntlesses approached at 19,000 ft unobserved.

At 10.22 the first of the Douglas SBD Dauntless dive-bombers, each armed with a 1,000 lb bomb, started their near-vertical dives on the unsuspecting carriers.

The *Kaga* was first, taking four direct hits from the twelve 1,000 lb bombs aimed at her. These four were enough, penetrating her flight deck and exploding in her hangars among the parked, fuelled and armed aircraft. The ship was almost immediately abandoned.

The flagship *Akagi* had a near miss, before being struck by two 1,000 lb bombs. Fuchida, sitting taking notes on the *Akagi*'s deck, had seen the first US aircraft diving. He yelled a warning to the command post, and the carrier's guns burst into life. He could see that the first bomb was going to be off-target, but guessed that the following aircraft would see this and adjust its aim. He was right. The first bomb missed the carrier by some 30 ft, but it created a huge geyser of black water which washed over the carrier's bridge, blackening the faces of everyone there.

Fuchida spreadeagled himself on the deck close to the island's superstructure as the second bomb fell, hitting the amidships hangar lift, and smashing through it into the hangar. The third bomb hit the flight deck to port, and smashed through this into the hangar. These hits were serious enough in themselves, but their impact was far worse than it might have been. In their haste to re-arm the aircraft of the second strike with torpedoes, the hangar crew had left the bombs, each of 1,750 lb, in the hangar rather than returning them to the ship's magazine. The US bombs hit stacks of them, setting them off in a chain reaction. On the flight deck, fully armed aircraft, each full of fuel, exploded in flames from the fire and the explosions below, and again a chain reaction occurred as each plane set its neighbour alight. Soon flames were sweeping across the flight deck, while the hangar had become a blazing inferno.

Fuchida went to the briefing room, where he found sailors bringing in the wounded, and amid the confusion he found that no one was moving the casualties to the sickbay. He asked one rescue worker about this, only to be told that the entire ship was on fire and no one could get through. He realized that he had left thirty-one sick comrades in the sickbay that morning, and that these were now hopelessly trapped. He tried to get to his cabin to salvage his personal belongings, but the fire and smoke turned him back.

Fuchida looked to see what was happening to the rest of the striking force. What he saw stopped him dead. Both the *Kaga* and the *Soryu* were huge balls of smoke and flame, although *Hiryu*, some distance ahead of the other carriers, seemed to be untouched. The *Soryu* had received three

A Japanese torpedo-bomber falls victim to heavy anti-aircraft fire before it can reach its target. (IWM NYP11545)

direct hits in a straight line along her crowded flight deck, and a bomb exploding in her hangar turned that into an inferno.

The order was given to abandon the *Akagi*. Nagumo wanted to go down with his flagship, but was persuaded that his duty lay in continuing the battle, and transferred his flag to the light cruiser *Nagara*. Fuchida broke both legs in leaving the *Akagi*, but was rescued and taken into the *Nagara*'s sickbay.

Another witness of the entire action was Ensign George Gray, the only survivor of *Hornet*'s torpedo-bombing squadron, VT-8. He had crashed within the Japanese fighter screen, and was hiding behind a seat cushion which had floated up from his sinking Devastator. He was picked up by a Consolidated Catalina 30 hours later, and described the Japanese carriers as burning 'like blow torches'.[5]

The speed and co-ordination of the attack had been impressive, with the first dive-bomber striking at 10.22, and the entire raid completed just four minutes later.

In a desperate attempt to salvage something from the defeat, Rear Adm Yamaguchi ordered a strike against the *Yorktown*. The aircraft took off at 11.00 from *Hiryu*. Just eight Aichi D3A 'Val' bombers got through the ship's AA fire and fighter screen, but they managed to drop three 500 lb bombs onto the carrier. The first bomb struck the deck among parked aircraft, setting them alight, a second hit the funnel and blew out the fires for five of the six boilers, while the third penetrated three decks and ignited her aviation fuel tanks. Prompt damage control saw the aviation fuel fire smothered with carbon dioxide, while the magazines were flooded as a precaution against the intense heat of the fire.

Early in the afternoon, *Hiryu* sent another wave of aircraft to attack the *Yorktown*. This was another much-reduced force, with just ten Nakajima B5N Kates and six escorting fighters. As soon as the aircraft were sighted, *Yorktown* stopped refuelling her aircraft, and as a further safety measure, drained her aviation fuel system. This meant that her fighter defences were dependent on just six Grumman F4F Wildcats on standby, with whatever fuel was left in their tanks. These aircraft managed to shoot down five of the torpedo planes, but four got within dropping range. The crippled ship could not manoeuvre easily, but she avoided two torpedoes before another two hit her on the port side. The ship was also struck by three bombs.

While her fighters landed on the *Enterprise*, the order was given to abandon the *Yorktown*.

Tomonaga had survived the sinking of the *Akagi* to lead the afternoon attack on the *Yorktown*. Yamaguchi was under the mistaken impression that the morning and afternoon attacks had been against two different carriers, and, believing that there were only two US carriers in the Pacific, he thought that the Americans were now without a strike capability. He organized a final all-out attack on the US fleet with aircraft from the other carriers which the *Hiryu* had recovered. As the aircraft were ranged ready to take off, Dauntless dive-bombers from the *Enterprise* and *Hornet* attacked, with four bombs hitting the desperately manoeuvring carrier, while there were another four near misses, so that aviation fuel fires were soon blazing on her flight and hangar decks.

Late that afternoon the abandoned *Soryu* blew up, about 190 miles north-west of Midway, to be followed fifteen minutes later by the *Kaga*, 40 miles away, as the flames reached her magazines. The *Akagi* was sunk in a torpedo attack by Japanese destroyers at dawn the following day. A destroyer torpedo attack on *Hiryu* was unsuccessful, as was an attack by B-17s from Midway, but the ship finally sank at 09.00, taking her captain and Yamaguchi with her. In all, the Japanese had lost 4 aircraft carriers, 258 aircraft and 2,280 men. The Aleutian raiding force was too far away to help.

Both sides incurred losses, especially the Japanese. This is Hiryu, with much of her flight deck blown away. The port-side island can be clearly seen. (IWM MH6492)

The *Yorktown*, badly crippled, was under escort by a destroyer on 7 June when the Japanese submarine *I-168* found them and sank both ships with her torpedoes.

Yamamoto, far away from the action, abandoned the operation, withdrawing westwards. Two heavy cruisers from the assault group collided at sea and fell behind the rest of the retreating Japanese fleet. On 6 June, aircraft from the *Enterprise* and *Hornet* attacked the two cruisers and sank one, the *Mikuma*, as well as severely damaging the *Mogami*, the other cruiser, and two escorting destroyers.

Comment

Just six months after starting the Pacific War the Japanese had lost their advantage, largely because they failed to take notice of the advice of

Yorktown was badly damaged, despite heavy anti-aircraft fire. She was eventually sunk by a Japanese submarine. (IWM OEM3672)

experienced naval airmen. Reconnaissance and intelligence were also poor. They had spent their energies after Pearl Harbor seizing territory, rather than destroying the US fleet, the one big obstacle between Japan and that country's ambitions.

Having decided to press ahead with the operation, they failed to concentrate their forces, since the combined firepower of Yamamoto's battleships and cruisers would have made the American dive-bombing attacks that much more difficult. Nagumo's indecision was another contributory factor in the eventual defeat. Had the aircraft of the second wave been allowed to keep their torpedoes, they could have been launched earlier, and there would not have been bombs lying around in the hangars.

The Japanese were now to suffer the consequences of their lack of organized shipbuilding and aircraft production, and of course aircrew training, with the war in mind. The starting date for the war was in their hands, and it can only be assumed that they reacted prematurely with their attack on Pearl Harbor.

BOMBING THE USA, 9 AND 29 SEPTEMBER 1942

With the exception of the Aleutian operation, designed to distract attention from the operation to seize Midway Island, the Japanese aircraft carrier force did not even get close to the US mainland. The USA was

*Crewmen found it increasingly
difficult to maintain their footing as
Yorktown listed heavily to port.
(IWM OEM3673)*

outside the range of land-based Japanese bombers, just as the Japanese
home islands were outside the range of US land-based bombers until the
closing stages of the war, by which time bases had been made available as
Japanese-held territory fell to the US advance across the Pacific.

A raid on the mainland of the United States would have been a daring
operation for the carriers, especially since it would have had to come after
Pearl Harbor, that supposed decisive stroke which would give Japan
breathing space in which to achieve its immediate wartime objectives.
Generally, it is believed that the mainland United States was not attacked
during the Second World War, but this is not strictly true. The Japanese
had a fleet of submarines capable of carrying one, sometimes two, aircraft
each, and it was these which they used for a raid on the US mainland.

Ships and Aircraft

The *I-25* was one of a small fleet of Japanese submarines capable of
carrying just one aircraft, a seaplane, which was housed in an extension to
the conning tower, and launched down rails laid on top of the hull.
Because of the lack of steam, the catapult relied on a rocket-driven shuttle.
There was also a small crane to hoist the seaplane back on board after its
flight.

The Yokosuka E14Y1 seaplane was a small single-engined biplane with
folding wings.

The Japanese made little use of their fleet of aircraft-carrying submarines, even though they had amassed quite a sizeable fleet. Although an attack on the Panama Canal was planned, it never took place and the two raids on the forests of Oregon seem to have been the only action. These submarines are moored alongside the tender Proteus *in Tokyo Bay. (IWM MH6694)*

The Action

The idea of a small-scale air campaign against the USA was the idea of a young Japanese naval officer, Fujita. His idea of bombing the vast forests on the west coast to start large-scale forest fires was approved by Adm Yamamoto, who had seen a report from the former Japanese Consul in Seattle, arguing that this would be the best way to alarm the Americans.

The coast of Oregon was chosen, not only because of the existence of substantial areas of forest, but also because it was well away from the major naval base at San Diego in California.

As with the raid on Pearl Harbor, the submarine *I-25* was able to approach the flying-off position through an area of bad weather. The submarine approached close to the coast of Oregon, and those aboard were able to see the coastline before surfacing.

Fujita, the pilot, recalled afterwards:

After putting on my flying suit I made my last minute preparations. I put a couple of locks of my hair, some finger-nail clippings and my will into a small wooden box. In case I did not return . . . these 'remains' would be delivered to my wife. Now everything was ready, my observer Okuda was in the plane and the catapult was lit. We zoomed over the Cape Blanco lighthouse toward the coast and then turned north-east towards the target zone. The sun bathed the eastern sky in red gold light. When we had travelled about 42 miles, I ordered Okuda to drop the first bomb over the huge forests. We flew another nine miles eastward and let loose the second bomb. When we reached Cape Blanco again, we veered south-west. Suddenly I saw two freighters. We flew directly over the water's surface to avoid detection. A couple of minutes later we were concealed by the skyline. Only then did we veer off to look for our submarine. Soon we were back on board.[6]

A second raid was made at night on 29 September, again bombing forests. No further raids were made because of bad weather.

Comment

This was a brave but futile attempt to undermine US morale. The forests obviously didn't catch fire, and after the bad weather were probably too damp to do so. Forest fires often happen due to negligence or natural causes in extremely dry weather, and given the scale of the operation, one can only assume that even if a major fire had started, it is unlikely anyone would have known it was the work of the Japanese.

Given the way the war was developing, it seems incredible that a more ambitious raid on, for example, the Boeing plant outside Seattle wasn't considered, although this would have required a far heavier raid than a submarine with a single aircraft could have mounted. Plans for a raid on the Panama Canal using aircraft launched from submarines were made late in the war, but never put into effect.

KAMIKAZE: THE MANNED MISSILE, OCTOBER 1944–AUGUST 1945

After the Battle of Midway the situation for the Japanese worsened. The war was far from over, but there could be no doubt that they were losing it to the superior tactics and strategies, military and industrial strength of the Americans, who also had one other significant advantage: the ability to innovate and to develop newer and better aircraft and weapons systems.

The steady advance by US forces across the Pacific really started in late 1943. By this time, new ships and aircraft were being delivered in quantity, along with a steady stream of new pilots. It would be wrong to suggest that naval air power alone was responsible for the US forces' success. There was much hard fighting ashore as soldiers and marines attempted to wrest territory from an enemy whose resistance was fanatical, even to the extent of committing suicide or shooting in the back those, including

As the war progressed, aircraft such as this Curtiss Helldiver dive-bomber joined the USN. (FAAM US MIL/199)

civilians, who attempted to surrender. The Japanese lacked good anti-tank weapons, so soldiers would strap on a satchel of explosives before throwing themselves under an advancing tank.

The Battle of Leyte Gulf in October 1944 was the biggest naval battle in history, a desperate attempt by the Japanese to make use of that wasting asset, their large surface fleet. They failed, losing even more carriers, while their battleships engaged the US escort carriers covering the landings, and then withdrew without inflicting serious damage.

At sea, the Americans were also demonstrating determination and professionalism in their submarine campaign against the Japanese. The Japanese failed to make proper use of their submarine resources, and also failed to institute a proper convoy system for their long lines of communication. As the war progressed, US submarine commanders not only patrolled the Pacific with increasing freedom, they also moved into Japanese coastal waters and even the inland sea, to the extent that the carrier *Shinano*, converted from the third and last giant battleship of the Yamato class, was sunk by the submarine *Archerfish* before the carrier could even enter service. The ship would have been a substantial addition to the fast-diminishing Japanese carrier fleet.

Accounts of the original *kamikaze* vary, not because of historical inaccuracy, but because several people had the same idea at around the same time, and there were variations on the theme. Today, the term is usually regarded as meaning suicide attacks by manned aircraft, but there were *kamikaze* troops and marine craft as well, while the usual means of destroying the high-flying Boeing B-17 Flying Fortress and B-29 Superfortress bombers was 'ramming' – in effect *kamikaze* fighter defences. This was necessary because the Japanese lacked aircraft capable of climbing to the bombers' altitude unless all their armament was stripped out to reduce weight.

The concept of suicide attacks had long been part of Japanese culture. One of the first to raise the matter was Adm Arima, but the idea was rejected by his superiors at first. Another advocate was Ensign Shoichi Ota of the Naval Air Technical Depot, who designed a human bomb following the invasion of the Marianas by US forces. Ota chose the name *Oka* for his weapon when it first appeared in September 1944, the Japanese word for cherry blossom, which falls at the height of its beauty, as the young warrior dying in battle. After toying with various other names for the project, including a 'Hornet' Corps, the term *kamikaze* later became widely used, the original *kamikaze* being the divine wind which had sprung up to prevent Japan being invaded by the Mongol emperor Khublai Khan in 1274.

Mitsuo Fuchida had the concept drawn to his attention by Adm Toyoda, who had been passed the idea from a Capt Eichiro Jo, with the endorsement of his superior, Adm Jisaburo Ozawa. Fuchida objected to the concept for two reasons. The first was that he felt that the young and inexperienced pilots likely to be assigned to the operation would lack a true strategic sense and would be unable to handle the project effectively. The second was that small numbers of aircraft on a single operation would be unlikely to inflict significant damage on the enemy, while they would be vulnerable to the defences of a substantial fleet. This was a good point, since the progress of the war on all fronts had shown that massed air attack was most likely to succeed, overwhelming the defences and dividing the enemy's fire.

The Aircraft

A wide variety of aircraft types were used on *kamikaze* missions, including the Mitsubishi Zero fighter, which could carry a 500 lb bomb. Japanese light bombers, both carrier-borne and land-based, were also pressed into service.

There was also the *Oka* rocket bomb already mentioned, a small rocket-powered aircraft which was carried close to the target by a larger aircraft, such as the twin-engined 'Betty' bomber, and could then fly for up to 11 miles on its five small rockets, before finally gliding or diving onto its target with a its 2,600 lb warload. The aircraft was of flimsy construction, and the need to be carried so close to the target was a major drawback, for the larger and therefore much less manoeuvrable 'mother' aircraft had to be able to get past US fighter defences. These were generally stationed some miles out from the target, not just to intercept Japanese attacks, but to do so while well clear of the increasingly accurate curtain of fire thrown up by the fleet's AA defences.

The Action

In many cases the *kamikazes* were squandered. As Fuchida had predicted, the pilots, mainly senior ratings and junior officers, usually went for escort carriers and destroyers, or a single *kamikaze* would aim at a large aircraft carrier, without causing serious damage. The preferred aiming point for the *kamikaze* attacks on the larger carriers seems to have been the join between the flight deck and the island, where they caused heavy casualties, but had they aimed for the hangar lifts, even on the armoured British carriers, they would have caused more damage. A massed *kamikaze* attack on the troop transports prior to an invasion would also have been more effective. Yet, when they did hurl themselves into troop transports, as at Okinawa, they were too late: the ships were empty.

The type of attack varied. If the *kamikaze* managed to evade the fighter defences, he had a choice. He could make a high-altitude attack from as high as 20,000 ft, in which case the aircraft could not dive at a very high angle of attack without speed and handling difficulties making accuracy difficult. Alternatively, he could dive at a high angle of attack from 3,000 ft or less, facing heavy and accurate AA fire. The manned suicide aircraft were not as accurate as might be imagined, and many were shot down or crashed on to their target in flames, their pilots either dead or painfully wounded.

The bombs carried by the *kamikaze* aircraft often failed to explode, usually because the pilots forgot to prime the weapon before making their final run towards the target. This need for priming was a refinement introduced after early missions had left pilots who hadn't found a suitable target to either crash their aircraft into the sea, or attempt to land back at their base with a live bomb under the aircraft.

Contrary to popular belief, there was feedback about the success of the missions, but this also served to mislead. True, the *kamikazes* died, but they were usually escorted by fighters which were also expected to report back. Whether or not the fighters were so heavily engaged fending off British and US fighters that they did not see what happened, or there was a subconscious desire to boost the reputation of those who had died, the one consistent theme from the escorts was exaggeration of the *kamikaze* successes. Poor ship recognition could also have been a factor, tankers often being mistaken for escort carriers.

The Japanese boasted that every *kamikaze* sank a ship, but this was an exaggeration. Even so, they were successful enough to cause the US Navy serious concern. At Leyte four escort carriers, or CVEs, were damaged and another, the *St Lo*, sunk. Overall, about 1 in 4 *kamikazes* inflicted damage and 1 in 33 sank its target.

In November 1944, when the US Third Fleet was operating east of the Philippines, *kamikaze* attacks sank a destroyer and damaged the aircraft carriers *Essex*, *Franklin*, *Hancock*, *Intrepid* and *Lexington*, as well as two light carriers, *Belleau Wood* and *Cabot*.

The worst day was 25 November, when the attacks reached a peak, 25 aircraft being deployed from five bases, escorted by 17 fighters. Although *Hancock*'s AA gunners shot down a *kamikaze*, burning debris struck the deck and started fires. *Intrepid* was hit by two *kamikazes* and put out of action, while *Cabot* was hit by one and damaged by another, which crashed into the sea close to the ship after being shot down. *Essex* had a narrow escape when the bomb on the *kamikaze* which crashed into her flight deck failed to explode.

In January 1945, off Luzon, the CVE *Ommaney Bay* was sunk, and another 3 CVEs were damaged, as well as 2 battleships and 4 cruisers. On 21 February, off Iwo Jima, the CVE *Bismarck Sea* was sunk, and the carrier *Saratoga* was hit six times, saved only after a struggle by her crew.

The British armoured carriers fared much better than the US warships, with their wooden flight decks. On 4 May *Formidable* was attacked by a *kamikaze* off Miyako in the Sakishima Gunto. Geoffrey Brooke was the Ship's Fire and Crash Officer:

Opposite: Faced with mounting losses, the Japanese resorted to the use of kamikaze *attacks. This sequence of pictures shows a* kamikaze *attack on the Royal Navy's carrier* Formidable, *with the aircraft about to strike, exploding on impact, the ship damaged and on fire, and then covered in smoke.* Formidable *survived, thanks to her armoured deck. (FAAM CARS F/127-30)*

The scene on Formidable's *deck after the fires had been extinguished following the attack of 4 May 1945. (FAAM CARS F/36)*

It was a grim sight. At first I thought that the *kamikaze* had hit the island and those on the bridge must be killed. Fires were blazing around several piles of wreckage on deck and a lift aft of the island and clouds of black smoke billowed far above the ship. Much of the smoke came from fires on deck, but as much seemed to be issuing from the funnel, which gave the impression of damage deep below decks.[7]

Five days later, on 9 May, *Formidable* was hit again, by another *kamikaze* which hit the after end of the flight deck and ploughed into the aircraft ranged there. A rivet was blown out of the deck and burning petrol poured into the hangar, where the fire could only be extinguished by spraying, with adverse effects even on those aircraft not on fire. In all, 7 aircraft were lost on deck and another 12 in the hangar, leaving the ship with just 4 bombers and 11 fighters.

Even these losses didn't compare with the normal hazards of life at sea. On 18 May an armourer working on a Corsair in the hangar failed to notice that the aircraft's guns were still armed. He accidentally fired the guns into a parked Avenger, which blew up and set off yet another fierce fire, destroying 30 aircraft, yet the ship was fully operational again by evening.

One US observer took a relaxed view of life aboard the British carriers: 'When a *kamikaze* hits a US carrier, it's six months repair at Pearl. In a Limey carrier, it's a case of "Sweepers, man your brooms!"'[8]

The Japanese viewpoint was different. Ryuji Nagatsuka trained as a pilot with the Japanese Army Air Force during the Second World War, starting his training after the massive early defeats suffered by the Japanese. After training, initially he was assigned to the 4th Sqn base at Ozuki, flying the Ki-45 Kais twin-engined fighter (also known as the *Toryu*, meaning 'slayer of the dragon'), which were designed to counter the high-flying Boeing B-29 Superfortress,

On 31 March 1945 Nagatsuka and his fellow pilots were ordered to appear before their CO, Commandant Suenaga:

'As you know,' he said at last in a grave voice, 'the army is short of pilots, petrol, planes and ammunition . . . in fact everything! We find ourselves at an impasse. There is just one last resort left to us: to crash on the decks of enemy aircraft carriers, as your comrades have done before you . . . I am compelled to ask you . . . to . . . to undertake this mission.'

It was an effort for him to bring out this phrase, which he hastily corrected:

'But of course you are free to choose. I will give you twenty-four hours to think it over.'[9]

Nagatsuka and his fellow cadets reckoned that they had a month to live while they were trained for their final mission. They were willing to become *kamikazes*, although he apparently had reservations. In the event, they didn't wait twenty-four hours, but instead went to see the Commandant immediately after breakfast the following morning. Their new group was officially named *Kikusui* group of the *Jun-no* Special Attack Corps, *Kikusui* denoting 'chrysanthemums floating on a river', and *Jun-no* 'the sacrifice to the Emperor'. There were 22 pilots in his unit.

Five days later there was another kamikaze *attack on* Formidable, *and again, she survived. (FAAM CARS F/39)*

Many kamikaze *aircraft never reached their target, or were already on fire as they reached it, succumbing to fighter patrols or to intense anti-aircraft fire, as with this Yokosuka D4Y3A Suisei, or Comet. (IWM HU63019)*

Fuel shortages meant that the training took more than two months, during which the cadets were all promoted to flying officer, and in early June, Nagatsuka went on leave to see his parents. Returning to his unit on 28 June, they were all told that they would be making their attack the following morning. He promptly went to write to his parents, breaking the news that he was a suicide pilot: 'My dear parents, I shall depart this life at 07.00 hours on the twenty-ninth of June, 1945. My whole being is permeated by your tremendous affection, down to the last tiny hair . . .'.[10]

The following morning, at 04.30, he started his last breakfast, a bowl of *sekihan*, a cup of soup, a little dried fish and an egg. After the briefing at 05.30, they were given a glass of sake, having just heard that four aircraft were unserviceable, so that the number of *kamikazes* would be just 18. They sang a solemn song. By 06.50 they were flying, with Nagatsuka flying the fourth plane in the first formation, in poor visibility. At 07.05, their leader made them turn back: the poor visibility meant that finding a target was impossible. Although they only had enough fuel for the outward flight, by careful handling of the aircraft, the first and second formations managed to return to their base.

At first, the Commandant seemed to accept that they were unlucky, but the non-appearance of the third section persuaded him that they had carried out a raid, and that those who returned were guilty of cowardice, so they were arrested. They were eventually offered fuel at the end of July with a chance to redeem themselves, although the Allied fleets were still out of range. As an alternative, Nagatsuka and his comrades were told that they were to ram US fighters. Delay followed delay, and they did not become airborne until 12 August, when their attempts to ram the US fighters were overtaken when the formation was attacked by Grumman naval fighters. Instead of ramming US fighters, Nagatsuka was shot down by one.

He heard the news of Japan's surrender while still in hospital.

The Japanese Oka, *or Cherry Blossom, was a purpose-built suicide weapon, which had to be carried close to the target by a bomber.*

Comment

The *kamikaze* campaign was both wasteful and inhuman. It did nothing to prevent the Japanese defeat, and indeed, it may have accelerated the process through denying the Japanese armed forces a pool of pilots of growing experience. The idea was born out of desperation, and at first alarmed the Americans, until they realized that their defences were capable of handling the attacks.

Despite the massed air attack at Pearl Harbor and elsewhere, the Imperial Japanese Navy showed little sign of appreciating the significance of this tactic as the war progressed, possibly due to manpower and equipment shortages.

SAFETY IN NUMBERS

O n 23 February 1942 Air Chief Marshal Sir Arthur 'Bomber' Harris took over as C-in-C RAF Bomber Command, replacing ACM Sir Richard Peirse, who moved first to the Far East and then, as the Japanese advanced rapidly, became Air Officer in Command, India.

Harris, whom we came across earlier as a young officer in Mesopotamia, had to fight many battles, if not for the survival of Bomber Command, at least for its status and prominence in the war effort. The other services were jealous of the resources being demanded by Bomber Command, lobbying for more tactical air support, or even to have the resources and manpower diverted to other needs.

The attitude of the other services was not altogether surprising. Bomber Command's losses and the early lack of impact on the enemy encouraged some to look for other ways of fighting the war. Harris was a proponent of massed bomber raids, and it was to be his idea that the RAF should mount the large 'Thousand Bomber Raids', even demanding that aircraft should be diverted from the Operational Training Units and Coastal

While the Führer himself never visited the scenes of air raids, Joseph Goebbels and Albert Speer, the Armaments Minister, did. Here is Goebbels in the Rhineland, seeing the devastation and learning of plans for reconstruction. (IWM HU40289)

Command to make up the numbers. This upset the Admiralty, which counted on RAF Coastal Command to help counter the German submarine menace, which was at its peak during 1942.

For his part Harris was blind to the needs and achievements of the other services. The effect on Britain – and indeed, on his own part of the RAF – of a complete cessation of fuel supplies was lost upon him. He wanted all bomber aircraft returned to Bomber Command, even those in North Africa, 'once the current situation had stabilized', ignoring the fact that Rommel was about to take Tobruk and that the Eighth Army was falling back towards Cairo and the Suez Canal. In a paper for the War Cabinet submitted on 28 June 1942, he posed the questions:

What shouts of victory would arise if a Commando wrecked the entire Renault factory in a night, with a loss of seven men! What credible assumptions of an early end to the war would follow upon the destruction of a third of Cologne in an hour and a half by some swift-moving mechanised force which with but 200 casualties withdrew and was ready to repeat the operation 24 hours later! What acclaim would greet the virtual destruction of Rostok and the Heinkel main and subsidiary factories by a Naval bombardment! All this and more has been achieved by Bomber Command: yet there are many who still avert their gaze, pass on the other side, and question whether the 30 squadrons of night bombers make any worth-while contribution to the war . . . The Army fights half-a-dozen battles a year. The Navy half-a-dozen a war. But poor Bomber Command! Every night that the weather gives us a breather even though our monthly sortie ration is always attained, every night that for such reasons we fail to stage and win a major battle, the critics rise in their wrath and accuse us of doing nothing yet again![1]

There was much truth in his comments about Bomber Command's successes, but the comments about both the other services were unfair: the Royal Navy had to fight to protect the convoys in fair weather or foul. Most nations seem to suffer from this bitter division between the fighting services – and those who have tried to establish a unified defence force have always failed. All too often, regardless of the service, senior officers, who should take a wider perspective, show themselves to be blinkered. Nevertheless, it is only fair to point out that much of this may have been a war-weary reaction to too much harping criticism – a reaction to the ill-informed and cruel comments of others.

THE BATTLE FOR ACCURACY: THE PATHFINDERS

Even as the numbers built up and more reliable and heavier aircraft replaced the unsatisfactory earlier types left over from peacetime, the RAF still had great difficulty in ensuring that targets were hit. Navigation was one problem, good bomb-aiming was another. Many aircrew felt that a specialized target-finding and marking force was the answer, and some had said so to Mr Justice Singleton when he prepared his report on bomber operations.

The idea eventually found adherents in the Air Ministry, at least by March 1942, when the Deputy Director of Bombing Operations, Gp Capt (later Air Cdre) Sidney Bufton, wrote to Harris with the proposal that six squadrons should be specially selected for this task. Although he discussed this with his group commanders, Harris was against the idea, believing that the creation of an élite force within Bomber Command would have an adverse effect on morale in the other squadrons. As a compromise, he suggested that each month the squadrons with the best post-raid bombing photographs would become the marker force for the next month, thus introducing healthy competition and fairness. Eventually, his own concern over accuracy and the pressure of the RAF's own overall chief, Marshal of the Royal Air Force Lord Portal, who supported Bufton's ideas, meant that he had to give way.

In this way the Pathfinder concept was eventually born, although Harris still had objections, not least because the proposed force would be taking a fifth of Bomber Command's establishment of 30 squadrons. A compromise to allay the fears of the bomber groups over losing their best crews to the Pathfinders was to allow each group to nominate a squadron. The new force formally came into being on 11 August 1942.

AIDS TO ACCURACY

The force came into existence at a time when Gee (see p. 76) had almost outlived its usefulness. In any case, many of the more experienced crews believed that Gee was only useful in the hands of an experienced navigator with special training. Two new aids were almost ready for service. While these were awaited, the Pathfinders were entirely dependent on their own abilities, and Gee, to provide the guidance which their comrades expected.

The first of these was Oboe, which was the British equivalent of the Lorenz beams used by the Germans in 1940, which the British had eventually been able to 'bend'. In Oboe, two ground stations were used, one being the 'cat', with the aircraft flying on a route which was in effect circular, enabling the aircraft to operate at a constant fixed range from the 'cat' station's audible signal. The 'mouse' station gave the signal for the aircraft to bomb the target.

Stirlings of 7 and 15 Sqns used the system for raids on the two German warships *Scharnhorst* and *Gneisenau* at Brest in December 1941, but while the early results were promising, the equipment was not ready for service until the end of 1942. The system was sensitive to jamming and its range could only be extended by aircraft flying higher, which meant that over the Ruhr, bombers would have to fly at 28,000 ft, which was beyond the capabilities of any bomber type with a worthwhile bombload at the time. The other major problem with the equipment was that any one 'cat' and 'mouse' could only control one bomber at a time.

Far more promising was H2S, a downwards-pointing rotating radar transmitter which scanned the ground over which the aircraft was being flown, changes in terrain being observable on a cathode ray tube. In this way, the navigator could detect the change from open country to a built-up area, but it was most effective when there was a sharp contrast, as occurred between water and a built-up area, in docks, for example. In the hands of a specially trained operator, H2S could be used for both navigation and bomb-aiming. Although the technique had been known as early as 1937, development had been shelved while priority was given to defensive radars. Although it had a range of 40 miles, one disadvantage was that the radar signals could be picked up by the Germans, making interception of the bombers by night-fighters easier. There was another snag: H2S had been developed for Coastal Command, and a wrangle broke out between its AOC, ACM Joubert de la Ferté, and Harris, as the former sought 200 sets by Christmas 1942, rather than having to wait until June 1943.

THE AMERICANS ARRIVE

The USA entered the Second World War following Pearl Harbor. Inevitably, it took time for forces to be deployed to Europe, and while the USAAF's bomber units were forming, supplies of equipment to the RAF were, of necessity, much reduced. Nevertheless, the combined force of the RAF and USAAF would provide an unbeatable threat to the Luftwaffe, and allow fresh initiatives to be taken, in the air as well as on the ground and at sea.

The first operational sortie for the Americans was in a joint raid with the RAF on 4 July 1942, when six Boston medium bombers of the 15th Bombardment Sqn joined six of the RAF's 226 Sqn on a raid against airfields in the Netherlands. One of the RAF's aircraft and two of the USAAF's failed to return. More than a month was to pass before the first official operational sortie by the US Eighth Army Air Force, when 12 Boeing B-17E Flying Fortresses of the 97th Bombardment Group, on this occasion personally commanded by Brig Gen Ira C. Eaker, made a daylight raid on the railway marshalling yards at Sotteville-les-Rouen. Another six B-17Es made a diversionary sweep, to confuse the defending forces, and the target's proximity to the Channel coast meant that for once, at this early stage in the US involvement in the war in Europe, a fighter escort could be provided by RAF Spitfires. All the aircraft returned safely after hitting the target with reasonable accuracy, which boded well for US involvement in the European theatre.

Over the weeks which followed, the USAAF made a further ten daylight raids, all with a reasonable degree of success and with the loss of just two aircraft. The first raid on Germany itself followed on 27 January 1943. While daylight raids meant that accuracy in navigation and bomb-aiming should be easier than at night, even allowing for the much larger defending fighter formations, there was one problem. The USAAF aircraft were using the Norden bombsight, which had performed well on tests in the deserts of North America, with clear skies and low humidity, but as the RAF had already discovered, was not so effective in the hazy skies of northern Europe.

The US build-up at airfields in the UK for operations in northern Europe seemed to be slower than expected, because this was far from being the sole theatre of war for the USA. Apart from the obvious demands of the war in the Pacific, although the Japanese had already lost any hope of victory even at this early stage, more than 800 British and US aircraft were needed for OPERATION TORCH, the Allied invasion of North Africa in November 1942, and for the campaigns which would follow this, culminating with the invasions of first Sicily and then mainland Italy. These delays were frustrating for Harris, who believed that if he could send '1,000 bombers over Germany every night, it would end the war by autumn'.[2] He pressed for a combined RAF/USAAF force of 3,000 bombers to be established.

By late 1942 RAF Bomber Command was growing rapidly in strength and experience. The introduction of the Pathfinders, under Gp Capt (later AVM) Donald Bennett, had contributed to greater accuracy. A true heavy bomber force had been created through the introduction to service of the Short Stirling and the still more potent Handley Page Halifax and Avro Lancaster four-engined aircraft. The best of these was the Lancaster. Bomb sizes had increased, with first the 4,000 lb Cookie and then the 8,000 lb Double Cookie. Larger bombs obviously caused far more damage, especially to hardened targets, but they also made accuracy even more important, for as one pilot put it: 'That's the worst of one big bomb; you go a long way to do your best; then you miss; then you have a five hours' bind on the way home. It is an infuriating business.'[3]

THE AIRCRAFT: ARRIVAL OF THE HEAVY BOMBERS

The aircraft used on the main heavy bomber raids remained much the same throughout the remainder of the war – the Short Stirling, Handley Page Halifax and Avro Lancaster.

The Short Stirling was the first British four-engined heavy bomber, making its first flight in 1939, and entering RAF service in 1940. It used four 1,600 hp Bristol Hercules radial engines, giving it a maximum speed of 280 mph and a bombload of up to eight tons. Its weakness was the position of the wing, which meant that the bomb bay was split into two, and when 4,000 lb Cookie bombs became available, the Stirling could not handle them.

More successful (after its initial teething problems) was the Handley Page Halifax. Another four-engined bomber, early versions used four 1,280 hp Rolls-Royce Merlin engines, but later models used Bristol Hercules radial engines. The maximum speed was 300 mph, and the aircraft had a range of up to 2,000 miles.

John Hudson was a Master Bomber. A former peacetime regular RAF pilot, he was one of the few able to contribute great experience to the rapidly expanded Bomber Command once war broke out. Even a pilot with his skill found some aircraft trickier than others. He didn't like the early Halifaxes:

As soon as he had bombed the average pilot, being harassed by flak all over the place, used to put 'em straight over into a steep diving turn, one way or the other, which was the quickest way out of the target area. On the Halifax if you banked over like that, it got steeper and steeper till the thing went over on its back and spun in. They couldn't understand why they were having such heavy losses.

One day a bod got into one of these spins when practising corkscrew evasion and couldn't get out of it. The plane went over and all sorts of queer things started happening. Fortunately he had a bit of height and by juggling the engines, switching some off, trying to boost it up with another

– he didn't know what he was doing – he managed to get out of it. Came back alive and told the tale. So they recalled all the Halifaxes, and if you look at the Mark II or Mark III you find that they've got huge square rudders. But they lost a hell of a lot of aircraft before they found out![4]

Safety was important, since it took eighteen months to train a pilot to a sufficient level of competence to take a Lancaster or other heavy bomber over enemy territory with a chance of returning safely. There were many factors. The first was that aircraft ideally had to cross the enemy coast, littered with AA defences, flying at least at 15,000 ft. This was no problem for a new Lancaster with its standard bombload, which could sometimes reach 22,000 ft, but it could be difficult for an older aircraft or as bombloads increased. Some pilots ditched part of their load. Another technique was for the bombers to rendezvous before crossing the enemy coast, so that a large formation would stream across at the same point, forcing the defences to disperse their fire and making fighter attack difficult because of the danger of collision and the concentrated fire of the bombers' guns.

The best of the three four-engined heavy bombers was the Lancaster, although it had an inauspicious background, having been developed from the Manchester, a twin-engined heavy bomber which had been prone to over-heating problems with its twin 1,760 hp Rolls-Royce Vulture engines. Manchesters were withdrawn from service in 1942, the same year that the Lancaster first flew, using four 1,466 hp Rolls-Royce Merlin engines. The Lancaster I had a bombload of 14,000 lbs, and a maximum speed of more than 300 mph. Almost any size of bomb seemed possible for the Lancaster, and before the war ended, it was carrying first the 12,000 lb 'Tallboy' and then, after some stripping down to reduce weight, the huge 22,000 lb 'Grand Slam' bombs. After modifications, Lancasters of 617 Sqn were able to deploy the huge 'bouncing bombs' used for the raid on the Ruhr dams. More than 7,000 Lancasters were built in the UK and Canada. The aircraft was offered to the USAAF for production under licence in the USA, but it was rejected because it did not have a heavy enough defensive armament for day operations.

Guy Gibson, probably the most famous Lancaster pilot, recalled:

Those who have seen a Lancaster cockpit in the light of the moon, flying just above the earth, will know what I mean when I say that it is very hard to describe. The pilot sits on the left of a raised comfortably padded seat fitted with arm-rests. He usually flies the thing with his left hand, re-setting the gyro and other instruments with his right, but most pilots use both hands when over enemy territory or when the going is rough. You have to be quite strong to fly a Lancaster.[5]

In winter, one of the many advantages of the Lancaster was a reasonably efficient heating system, placed well forward in the aircraft by the wireless operator's position, who was permanently roasted as a result. At the same time, the navigator, further forward, shivered, and not much heat reached the rear gunner, whose position was especially cold if the gunner had cut out a panel of perspex to ensure a clear view at all times. The pilot and flight engineer, sitting together, had the luxury of a window which opened.

Heated suits arrived later in the war, but these didn't always work. It was not unknown for coffee from Thermos flasks to freeze, as did sandwiches and, more seriously, guns.

Baling out was a problem, because parachutes had to be found and put on. Worse still, if the bale-out was over the sea, the gunners had to find their Mae Wests, which were too cumbersome for them to wear while sitting in their cramped turrets. Rear gunners often chose to remove the doors at the back of their turrets to prevent them being trapped while the aircraft made its final plunge earthwards.

The large and lumbering Lancasters had to be thrown about the sky to avoid flak from the ground or, even more lethal, an attacking fighter. The ability to send the aircraft into a corkscrew dive to starboard or port, or to side-slip, was vital. If the pilot couldn't see what was happening, the gunners, either the rear or the mid-upper, would have to shout instructions. For this reason, the rear gunner was often the first target for a fighter pilot. A pilot who was concerned that his aircraft might break up was almost certain to be shot down, and generally, Lancasters didn't break up unless they had taken heavy battle damage.

Baling out was a hazard in itself. It is generally believed that the crew of a damaged aircraft had a 1 in 5 chance of getting out alive. The aircraft would probably be damaged and filled with smoke, and perhaps flames as well, possibly out of control despite the valiant efforts of its pilot. The crew had to extricate themselves from whichever position they had jammed themselves into, find their parachutes and put them on, find the escape hatch and then jettison it, possibly while wounded themselves. Sometimes they could spare a hand or an arm to help a wounded comrade, sometimes they couldn't reach them through smoke and flames. Once out, there was danger from ground fire or other aircraft. Most crews tried to avoid baling out over a target zone for fear of being attacked and even murdered by angry civilians or troops, or for fear of being sucked into the flames of a firestorm.

Incredibly, a small number managed to carry civilian clothes with them for an attempt to evade capture. If shot down over occupied territory rather than Germany itself, the chances of making a successful home run were reasonably good, provided the airman could evade capture during the first few hours after baling out.

START OF THE HEAVY BOMBER OFFENSIVE: DAYLIGHT RAID ON AUGSBURG, 17 APRIL 1942

While the RAF was committed to night-bombing raids, there were exceptions to this policy from time to time. One reason for this was the need for precision bombing, always easier in daylight than at night, and another was to tie down as much of the enemy's fighter strength as possible, especially after the Air Staff issued Directive No. 22, which required both Bomber Command and Fighter Command to put pressure on the Luftwaffe's fighters in Northern Europe to prevent it being used to reinforce other fronts – at this time there was a real need to relieve pressure on Allied forces in North Africa and Malta.

'Bomber' Harris accepted this, and decided upon a target in southern Germany, to be reached by a circuitous route which would keep the Luftwaffe guessing about the target, Augsburg, which had a worthwhile concentration of heavy industry, including the MAN diesel engine works. Schweinfurt had been considered and rejected, since the route would be over the Rhine, heavily defended and also threatening range problems, while Nuremberg was also rejected because of the heavy AA defences in the area. The idea was that the attacking force would either be escorted outwards by fighters through the worst of the German defences, or that there would be diversionary operations, and they would return under cover of darkness.

The Aircraft
The Avro Lancaster is described on p. 115.

The Action
The need for precision meant that the chances of finding sufficient skilled navigators in a single squadron were slim, so seven of the new Avro Lancaster heavy bombers were chosen from each of two squadrons, 44 from Waddington, which had been the first to operate the aircraft, and 97 based at Woodhall. Command of the raid was given to Sqn Ldr J.D. Nettleton, RAF. For the raid, low-level flying would be necessary, and three days of practice started on 14 April.

Sqn Ldr John Nettleton of 44 Sqn was awarded the Victoria Cross, Britain's highest decoration, for his part in the raid on Augsburg. (IWM CH5669)

Sqn Ldrs John Nettleton and Whitehead, both of 44 Sqn. (RAFM P019728)

During the late afternoon of 17 April 12 of the allocated aircraft took off, while 30 Boston light bombers mounted diversionary raids, and 500 fighter sorties were also mounted over northern France to distract the Luftwaffe. The operation soon ran into trouble, as a strong force of Messerschmitt Me109s found the Lancasters, and in a running battle, four were shot down while the force was still over France. The remaining eight continued towards the target, the machine assembly shop at the MAN works, where another three were shot down, but although damaged, the remaining five aircraft eventually returned home safely, including Nettleton's own aircraft. He was subsequently awarded the Victoria Cross for his leadership of the raid.

The raid was successful, the force scoring hits on the machine assembly shop, as planned, but with losses of almost 60 per cent this was obviously not to be the preferred tactic for the future. Nevertheless, Nettleton made a radio broadcast afterwards in which he said: 'The war can't be finished without attacking the enemy.'[6] Unfortunately, this brave man was lost leading his squadron on a raid over Turin fifteen months later.

Comment

The heavy losses likely to be inflicted on a small bomber force once over enemy territory, outnumbered by defending fighters in addition to ground fire, was a lesson which seemed to take a long time to learn. Small forces of bombers were always vulnerable, with the occasional exception of fast light bombers such as the Mosquito.

COLOGNE: THE FIRST 'THOUSAND BOMBER RAID', 30–31 MAY 1942

The British bombing strategy evolved as the war progressed. For example, Rostock was one of the early targets to receive repeat visits from Bomber Command, with the assault spread over four nights. The first two nights (23/24 and 24/25 April) were disappointing, but the third and fourth nights yielded devastating results, despite a massive increase in AA measures. One notable success was the damage inflicted on the Heinkel factory, which disrupted production for weeks.

Another of the more successful early raids had been against Cologne on the night of 13/14 March 1942. The city occupied a good strategic position, but it was also famous for many architectural treasures, not least the great cathedral. Bomber Command had sent 134 aircraft on this raid, one of the few on which the infamous and unreliable Avro Manchester was deployed, and subsequent reconnaissance showed that half the aircraft dropped their bombs within 5 miles of the target. One rear gunner aboard a Manchester of 83 Sqn recalled: 'Across the centre of the city, I saw flares illuminating every detail of the towers, turrets and buttresses of the cathedral. Here let me say at once that Whitey and Bill had previously discussed their run-in with care to avoid bombing this ancient building, and as far as I could find out so did every other crew who attacked Cologne that night.'[7]

The new navigational and bomb-aiming aids were not always successful because not all of the crews used the systems properly or had full confidence in them, and training so many in a short time was an insurmountable problem. On one raid against Essen, 20 marker aircraft using Gee were instructed to drop their flares 'blind' if need be, since this target was notorious for being obscured by industrial haze, but only 11 did so. Even before they could interfere with the signals, the Germans used dummy flares and fires to divert the following bombers into dropping their bombs out of harm's way.

The heavy losses inflicted on a small bomber force once over enemy territory, outnumbered by defending fighters even before facing heavy AA defences, and the need to create sufficient impact on the Germans both pointed in the direction of mass bombing raids, so the idea of the 'Thousand Bomber Raids' was born. Gathering together the necessary aircraft meant that training squadrons and Coastal Command units would be necessary, but in any event, part of the training for bomber aircrew had been on leaflet- and mine-dropping operations over enemy territory, so their participation in a bombing raid was not as revolutionary as it may seem. The target would have to be one on which Gee could be used, and eventually a short list of two was drawn up: Hamburg and Cologne. It was decided that the submarine pens at Hamburg would encourage the Admiralty to release the required Coastal Command units, which although part of the RAF, were directed

Flg Off Leslie Manser of 50 Sqn was awarded a posthumous VC for his part in the raid on Cologne during the night of 30/31 May 1942. (IWM CHP 796)

by the Admiralty in the fight against German submarines. Cologne would be the alternative target should weather conditions over Hamburg be too poor for accurate bombing.

To ensure secrecy, a cover was necessary, and this took the form of OPERATION BANQUET, the RAF's response to a German invasion of Britain, although by this time, May 1942, such an event was improbable. Despite taking the submarine pens at Hamburg as the target, on 25 May the Admiralty withdrew the promise of the Coastal Command units, forcing Bomber Command to look again at the aircraft available, finding 916 out of Harris's target figure, the magical 1,000. In desperation, all aircraft and crews involved in conversion training – indeed almost anyone who had graduated into a bomber aircraft from purely training types – were ordered on to the raid.

The Aircraft

The aircraft used on the first 'Thousand Bomber Raid' were a mixture of the types then in front line service, including the Stirling, Halifax, Manchester and Lancaster heavy bombers, with the numbers boosted to the target figure by the inclusion of Wellingtons.

The heavy bombers are described on pp. 114–15, but at the outbreak of war in 1939, the Vickers Wellington, designed by Sir Barnes Wallis of 'bouncing bomb' fame, was the RAF's heaviest bomber. First introduced in 1937, this medium bomber remained in service throughout the war on both

Bomber Command and Coastal Command duties. A twin-engined mid-wing monoplane with a single-fin tail, the aircraft had nose and rear turrets, and used the sturdy geodetic structure pioneered in the Vickers Wellesley. As with many wartime aircraft power plants varied, with the earlier models using two 1,000 hp Bristol Pegasus radial engines, while later versions used 1,500 hp Bristol Hercules radials, giving a maximum speed of 250 mph, a range of up to 1,250 miles, and a bombload of up to 4,500 lb. Despite the arrival of the four-engined 'heavies', the first 'Thousand Bomber Raid' had almost 600 Wellingtons on the force, making it the most numerous type by far.

In RAF service the Wellington was nicknamed the 'Wimpey', after the character in the famous 'Popeye' cartoons, J. Wellington Wimpey. In silhouette from abeam, the aircraft also had a distinctive 'wellington boot' profile.

The Action

The target for the first of these massive raids was Cologne, for which 1,050 bombers took off on the night of 30 May 1942, using no fewer than 55 airfields in the east of England. While many serving in the RAF during the war years believed that senior officers never had first hand experience of operations unless they had enjoyed rapid promotion, on this raid the Air Officer Commanding No. 3 Group, AVM J.E.A. Baldwin, was flying in one of his Stirlings as an observer.

First over the target were Short Stirlings of 15 Sqn, finding dummy fires outside the city but nevertheless avoiding these to drop their bombs on the

Albert Speer, an architect by profession, proved to be a production genius when he took over from Dr Todt as Minister for Weapons and Munitions. He was also a chronicler of the impact of Allied bombing. (IWM HU40131)

three target points in the city centre. Before long the city was ablaze and a massive firestorm seized hold. Given the large force deployed, the raid continued for some time, about ninety minutes in all. A Halifax pilot in 76 Sqn recalled: 'We took off at about 10 pm – the final wave to bomb – and I could not simply believe my eyes at the Dutch coast at what I saw 100 miles ahead of us. It was a gigantic fire that an hour before had been the city of Cologne. There it was, on fire from end to end, with still another 300 bombers to deliver their load.'[8]

Another account of the raid comes from a letter written by a Wellington rear gunner, one of those from an operational conversion unit:

On the Cologne show we had a nice quiet journey out. Coming into Cologne you knew exactly where you were, the place was absolutely lit up and huge fires all over the show. We were running in to bomb when we were caught by searchlights and then the flak started all around us. We dodged and dived till we got out of it at 7,000 feet and then ran up and bombed then stooged as hard as we could for home. Everything was quiet for about ten minutes when suddenly a master searchlight came straight on us followed immediately by flak absolutely all around us. The plane went straight into a power dive and I nearly thought we were hit till the cool voice of the pilot came over 'OK Chaps?' Anyway, we dived and weaved down to 3,000 [ft] and managed to get out of it and stooged the rest of the way over occupied Europe at that height. The plane had four shell holes in it and we thought it an exciting trip.[9]

Later waves of aircraft found the target obscured by smoke, making aiming difficult, which was made even harder by the buffeting aircraft received from the great uprush of hot air from the fires.

One benefit of overwhelming the enemy's defences with such a large force was that losses were relatively light. Out of 1,050 aircraft, 890 claimed to have found the target, while 40 failed to return, with another 12 so badly damaged that they had to be scrapped and 33 seriously damaged. Cologne received 540 tons of high explosive and 915 tons of incendiaries. It took some days before a worthwhile reconnaissance could be mounted over the city because of the fires which continued to rage, but it soon became clear that the raid had been a major success.

Bomber Command received praise from Churchill, as might be expected, but perhaps the praise which meant most was from 'Bomber' Harris's opposite number in the USAAF, Gen 'Hap' Arnold:

As Commanding General of the US Army Air Forces I desire to extend my congratulations to you, your staff and combat crews for the great raid last night on Cologne. It was bold in conception and superlative in execution. Please convey to your officers and men my admiration for their courage and skill, and say that our air forces hope very soon to fly and fight beside them in their decisive blows against our common enemy.[10]

Given such support, Harris decided to mount another operation the following night, this time against Hamburg. Bad weather meant that this had to be cancelled, and there was insufficient time to prepare for an alternative target. Anxious to strike again while the aircraft and their crews were assembled at their airfields, Harris opted for Essen the following night, 1/2 June. Given the losses and damaged aircraft from the Cologne raid, and the continued absence of Coastal Command aircraft, 956 aircraft took off on this second raid, of which 767 claimed to have found the target, while 31 failed to return. Aware that many of the aircrew at debriefing had seemed doubtful about their performance, prompt photographic reconnaissance of Essen was ordered, which found that damage had indeed been light, but that Duisburg, Mulheim and Oberhausen had been attacked by many of the bombers instead. The industrial haze of the Ruhr had helped protect the chosen target once again.

On the third 'Thousand Bomber Raid', on the night of 25/26 June, 1,006 aircraft took off for Bremen, including 102 Coastal Command Hudsons and 5 Bristol Blenheims from Army Co-operation Command. Weather over the target was far worse than expected – a persistent problem during the war years, when weather reporting and forecasting, especially over longer distances, was far more difficult than in the modern satellite age, and at best dependent upon good weather reconnaissance aircraft operations. Once again, as at Essen, the results were disappointing in terms of damage to the target, with many aircraft dropping their bombs well off the mark, although there was some damage to the town and to the Focke-Wulf aircraft factory. Aircraft losses were also disappointing: 49 aircraft failed to return, and of these, no fewer than 21 of the 24 aircraft of 91 Group OTU were lost with their inexperienced student crews. This was a blow to Harris, who, after the great success at Cologne, had seen the raids as the way forward, with two or three 'Thousand Bomber Raids' each month, the operational units spending the period in between such operations divided between a number of more modest operations 'to keep the pot boiling' and boosting the efforts of the OTUs through helping to train crews. With the support of Portal, he had suggested that a list of as many as thirty major German cities be drawn up for 'Thousand Bomber Raids'.

Comment

The 'Thousand Bomber Raids' were obviously the way forward, since even before the first Pathfinder units were formed, the more experienced crews were able to guide the others to the target. Once over the target, the defences were overwhelmed by having to divide their fire, and for night-fighters, the massed firepower of the massive bomber formation presented a serious hazard.

The Admiralty's attitude may seem hard to understand, but the damage a German U-boat pack could inflict on a convoy in a single day at this stage of the war would have outweighed any strategic advantage gained by an air raid. Not until the advent of the escort carrier could the Admiralty even consider releasing the most effective antidote to U-boat attack – air power.

While the massive force was stood down, Harris decided to mount another raid during the June full moon, and pressed the Prime Minister to order the Admiralty to release Coastal Command aircraft, which Churchill duly did. Instead of the 250 or so aircraft expected, the Admiralty offered just 100 Lockheed Hudsons and a Wellington squadron manned by Free Polish airmen regarded as being temperamentally unsuited to Coastal Command work, and which the Admiralty were hoping to swop for another Wellington squadron. Again, the training units had to be raided to make up the numbers.

There were other problems. Many of those at the OTUs were not raw students, but experienced bomber crews sent to the OTUs for a rest between tours. They objected to being sent on raids over Germany, and some even made themselves absent without leave.

There was considerable strain on bomber aircrew. At the outset, they were at their most vulnerable during the first five operational sorties, out of a tour of 200 flying hours or thirty sorties. During this period, aircrew who survived ten sorties usually completed their tour. As the war progressed, the loss rates for the more experienced crews started to mount, until they were almost as high as for the novices, although the RAF's senior medical officers could not be sure whether this was due to fatigue, stress, or overconfidence.

THE AMERICANS ARRIVE: ROUEN, 17 AUGUST 1942

Preparing for the possibility of US involvement in what was at first a European war, the United States Army Air Corps, as it then was, had designated 154 targets which would cripple Germany's military strength, appreciating that the key to success lay in the destruction of the Luftwaffe. Among others, the steel industry had been regarded as a primary target, although it was soon realized that the steel furnaces themselves would be a hard target, difficult to destroy with the bombs available. Energy and transport targets were then substituted, since the steel industry needed electricity. It was also appreciated that transport targets could be difficult to hit, and that railway lines could be relaid fairly quickly. In the end, the targets which received priority were to be those linked with oil production, synthetic rubber, ball-bearings and aircraft production.

The availability of British airfields was initially seen as a problem which would affect implementation of the Air War Plans Department (AWPD) 1, which relied heavily on strategic bombing to neutralize the enemy's war effort. The idea came up of having two crews each for the B-17 and B-24 bombers, to be based in England, and developing the huge Convair B-36, which could operate from the USA with a 4,000 mile radius of action. A major factor in developing the B-36 was the pessimism of those Americans who believed that they might have to fight Germany after German occupation of the British Isles. In addition, when it was ready, 24 groups of the new B-29 would be deployed, split equally between bases in North Africa and in Northern Ireland. In the end, the British made sufficient bases available, and others were built. Despite the unrivalled industrial muscle of the USA, there were shortages. The US Navy had come to realize the shortcomings of the flying boat for maritime reconnaissance, and couldn't build enough aircraft carriers for this role, so arguments broke out over the allocation of the B-24 between the USAAF and the US Navy.

Brig Gen Ira C. Eaker who commanded the US Eighth Air Force's Bomber Command under Lt Gen Carl Spaatz, was a fighter pilot by training and experience, but he was chosen by the head of the USAAF, Gen 'Hap' Arnold, because he believed that bombers needed the fighter spirit. He founded his

The crew of one of the USAAF Boeing B-17 Flying Fortress bombers which took part in the first all-American raid of the war – the attack on the railway yards at Rouen in northern France on 18 August 1942. (IWM HU66787)

headquarters in March 1942, and within two months, eight RAF bases had been extended and were ready for occupation by the USAAF.

The Americans believed in daylight raids for many reasons, including the heavy defensive armament of their aircraft, the Norden bombsight, and because they felt that round-the-clock attack in conjunction with the RAF would force the Germans to pull more and more manpower into AA defences and what might be described as civil defence.

Conflict existed within the US armed forces over the emphasis being placed on winning the war in Europe, when many believed that Japan should receive prior attention.

The First USAAF combat unit to arrive in Europe was the 97th Bombardment Group on 1 July 1942, accompanied by the 1st and 31st Pursuit Groups. The 97th had been on standby in the west coast of the USA for the Battle of Midway. The arrival of these three units together was no coincidence – the fighters needed the guidance of the bombers when crossing the North Atlantic via Labrador and Iceland.

The Aircraft
Developed from the prototype Boeing 299 (the manufacturer's first four-engined bomber, which had first appeared in 1935), the B-17 was to form the backbone of the USAAF's bomber force in Europe. The name 'Flying

Fortress' reflected the very heavy defensive armament, with up to 20 machine-guns, to allow the aircraft to operate outside the protection offered by the fighters available during the first months of the USAAF's involvement in Europe. While specifications varied, typically four 1,250 hp Wright Cyclone radial engines powered a B-17, giving it a maximum altitude of 35,000 ft and a speed of up to 280 mph, although these performances reduced the bombload from a theoretical maximum of 16,000 lb to 4,000 lb.

The RAF used the B-17 for a short period, their first operational sortie being on 8 July 1941 on a raid against Wilhelmshaven, and the last being on 25/26 August against Emden. Pilot Officer Mulligan had fond memories of flying a Boeing B-17 on a number of operations, concluding with the Emden raid:

A USAAF Boeing B-17E in flight. (RAFM P09574)

I was in a Fortress which was attacked by seven fighters when we were returning from Brest. Three minutes after our bombs had gone, the fire controller called out that there were seven enemy fighters coming up from the starboard quarter a thousand feet below. They closed in and there was almost no part of the Fortress which was not hit. Some of my friends in the crew were killed and others wounded. The petrol tank was punctured, bomb doors were thrown open, flaps were put out of

USAAF Boeing B-17Gs of the 91st Bombardment Group dropping bombs – although the location is unknown. (RAFM P017513)

action, tail tabs shot away, tail-wheel stuck half down, brakes not working, one aileron was only just slightly good, the rudder was almost completely out of control. The centre of the fuselage had become a tangled mass of wires and broken cables. A square foot of the wings had been shot away, and still the pilot managed to land the Fortress on a strange aerodrome . . .

Another time we were coming away from Oslo and part of the oxygen supply failed and the pilot had to dive down swiftly through 19,000 feet. He pulled out and the Fortress landed safely at base.[11]

The Consolidated B-24 Liberator was the most widely used of the US four-engined heavy bombers. A high-wing aircraft powered by four 1,200 hp turbo-charged Pratt & Whitney R-1830 radial engines, it could carry up to 5,000 lb of bombs and had a radius of action of up to 1,700 miles, while it could cruise at 25,000 ft. This meant that the Liberator saw intensive use in the Far East, where distances to the targets from the available bases initially involved long flights, and it was also a popular maritime reconnaissance aircraft.

The Action

Originally set for 10 August 1942, the raid on Rouen was the first USAAF heavy bomber operation in Europe, with the 97th Bombardment Group despatched to bomb the railway marshalling yards at Sotteville. Bad weather delayed the operation until 17 August. There were also disagreements. Spaatz wanted to fly on the first mission, with Eaker flying on the second. The RAF protested vigorously, pointing out that although the Americans had designated successors if they failed to return, if they were captured, they had all the Allies' secrets, and if they died, it would still take a long time for their designated successors to acquire this knowledge. Spaatz agreed, but Eaker persisted, and in the end flew on this first mission, in *Yankee Doodle*, one of six aircraft in the second wave of the attack, which had just 12 aircraft altogether. The operation was escorted by four squadrons of RAF fighters – a reflection of the closeness of the target.

The 12 B-17s took off at 11.00. Over the target, about half the bombs fell on the railway, but many others landed on the town itself. Eaker was concerned about French casualties, but he was soon reassured by the leader of the Free French, Gen Charles de Gaulle, whose reaction was that everyone was delighted that the Americans were now operational, and that casualties were to be expected.

Throughout the war British senior officers flying with their bomber squadrons seemed to be especially unlucky, many being lost on their rare missions. On the other hand, Eaker came back with many ideas which might have taken longer to gather had he not taken part in an actual operation. He realized that training of bombardiers (bomb-aimers) and gunners needed to be improved, while tighter formations were necessary so that the bombers could cover each other. He also felt that crew comfort needed to be improved, and proposed a 25,000 ft limit on the B-17 because of the –44°F temperature at this altitude, which was enough to freeze oxygen masks and halve crew efficiency.

Comment

It would be unwise and unfair to expect too much of the first raid by any air force, but the American enthusiasm to learn the facts at first hand and quickly was notable.

LILLE, 9 OCTOBER 1942

The USAAF spent its first few months in the European theatre on operations over enemy-occupied territory while the crews refined their techniques before operations over Germany itself. This incremental approach to the bombing campaign also reflected the still relatively small number of aircraft available, and the fact that the greater distances inherent in operations over Germany would effectively mean fighting all the way to the target and back again, against the formidable Luftwaffe day-fighter force.

The main targets included communications and oil facilities, and the U-boat pens.

The Aircraft

The aircraft included Boeing B-17s and Consolidated B-24s (see pp. 125 and 126).

The Action

On 9 October the US Eighth Air Force's 301st Group sent 108 B-17s plus a number of B-24s from the 93rd Group to Lille in northern France, to bomb the Chemin de Fer du Nord's railway carriage and wagon works. The force was escorted by three squadrons of RAF Spitfires and another three squadrons of USAAF P-38s.

The raid was led by the Commander of the 301st Group, Col R.R. Walker. Little opposition was met on the outward flight to the target, although some difficulty was encountered in finding the target, which forced the formation to make 180° turns, delaying arrival and giving the Luftwaffe's fighters time to become airborne. Over the target, bombing was made more difficult by aircraft having to take evasive action to avoid mid-air collisions. The full force of AA fire was not felt until after the bombs had been released, by which time they also came under fighter attack from Fw190s. Despite the confusion and the fact that the operation was taking place in broad daylight, just four aircraft were lost, although the crew of one of them was rescued from the English Channel.

In the confusion of the battle between the fighters and bombers, the Eighth afterwards claimed to have shot down 56 Luftwaffe fighters, which the British press refused to believe, even after the figure was later adjusted to 48. After the war the true number was found to be ten, of which four were shot down by British fighters. Worse still, only nine bombs fell close to the target, with most falling on civilian areas, which suffered serious casualties. After a further two operations, the 301st was transferred to North Africa.

Comment

This operation set the pattern for USAAF activity over Europe, and as one of the first, it showed a high level of success, with low losses, and even shooting down six of the Luftwaffe's fighters on one operation was an achievement. The high initial fighter kill claimed was doubtless an example of the 'fog of war', with many gunners claiming the same fighter in good faith, since they had all fired at it.

Civilian casualties in enemy-occupied Europe were something the Allies always tried to avoid, although the Free French on more than one occasion stated their acceptance that some civilian casualties were inevitable.

RAID ON THE SCHNEIDER ARMAMENTS WORKS AT LE CREUSOT, 17 OCTOBER 1942

The vast Schneider armaments factory at Le Creusot, almost on the border between occupied and Vichy France, presented a vital strategic target. The Germans had lost no time in converting as much industry in occupied Europe as possible to the war effort. The Schneider works was a major industrial complex, with some 10,000 workers producing armoured vehicles, guns and railway locomotives. The target had been beyond the reach of the earlier bombers, being almost on the Franco-Swiss border.

Increased attention was also paid to tactics which would help to reduce the risk from fighter attack. Gibson, by now with 106 Sqn in No. 5 Group, was among those trained in mass low-level formation flying. Initially flying in squadron strength, as proficiency in station-keeping and navigation increased, the aircraft were flown in wings and then finally in group strength, known colloquially as a 'group gaggle'. These exercises were conducted at heights of no more than 300 ft, wing tip to wing tip. To add realism to the exercises, mock attacks were carried out by RAF fighters. This proved to be a hazardous business for the fighter pilots, who found it difficult to get out of the bombers' slipstream once they managed to penetrate the formation, and several aircraft were lost in this way.

At 1,700 miles, the raid on Le Creusot would be the longest trip at the time for RAF Bomber Command.

An Avro Lancaster Mk I of 44 Sqn taking off for a raid on Friedrichshafen in June 1943. (RAFM P016432)

The Aircraft

This was another operation for the Avro Lancaster (see p. 115).

The Action

For the attack on Le Creusot, No. 5 Group was chosen, and sent a force of 94 Lancasters to the target, 10 of them from 106 Sqn, together with the aircraft of 57 Sqn. Another six aircraft were deployed against the power station at Montchanin, both as a diversionary raid and because this was an important target in its own right. Two of the aircraft assigned to the Montchanin raid were from 106 Sqn, one of them flown by Guy Gibson and the other by Sqn Ldr J.V. Hopgood.

As always, getting the force safely to and from the target exercised the minds of the RAF's planners. It was decided that the safest route was for the aircraft to fly out into the Atlantic, before turning and flying more than 330 miles to the target at low altitude. To do this, the aircraft would have to refuel at a base in the south of England on the outward flight, and RAF Coastal Command was instructed to increase the number of anti-submarine sweeps over the Bay of Biscay so that U-boats would remain submerged and unable to give early warning of the bomber force's movements. The navigators were given strip maps for the 1,700 mile round trip, while the aircraft were fitted with the new navigational aid, Gee, to enhance the accuracy of the bombing.

The aircraft for the raid on Le Creusot took off soon after midday, taking a long diversionary course as they flew outwards to avoid German fighters. The route took the aircraft over Land's End, at the extreme south-west tip of Cornwall, far out over the Bay of Biscay, before turning back towards the coast of France, crossing this well south of the Brittany Peninsula by the Ile d'Yeu, and then flying some 250 miles over occupied France to the target. The outward flight was at altitudes of 50–500 ft before climbing up to 4,000 ft as they closed on the target. They arrived as darkness descended, but found little difficulty in identifying the factories, workshops and warehouses. The ensuing raid lasted for nine minutes, with well over 200 tons of high explosives and incendiaries well placed so that huge fires broke out and explosions could be heard over a wide area, and within minutes the entire town was covered with dense, black smoke.

The attack on the Montchanin power station was made from 500 ft, with each aircraft dropping ten 500 lb bombs, straddling the target so that the resulting damage took two years to repair. Gibson recalled: 'Our two aircraft then circled the target and between them fired 1,000 rounds of ammunition into the transformers – a satisfactory and spectacular operation, which brought forth vivid blue flashes each time a bullet hit a vital spot.'[12]

The aircraft on both raids then took the shortest route home, flying independently, with many having to be diverted to bases in the South of England due to bad weather. Only one enemy fighter was encountered during the entire operation, and this was by an aircraft limping home on three engines. All of 106 Sqn's aircraft returned safely, although Gibson's had some holes, as had Hopgood's, which had been damaged by the blast from his own bombs.

No. 57 Sqn, by this time also part of No. 5 Group, had started to convert to the Lancaster in August 1942, moving to a new base at

Scampton. The squadron was ready to take part with the other eight Lancaster squadrons in No. 5 Group on 17 October.

On the day, just two of the aircraft failed to return, neither of which belonged to 57 Sqn. Two of its aircraft returned early, one with jammed guns, and another after becoming detached from the rest of the force over the Isles of Scilly, off the extreme south-west tip of Cornwall. There were other problems, two aircraft being damaged and their crew injured when they encountered a flock of birds.

Comment

Despite mounting a daylight operation, all went well, and this was a classic example of precision bombing, with very light losses. Heavier aircraft with a longer range and the use of heavier bombs meant that bombers had become a force to be reckoned with when handled by skilled crews.

GENOA AND MILAN, 16/17 AND 18 OCTOBER 1942

Despite the distance from their bases in England, raids on the major cities in northern Italy were popular with the RAF's bomber crews. This was because the Italian air defences were far lighter than anything encountered in German-occupied Europe, let alone over the Reich itself. Even the route over France was too far south for effective intervention by German fighters. Italy was a target well worth attacking, because effective intervention by the bombers could ease the pressure on the Allies in North Africa and on the beleaguered island of Malta, and help to reduce German and Italian attacks on the Mediterranean convoys.

Genoa, Turin and Milan were all significant targets, with the Italians obligingly having almost all of their major manufacturing industry in the north – even more so in 1942 than is the case today. The bomber crews were told at the briefing:

> The targets, of course, are all in the dock area where units of the Italian fleet are sheltering. You may wonder why we have been suddenly switched from Germany, and why you are going here tonight . . . Well, all I can say is that you may, for all I know, be taking part in a large operation in the Mediterranean. For the first time in history you may be supporting land operations, hundreds of miles away . . .[13]

The Aircraft
Once again, this was a raid for the Lancaster (see p. 115).

The Action
The squadron went, and as Wg Cdr Guy Gibson put it: '. . . we all came back. It was a good prang. The Pathfinders lit the targets just like daylight. We all watched our incendiaries burn merrily away on the concrete roofs of the Genoa houses. We watched our block busters disintegrate the buildings on the dockyards. And when we came back we all decided that Genoa was pretty cushy.'[14]

The major Allied offensive in the Western Desert started the next day.

The Milan raid was conducted in daylight. One pilot on the operation suggested that in addition to the damage they were going to do, he thought that the whole idea was to show the Italians that the RAF was supreme on the Western Front.

One advantage of operations against Italy was that the route was too far south for the Luftwaffe to mount effective fighter operations, the aircraft flying for the most part over Vichy France. The bombers crossed the Sussex coast at Selsey Bill at very low level, and flew towards a point between Cherbourg and Le Havre. They had been led to expect a warm front lying across France which would give cloud cover, in which the bombers were to hide. As so often happened, the weather was different from the forecast, and the bombers arrived over the French coast in bright sunshine. They could see the clouds in the far distance, and had gone a long way into France before the safety of the blanketing white mist could be reached. There was some AA fire over the French coast, but as Gibson put it:

Three officers of 106 Sqn waiting to take off for a raid on Berlin in 1942. Left to right: an American volunteer with the RAF, Flt Lt Don Curtain, Wg Cdr Guy Gibson, and Flt Lt D.J. Shannon. (IWM HU63349)

I think that they were all surprised to see a hundred bombers supported by Spitfires flying so low. Then we heard the Germans chattering away on the RT. We heard the controller say: 'Hello, all German aircraft, the British bombers are too far south, you must land at the nearest bases.'

On we flew, this bright sunny day; it was getting warmer and warmer as we flew south . . . we were carrying movie cameras and took many interesting pictures of little French villages, and some rather charming French people who were all waving to us. One charming family group I remember stood in front of their white cottage – a young man, a little blonde daughter, about seven years old, and a sweet wife; at least she looked sweet from 100 feet, with her blonde hair flying in the breeze; they were all waving like mad. Another time we saw a flock of what I thought at first were geese . . . Johnny told me they were nuns.[15]

They flew for three hours before climbing up over the Alps, and gathered into a fighting formation over Lake Annecy, before making their final approach to Milan, still some 60 miles away:

. . . dropping our cookies from 3,000 feet The sun was still well up . . . The confusion in Milan was something to be seen. A few flak guns fired spasmodically; private cars ran on to the pavements; people rushed to shelters . . . But it was no use, the boys behaved like real gentlemen. They all went for military objectives, and they did a lot of military damage. As far as I know not one civilian establishment was hit.[16]

Flying back over the Alps, the bomber crews were treated to a beautiful sunset, and attracted the interest of an Italian fighter, a biplane, Gibson

Another 106 Sqn trio, again with Wg Cdr Guy Gibson, this time flanked by Sqn Ldrs John Searby (left) and Peter Ward-Hunt, with one of the squadron's Lancasters in the background. (IWM HU63357)

recalls, with just two guns, as opposed to the six of each Lancaster. The fighter pilot decided to keep his distance.

There was a follow-up raid on Milan by a Halifax group that night, and before the end of the month, Genoa was visited on two consecutive nights. This all built up to the Allied invasion of North Africa on 8 November 1942, OPERATION TORCH.

Comment

The raids on Italy were timely, and successful, in as much as losses were light. They also served to remind the Italians, at a crucial stage of the war in the Mediterranean, that they were not beyond the reach of the RAF's bombers. Undoubtedly, damage was done which helped the war effort, but these targets were visited too rarely, and never in sufficient force or in such quick succession, to make a major difference.

ATTACKING THE SUBMARINE PENS, OCTOBER 1942–JANUARY 1943

The German U-boat fleet continued to grow during the early years of the war, and in 1942, the numbers operational grew from 90 to 96. The effect on Allied shipping was disastrous, with 108 ships being sunk in August alone. September was worse still.

Churchill demanded action, including additional B-24s for anti-submarine patrols. Eisenhower took a different view, demanding in late October that the US Eighth Air Force treat the submarine pens as a priority target, to protect shipping bound for North Africa. The aircraft industry was to be the second item on the priority list.

The Aircraft

Once again, these operations were carried out by Boeing B-17s and Consolidated B-24s.

The Action

On 21 October the US Eighth Air Force started its campaign against the submarine bases, dropping 31 tons of bombs that day. Accuracy was good, despite heavy opposition from German fighters, but the bombs failed to penetrate the massive reinforced concrete pens. A solution was to modify aircraft to carry two armour-piercing 5,000 lb Disney bombs, one under each wing. This was not an ideal solution, one pilot describing the bombs as 'about as consistent as a fart in a windstorm',[17] while another said that flying a B-17 while carrying these bombs was 'like trying to tap-dance on a billiard ball resting on an ice cube.'[18]

Despite the USAAF belief before the war that no structure could resist a 4,000 lb bomb, even these massive bombs were ineffectual, and the raids soon stopped. It was not until the appearance of the massive 12,000 lb Tall Boy and 22,000 lb Grand Slam earthquake bombs later in the war that the Allies were to possess weapons truly capable of dealing with such targets.

The raid on 9 November on the U-boat pens at St Nazaire used many crews who were inexperienced. Twelve B-24s attacked from 18,000 ft, while 31 B-17s operated at 7,500 ft and 10,000 ft. The B-17 force suffered badly from heavy AA fire, which was very accurate, so that 3 aircraft were lost and another 22 badly damaged. Just 75 of the 344 bombs dropped landed close enough to the target to appear on post-raid reconnaissance photographs.

Despite this poor result, raids continued until 3 January, 1943, with another six raids against St Nazaire and Lorient, presumably for political reasons since the USAAF had realized that the missions were futile. Fortunately, flying at higher altitude kept losses to around 5 per cent, which the USAAF considered manageable.

Comment

That the U-boat pens were an important target cannot be denied – 1942 was the worst year of the war for Allied merchant shipping losses, which threatened both the British war effort and participation in the conflict in North Africa. The problem was that the bomb technology and the weight of the individual weapons were both inadequate for the task in hand. Perhaps the B-17s and B-24s would have been better off mining the approaches.

NORTH AFRICA

As experienced air groups the USAAF 97th and 301st were transferred to the US Twelfth Air Force for operations in, and later from, North Africa.

The RAF had been operating in North Africa since early in the war, initially scoring considerable successes against Italian forces, although, as with the ground forces, the British found the Germans a formidable foe, forcing them back towards Egypt and the vital Suez Canal. Suez had been seen as important by the British for the reinforcement of their forces in India and the Far East, but by this stage of the war, the canal was mainly used to reinforce and supply British forces in the eastern Mediterranean, since the sea route across the Mediterranean was barely usable, and then only for heavily protected fast convoys to Malta, which suffered grievous losses.

The Aircraft
In North Africa operations were mainly in support of ground forces, so the older and lighter Wellington bomber was in widespread use, rather than the 'heavies' operated from bases in England against Germany and enemy-occupied Europe.

The Action
The Allied invasion of North Africa, OPERATION TORCH of 8 November 1942, was an undoubted success, and one which was much needed after the earlier débâcle of the raid on Dieppe. Forces landed on the Mediterranean and Atlantic coasts of Morocco, and in Algeria, then a French colony.

There was drama and heroism among the British bomber squadrons in North Africa, including 142 and 150 Sqns of No. 330 Group, engaged on night-bomber operations. Operating from Blida, 35 miles south-west of Algiers, they used Wellingtons. On one operation Flt Lt Ronnie Brooks had a hung-up bomb, which they could only release by dangling the wireless operator over the bomb bay, holding him by the heels, while he attempted to release the bomb using an axe – fortunately, he was successful just as the aircraft passed over its target.

On 18 January 1943 Sqn Ldr J.F.H. Booth was again over the docks at Bizerte. Two sticks of bombs were dropped without incident, and as they circled, watching the other aircraft in the formation making their attacks in the moonlight, they were discovered by a Ju88 night-fighter, which managed to hit the bomber's starboard engine on its first pass. The Ju88 made three more attacks, hitting the bomber's hydraulics and its instruments, and setting a portable oxygen bottle on fire, with the risk of an explosion. On its next attack, the rear gunner scored hits on the fighter, and the pilot broke away, doubtless believing that his prey was disabled beyond recovery.

Booth ordered his crew to bale out immediately, in case the oxygen bottle blew up. Instead, the acting flight engineer, LAC J. Skingsley, attempted to smother the blaze, and when this failed, picked up the bottle with his bare hands and threw it out of an escape hatch, suffering severe burns.

Comment
This was all typical of combat in support of ground forces, with a wide variety of targets, including bombing attacks against the enemy's

communications, an essential element in a war of this kind in which both sides had extended lines of communication. What raised this above the routine even of war was the exceptional bravery of Skingsley in throwing out of the aircraft a burning oxygen bottle, which could have exploded at any moment. It is a shame that the poor man didn't receive a Victoria Cross.

ATTACKING THE SUBMARINE MENACE: ST NAZAIRE, 3 JANUARY 1943

During 1943 the balance of power changed, and no longer did the Axis powers dictate the pace, timing and location of events. The Allies had taken the initiative and put the enemy onto the defensive. At the end of 1942, Germany might still have won the war, or perhaps forced a stalemate, although the Japanese position was less certain, but by the end of 1943, defeat was simply a matter of time.

Nevertheless, not everything was going in the Allies' favour. For the USAAF, the problem was that by this time, German fighters had gained the measure of their opponents. They had realized that the early marks of B-17s and B-24s, so heavily armed in many respects, lacked nose turrets, so they were vulnerable to head-on attacks. Fortunately, this weakness was soon remedied by modifications to aircraft in service, and by improvements to later marks.

Meanwhile, at the beginning of 1943 the US Eighth Air Force was reorganized. In its new form, it consisted of Bomber, Fighter, Air-Ground Support and Service Commands. The Bomber Command consisted of three wings, two of which operated B-17s after the B-26s had been replaced with these aircraft in one of the wings, while the other wing operated B-24s. Eaker had been promoted to Major-General, and had replaced Spaatz as the Eighth AF's commanding general the previous November, and his post at Bomber Command had been taken over by Brig Gen Laurence Kuter, who had been head of the Eighth's First Bombardment Wing. Each of the wings consisted of four groups.

Kuter felt that while a single group lacked the defensive capacity to operate safely over enemy territory without fighter cover, the full wing of four groups was too cumbersome to formate on a single leader. As a solution, he proposed, and Eaker approved, combat wings with two or three groups. There were other changes as well.

Meanwhile, it was business as usual. The German submarine fleet had inflicted heavy losses on Allied shipping throughout 1942, with almost 5.4 million tons of shipping lost in the North Atlantic and North Sea. These losses were to be cut drastically during 1943, with a cut of two-thirds due to improved maritime reconnaissance and the arrival of escort carriers, but this still left the submarine pens at St Nazaire on the French Biscay coast at the mouth of the Loire as a tempting target. Nevertheless, bombers had to get to and from the target safely.

The Aircraft
The familiar Boeing B-17 was used on this raid.

The Action

On his first mission to the submarine pens at St Nazaire, on the third of January, Brig Gen Hansell flew with a crew from the 91st Group . . . He was distressed by the poor organization of the four groups, particularly because the formations did not relate to one another, and each was different.

Spitfires covered the bombers up to their fuel limits and then had to leave for home. German fighters, which stayed away from the formations until the escorting British fighters had to depart, then drew ahead, turned 180 degrees, and made head-on level attacks.

Hansell watched with concern as German fighters bored in where the B-17 defensive firepower was weakest . . . the fighters seemed bent on head-on collisions . . . Hansell watched the Fw190s and Me109s come in with yellow blinking lights on their wings as German pilots fired cannon.

As German fighters tore through their formations, Hansell noted that his gunners had opened fire too soon and fired with extremely poor accuracy . . . the Germans knew that the top turret guns on the Fortresses could not be depressed below the horizontal, so they made their attacks at the same level or slightly below the bombers. Once a Flying Fortress was crippled, fighters pounced on it . . . the bombers never faltered, even when seven out of eighty-five B-17s . . . plummeted to earth . . . Unfortunately, courage was not sufficient to achieve bombing accuracy, which was too erratic for serious damage to the target.[19]

Hansell set about achieving standardized formations and tactics. This initially led to arguments between the different group leaders, and eventually he settled on a compromise between the formations used by 305th and 306th groups. The new formation became known as the 'combat box', and consisted of three squadrons, each of six aircraft. The second squadron flew higher than the leading squadron, and the third flew lower than the lead. This improved the field of the firepower, although the leading squadron was still vulnerable to frontal attack. Eventually, even very large formations flew as three groups of 18 aircraft each, giving a wing of 54 aircraft. To improve bombing accuracy and defence against fighter attack, only the leading bombardier used his bombsight, and the other aircraft had to drop their bombs on his command, while the bombsights were removed from all but the leading and deputy leading aircraft and replaced by twin .50 calibre guns, which overcame the B-17's fatal weakness.

It was also necessary to convince the pilots that they should use their automatic pilots, although these had first to be provided with better lubricants, and even heaters, to overcome sluggishness at high altitude – this enabled the bombardier to effectively fly the aircraft once the bombsight was linked to the automatic flight control system. Bombing accuracy began to improve, from just 24 per cent of bombs landing within 1,100 ft of the aiming point in early 1943 to 24 per cent landing within 800 ft by the end of the year.

Comment

Once again, the presence of a senior officer on a major raid enabled an objective and constructive appraisal of the tactics employed. The USAAF knew that it had to learn fast, and decisive action always followed. Not that implementing the changes was always easy.

For example, appalled by the poor standard of gunnery when he took over 364 Sqn within No. 305 Group, the squadron's new commander, Maj (later Col) Henry Macdonald, decided to provide gunnery practice for his crews whenever no operations were planned. He flew an A-20 Boston light bomber towing a target 1,000 yd behind the aircraft. On his second gunnery exercise, the target reel jammed while playing out, and stuck at 400 yd. Unable to warn the bombers because his radio was not working, Macdonald decided to continue, believing that 400 yd was a safe enough margin. He was wrong. On his sixth pass by the bomber formation, a burst of fire swept through the A-20, smashing the windscreen, while another shell struck Macdonald in the back. In severe pain, he managed to land his aircraft safely, even though one of the tyres had been burst by the gunfire. As if this wasn't enough, once he was loaded into an ambulance, the American driver, unfamiliar with the British vehicle, reversed it into the tail of his aircraft, causing considerable damage.

CHAPTER EIGHT

COMBINED OPS: THE POINT BLANK DIRECTIVE

While there were doubts at first about the ability of the USAAF daylight raids over Germany to enjoy the same relative immunity from fighter attack as they had enjoyed over France, the level of success began to persuade many that a policy of RAF raids by night followed by USAAF raids by day could work. The heavy defensive armament of the B-17, even though at some cost in bombload, did seem effective, although eventually this was on operations which enjoyed fighter escorts for most, if not the whole, of the way there and back again, whereas at this stage of the war, before the appearance of the long-range escort fighters, the bombers would literally have to fight their way to and from the target.

The RAF still managed to provide the occasional daylight raid when conditions seemed to be right, and No. 2 Group's Lancasters were usually

The bomb bay and wing bomb cells of this Halifax Mk II of 138 (Special Duties) Sqn at RAF Tempsford had a full load of fifteen 500 lb bombs ready for a 'Thousand Bomber' raid in June 1942. The squadron was one of the units called upon to make up the numbers for these operations. (IWM HU54485)

allocated those tasks which weren't suitable for the fast 'hit and run' tactics of the lighter de Havilland Mosquito. For example, on 11 July 1942 a force of 44 aircraft had been deployed against the U-boat pens at Danzig, involving a 1,500 mile round trip, the longest then undertaken by Bomber Command aircraft. Intending to fly at low level, the presence of cloud encouraged them to fly at a higher altitude so that their movements would be less obvious to ground observers, but this made navigation more difficult, so almost a third of the aircraft failed to find the target. Contrary winds also meant that the force reached the target not just before sunset, as intended, but after dark. One bomber pilot recalled that most of the aircraft arrived over Danzig when it was pitch dark. Typical of many, unable to indentify the docks or the streets of the town, they targeted a small ship in the outer harbour but missed it by 20 yd from 1,000 ft. Just two Lancasters were lost to ground fire, but little damage was done.

Gen Ira Eaker, in command of the USAAF's Eighth Air Force, was unconvinced about the wisdom of raids over a wide variety of targets, taking a view that it was better to saturate certain targets:

On 12 April Eaker presented his 'Combined Bomber Offensive', more familiarly known as the Eaker Plan, and his approach was somewhat different from that of Harris's. His premise was that it 'was better to cause a high degree of destruction in a few really essential industries than to cause a small degree of destruction in many industries', and to this end the American Air Staff had selected six key systems – submarine construction yards and bases, the aircraft industry, ball-bearings, oil production, synthetic rubber and military transport. This faithfully followed the Casablanca Directive, and within these systems the Americans had identified 76 specific targets.[1]

The Combined Bomber Offensive target priorities for the RAF and the USAAF initially gave first priority to the destruction of the German aircraft industry, followed by the ball-bearing industry. Later, oil production was to be the top priority, followed by rubber production. Nevertheless, other factors meant that the commanders of the air units could not simply set a list of targets and plan operations according to the priorities, so they were frequently diverted to targets to meet changing demands. A good example of this was the need to restrict the operations of the Kriegsmarine, and Harris had ensured that regular mining sorties were conducted throughout much of 1942, especially during the run-up to OPERATION TORCH. Now the rule was that mining was to be conducted by all groups, not just No. 5 Group, whenever the weather was too bad for an attack over the Continent. Mines had proved effective, and before the North African landings had often delayed U-boat sailings. Harris was convinced that mines were more effective than attacking the U-boat bases, and was probably correct at this stage of the war. The Germans probably took the same view, since flak ships and, whenever possible shore-based AA batteries were installed around the more important positions, so that mine-laying sorties became increasingly hazardous, having earlier in the war been almost a soft option.

The RAF doubted that the Americans could carry out such raids in daylight, but the US view, based on operations over France and a limited

The American commanders, faced with the problems of defending their formations on daylight raids, spent much time devising good defensive formations. These Martin B-26 Marauder medium bombers show one such formation, the box. (IWM EA19186)

number of raids over Germany since January, was that it would be possible to operate at 20,000–30,000 ft and still bomb precision targets. They also believed that a minimum of 300 bombers would be required on each raid, requiring a minimum of 800 aircraft to be based in the UK. The Americans also agreed with Harris's target of a joint force of 3,000 bombers:

> . . . the plan called for some 950 heavy bombers to be in the United Kingdom by 1 July, 1943; 1,200 by 1 October; 1,750 by 1 January, 1944, and 2,700 by 1 April, 1944. In addition, US medium bomber strength would rise from 200 to 800 over the same period. Although, unlike Harris, he did not openly claim that the offensive could win the war, Eaker believed that without it a cross-Channel invasion was not possible, and it would work only if he had the required bomber strength.

However, the word 'Combined' had been used in the title of the plan, and Eaker recognized the growing power of Bomber Command; he also recognized that its attacks on the morale of the German work force could be harnessed to the American effort: 'There is great flexibility in the ability of the RAF to direct its material destruction against these objectives which are closely related to the US bombing effort, which is directed towards the destruction of specific industrial targets. It is considered that the most effective results from strategic bombing will be obtained by directing the combined day and night effort of the US and British bomber forces to all-out attacks against targets which are mutually complementary in undermining a limited number of selected objective systems. All-out attacks imply precision bombing of related targets by day and night where tactical conditions permit, and area bombing by night against the cities associated with these targets.'[2]

The RAF shared Eaker's vision of the combined bombing campaign, although it also stressed the need for some flexibility in the plan, and in practice this is what happened. The combined bombing offensive was soon given the title POINT BLANK. The US offensive was in four stages. During the first half of 1943, they were primarily concerned with targets within fighter range, including U-boat installations on the French Atlantic coast. The second stage would start in the third quarter of the year, with penetrations into Germany to a depth of around 400 miles, with the main emphasis on aircraft factories, and especially those producing fighters. The fourth quarter of the year would see other targets being attacked, although pressure would be maintained on the aircraft factories, to prevent these being rebuilt. The fourth stage would occur at the start of 1944, and pave the way for the forthcoming invasion of northern France. The emphasis on curbing fighter production was due to the growing threat from Luftwaffe fighters, which were affecting night- and day-bomber operations.

The heavy defensive formations of the USAAF units and their high flying aircraft led to desperate measures among defending German and Japanese pilots. While ramming aircraft was never official German policy, Sgt Dick Williams of the USAAF managed to shoot down one German fighter which did attempt to ram his aircraft. He is seen here posing by his turret, the ball-turret of a B-17 Fortress. (IWM HU63058)

Harris had also been given permission to attack German cities with a population of 100,000 or more. The first of these attacks had been with 442 bombers sent against Essen on the night of 6/7 March, the largest industrial centre in the Ruhr, Germany's industrial heartland.

The raid against the Bremen Vulkan shipyard at Vegesack, near Bremen, on 18 March 1943 was intended as a further blow to the Kriegsmarine. In the lead was the 303rd Bombardment Group, whose lead bombardier was Lt Jack Mathis, USAAF, responsible by this time for bomb-aiming for all the following aircraft. As the aircraft started its bombing run, it ran into heavy flak, the aircraft shuddering as shells exploded nearby. Mathis called for the bomb bay doors to open, but as he synchronized his bombsight, flak burst through the bomb-aimer's position, hitting Mathis and throwing him back against the aircraft's navigator. Mortally wounded in the abdomen and with a shattered arm, Mathis crawled back to the bombsight, which hadn't been damaged. Bleeding profusely, he knelt and resumed the task of leading the formation on to the bomb-release point. He released his aircraft's bombs, and called out: 'Bombs . . .', and that was all. The navigator completed the call 'away'.[3] Mathis had died from his wounds at the moment he had released the bombs.

By this time the Pathfinder units were using H2S, which could show on a cathode tube images of urban/rural or land/sea contrast, and was

The other American heavy bomber in the European theatre was the Consolidated B-24 Liberator. Here a formation of B-24Hs and Js of the Eighth Air Force's 34th Bombardment Group (Heavy) crosses the French coast on a daylight raid during the summer of 1944. (IWM HU59880)

particularly effective over targets where a city had a water frontage. A good example of this arose later in 1943, when 12 USAAF B-17s used both H2S and the US equivalent, H2X, for a successful raid on Wilhelmshaven. The new MkXIV bombsight was also giving Bomber Command shorter runs into the target, reducing the period when the bombers were at their most vulnerable. Harris also broke the rules, replacing the original turrets in many of his aircraft with a new design capable of taking heavier .50 calibre guns, which were far more effective against German fighters than the original .305 guns.

Damage to another major German industrial organization came on 20/21 July, when the former Zeppelin plant at Friedrichshafen, on the shores of Lake Constance, was attacked, using some of the still limited supply of H2S sets fitted to Pathfinder aircraft. The attack was reasonably successful, destroying half the plant, and might have been more successful still had the maps provided so that the crews could recognize the target area from the H2S image been more up to date. Losses amounted to just 4.6 per cent, despite the short summer night which meant that the aircraft had to continue to North Africa after the raid.

On another occasion the USAAF sent 107 aircraft to bomb the Focke-Wulf plant at Bremen, losing 16 bombers, with another 46 seriously

A twilight view of another of the 34th's B-24H Liberators. (IWM HU59871)

The last moments of a B-24, burning furiously over Austria. Heavy defensive armament could not guarantee the protection of the USAAF's aircraft. (IWM EA36158)

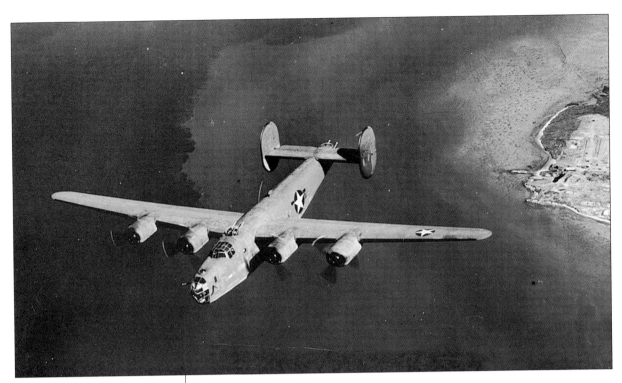

A Consolidated B-24 Liberator over the sea. (IWM OEM6010)

damaged. Nevertheless, the raid caused so much damage that the Germans were forced to move production to Marienburg, outside the range of the USAAF's bombers.

Meanwhile, the RAF had been back over the Ruhr, treating Wuppertal so roughly with 700 bombers that five out of the six main factories were destroyed.

THE BATTLE OF THE RUHR, 5 MARCH–10 JULY 1943

ESSEN, 5/6 MARCH 1943

By 1943 RAF Bomber Command was ready to step up the offensive. It had the right aircraft with the incomparable Lancaster and much-improved Halifax, as well as the Mosquito. Added to this, there were many US types, including Liberators, with many more of the latter in Coastal Command, and many of the US medium bombers. The Pathfinder concept had proved itself, while navigational and bombing aids were all much improved, including the MkXIV bomb-sight, which even allowed some slight changes in course for evasive measures during the run-in to a target.

In addition to the use of equipment such as Gee, and the development of more advanced navigational equipment such as H2S, which had entered service at the end of 1942, the RAF had also amassed a great deal of intelligence regarding German defences by this time. It had gained details of the Würzburg radar and the Kammhuber Line of radar, AA defences and night-fighter zones, stretching across Germany from the Baltic to Switzerland. Bomber Command's Operational Research Section (ORS), had

developed a technique known as 'streaming', in the belief that each air defence radar could only direct night-fighters onto one bomber at a time, so that bombers passed over any given point in the air defence network in a concentrated stream, with ten bombers crossing each point every minute, despite the very real risk of collision in the dark night skies. The 'given point' was a box, 3 miles long, 5 miles wide and 2 miles deep. Dr Basil Dickins, Head of the ORS, explained: 'We had to reduce it all to mathematics, and work out the actual chance of a collision. And it became quite obvious to us at ORS that while a collision was a half per cent risk, the chances of being shot down by flak or fighters was a three or four per cent risk. So we could allow the collision risk to mount quite a bit, provided that in doing so we could bring down the losses from other causes. . . .'[4]

The time was right to mount massive attacks on German industry and communications, and against the often difficult and heavily defended centres in the Ruhr, sometimes referred to as 'Happy Valley' by RAF crews. The first major raid of what was to become known as the Battle of the Ruhr, which was to last four months, came on the night of 5/6 March, 1943. The Ruhr was the principal area not just in Germany, but indeed the whole of Europe, for the production of coal, coke, iron and steel, with vast chemical and metallurgical industries as well. This was not another 'Thousand Bomber Raid', but the force of 442 bombers, of which 303 were heavy bombers, deployed against Essen's massive Krupp works was large enough. Krupp was a major industrial concern which produced railway locomotives, guns, shells and fuses. Essen was a popular target for the planners at Bomber Command, but not for the crews. However, there could be no doubt that a programme of successful raids on this area would seriously affect Germany's ability to wage war.

The Aircraft

Most of the aircraft, Lancasters, Halifaxes and Liberators, have been described already, but another aircraft used on this raid was the de Havilland Mosquito. Known affectionately as 'the wooden wonder', the de Havilland Mosquito had been a venture by the manufacture to use a non-strategic material, wood, to build a high-performance aircraft. Although here the aircraft is seen in its light bomber role, the versatile Mosquito was also used for reconnaissance, occasionally as a long-range escort fighter, as a night-fighter and even, for the new British state airline, BOAC (British Overseas Airways Corporation), as a light transport, carrying ball-bearings from Sweden over enemy-occupied Norway.

The aircraft had been proposed as early as 1938, but it was not until the end of 1939 that de Havilland were allowed to develop a prototype, and when 50 were ordered the following year, the order was subsequently cancelled. First flown in November 1940, the aircraft eventually managed to enter RAF service a year later, and soon its impressive performance and flexibility ensured its future. Two 1,230 hp Rolls-Royce Merlin engines gave a top speed of 380 mph, and up to 2,000 lb of bombs could be carried over long ranges, but the aircraft could also carry a single 4,000 lb Cookie, a unique achievement for what was officially a light bomber. Later versions could exceed 400 mph with more powerful Merlins of up to 1,720 hp. The two-man crew, pilot and navigator, sat side by side, with

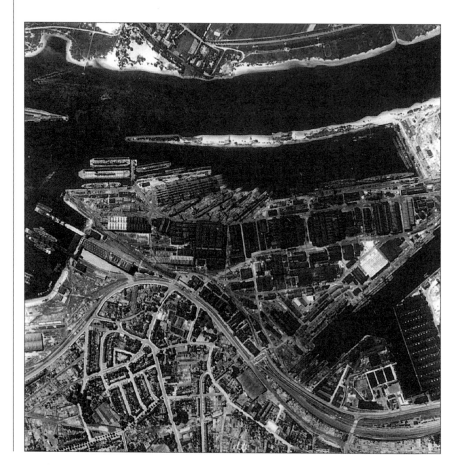

Another major port to receive attention from the RAF was Bremen – this is a reconnaissance photograph. (IWM MH30200)

the navigator also acting as bomb-aimer or, on night-fighters, radar operator. The aircraft demanded that its pilots should not be over-confident on the one hand, or hesitant on the other. It was extremely popular with its crews, and many regard it as the most beautiful aircraft ever built.

In RAF Bomber Command service this fine aircraft flew not only on light bomber missions, often on 'hit and run' and precision raids, but also as a Pathfinder. This was despite early objections by the authorities, one of whom explained to Gp Capt (later AVM) Donald Bennett, the Pathfinders' leader, that they could not have the aircraft since it could not be flown at night because the exhaust flames were so bad that they blinded the pilot and navigator. Bennett retorted: 'I'm very sorry, but if I'd known I'd never have done it, as I have for the past six or eight days every night.'[5]

One pilot recalled that:

The Mosquito was the cat's whiskers. We would have been well away at the beginning of the war with a few Mosquito squadrons. We could have hit Berlin for a dozen in the first few weeks – you could afford to fly one of those things in daylight.

In winter we could take off at about four o'clock in the afternoon, in the dusk. By the time we got over the Dutch coast heading towards the target . . . you were up at about thirty thousand feet, pretty safe, away from everything . . . We'd collect over the target, drop a load of four-thousand cookies . . . down they'd go fairly accurately, and back everybody would steam. Used to take about three and three-quarter hours, roughly, and you'd be back in the mess by half past eight, having a normal dinner.[6]

Joseph Goebbels visiting a blitzed German city in August 1943, attempting to raise civilian morale. (IWM HU55382)

The Action

As was usual with targets in the Ruhr, and especially Essen, the target was obscured by heavy industrial haze, despite the clear night. Anticipating difficulty, the raid was led by eight Mosquitos of 109 Sqn, equipped with Oboe.

The Mosquitos' role was to mark the way to the target with yellow marker flares, starting at 15 miles out – which in this case was the centre of Krupp – giving the main force both a navigational aid and a warning that the target was imminent, and then to drop red target incendiaries on the Krupp works at three-minute intervals, starting at 19.00. Following the Mosquitos were 22 Pathfinder Lancasters, dropping green target incendiaries on the reds, flying in at one- and two-minute intervals. These aircraft were followed by the main bomber force, flying in three waves, Halifaxes, Stirlings and Wellingtons, with Lancasters in the rear, concentrated so that the last Lancaster was to have dropped its bombs within 40 minutes after target marking had been completed. The bomber crews were instructed to aim at the red incendiaries, and if these could not be seen, to aim for the green incendiaries.

The main force which followed dropped bombloads which were generally one-third high-explosive and two-thirds incendiaries, aiming for the red indicators, and if these could not be seen, aiming for the green indicators. The entire raid took just 38 minutes, with 1,054 tons of bombs dropped.

This was the first raid to seriously damage the Krupp works, and the nearby Goldschmidt Company and Maschinenbau Union were also badly damaged, along with a gas works, power station and the main tram depot. The huge fires laid waste an area of 160 acres and made 30,000 people homeless, many of them Krupp workers.

Perhaps the best comment on the success of this raid came from the German Minister of Propaganda, Joseph Goebbels, who recorded:

> During the night Essen suffered an exceptionally severe raid. The city of the Krupps has been hard hit. The number of dead, too, is considerable. If the English continue their raids on this scale, they will make things exceedingly difficult for us. The dangerous thing about this matter, looking at it psychologically, is that the population can see no way of doing anything about it. Our anti-aircraft guns are inadequate. The successes of our night-fighters, though notable, are not sufficient to compel the English to desist from their night attacks. As we lack a weapon for attack, we cannot do anything noteworthy in the way of reprisal.[7]

Further attacks followed, although not as frequently as later in the war, taking place on 12/13 March, 3/4 April and 30 April/1 May, so that during the two months, there were 1,552 bombing sorties against Essen, dropping a total of 3,967 tons of bombs. Production at Krupps was very seriously damaged.

Goebbels wrote, after the night of 12/13 March: 'Later in the evening the news reached us of an another exceedingly heavy air raid on Essen. Twenty-five major fires were raging on the grounds of the Krupp plant alone. Air warfare is at present our greatest worry. Things simply cannot go on like this. The Führer told Goering what he thought without mincing words.'[8] This was before he had visited the city to see the damage for himself, which he did on 10 April:

> We arrived in Essen before 7am. Deputy Gauleiter Schlessmann and a large staff called for us at the railway station. We went to the hotel on foot because driving is quite impossible in many parts of Essen. This walk enabled us to make a first-hand estimate of the damage inflicted by the last three raids. It is colossal and indeed ghastly. This city must, for the most part, be written off completely. The city's building experts estimate that it will take twelve years to repair the damage . . . Nobody can tell how Krupps can go on. Everyone wants to avoid transplanting Krupps from Essen. There would be no purpose in doing so, for the moment Essen is no longer an industrial centre the English will pounce upon the next city, Bochum, Dortmund or Düsseldorf.[9]

Out of the entire force all but 58 aircraft claimed to have bombed the target, although only 39 out of 293 bombing photographs taken actually showed the ground. Subsequent analysis indicated that 153 aircraft, about 40 per cent of the main force, had been within the target area, demonstrating the effectiveness of Oboe, since this was the best effort yet on any Essen raid. Inevitably, there were some losses, 14 aircraft failing to return.

The next target was Nuremberg, outside the range of Oboe, and a chance to use the new H2S. On 8 March 1943, 298 heavy bombers were deployed for this raid, with no fewer than 157 of these being Lancasters, with another 36 aircraft as Pathfinders. The Pathfinder force was divided into two, the first 14 aircraft to use green target incendiary markers, and the remainder as a back-up force, which was to use red target incendiary markers; all were equipped with H2S. In the event, 6 of the first 14 aircraft had malfunctioning H2S sets, and visibility over the target was not good, so the green markers were scattered. In the circumstances, it was a worthy effort which saw 142 aircraft dropping their bombs within 3 miles of the target aiming point, and reconnaissance photographs taken on 10 March showed that considerable damage had been inflicted on industry. Just seven aircraft were lost, despite the long flight over occupied Europe and Germany itself.

Further attacks followed, with raids on Essen and Duisburg before the end of the month, but many more raids were being made east of the Ruhr, including Berlin on two occasions, and Munich and Stuttgart, all of which required the use of H2S, even though it was more effective as a navigational than as an aiming device – Oboe was far superior in this respect, but was limited in range. In April, the pressure was maintained, with another three raids on Duisburg, as well as two each on Kiel and La Spezia in Italy, and there were isolated raids on Frankfurt, Kiel, Rostock and Stuttgart. On the night of 16/17 April, a double operation was mounted, when 327 aircraft were sent against Pilsen and another 271 against Mannheim, but the losses were heavy, 37 being lost on the Pilsen raid and another 18 on the Mannheim raid – an unacceptable rate of almost 10 per cent, largely due to the clear moonlit night. A bomber's moon was almost invariably a night-fighter's as well.

Attention switched back to the Ruhr in May, since the short nights of the northern summer meant that longer-distance targets became riskier, although this did not stop a raid on Pilsen, home of the Skoda works. The number of aircraft deployed was rising again, and not far short of the thousand mark, but this time the heavy bombers were in the majority, with more than 500 available, giving a much heavier bombload. On the night of 23/24 May 826 aircraft, including many Wellingtons, were launched against Dortmund.

Visits to the Ruhr were unpopular with the bomber crews because of the heavy AA defences. The pressure built up as the number of hours and sorties mounted, many feeling that perhaps their luck would run out before the end of their tour. Robert Raymond, a US volunteer flying as a Lancaster captain, explained:

My crew have the jitters, being now so near the end of their tour and anxious to survive it. I talked to them en route to base while low over the sea. I told them that as long as they flew with me, we would continue to do our best over every target. My conscience won't let me do anything else. They agreed to stick to it instead of dropping the load outside the defended areas as we see some planes do. I know how they feel. They're tired. Griffiths is particularly nervous of late. He's only nineteen. So young.[10]

Eventually, it had to be agreed that while the first tour would remain at around 30 trips, second tours would be just 20 trips. Pathfinders were supposed to have 60 trips per tour, but during 1943 this was reduced to 45, only to be increased again to 60 once the difficulty in training sufficient replacement crews became apparent.

There were six raids on Essen during the spring of 1943, with as many as 700 bombers being used on one occasion. They can be counted among some of the most successful of the war, especially the attack of 25/26 July, the last of the series of raids against the city. The main target in Essen continued to be the giant Krupp works. Damage was so severe that the largest building, a locomotive factory, was not completely repaired before the war ended. Production of guns was halved. Shell and fuse manufacture was stopped for some time. The German armies, increasingly beleaguered on the Mediterranean and Russian Fronts, were in desperate need of guns and munitions.

Unusually, the Krupp works had been at the centre of Essen, unlike many other German cities, where heavy industry tended to be on the outskirts. Given the state of bomb-aiming technology at the time, this made the plant easier to target. The owner, Gustav Krupp von Bohlen und Halbach, visited the devastation, and was so shocked that he suffered a stroke.

Bad weather prevented a successful raid on Düsseldorf in May, but the greater part of the city, with its many corporate headquarters, was destroyed on the night of 11/12 June.

Comment

At the end of the Battle of the Ruhr Lord Cherwell, the British Government's Chief Scientific Adviser, was able to reassure Churchill that bombing accuracy had improved. In 1941 RAF Bomber Command had managed to get just a fifth of its bombs within 5 miles of the target, but by 1943, almost 70 per cent were within 3 miles. Harris claimed: 'Nothing like the whole succession of catastrophes which overcame the cities of the Ruhr and North-West Germany in the first half of 1943 had ever occurred before, either in Germany or elsewhere. It was an impressive victory.'[11]

There can be little doubt that the raids on the Ruhr were extremely successful, and with the 'Thousand Bomber Raids' showed that the RAF had overcome its early difficulties to provide an effective bombing strategy. By 1944 production of tanks would be down to 17,625 against planned production of 38,400, while for day- and night-fighters it would be 25,822 against 57,600, and when production of all aircraft types is taken into consideration, there would be 39,925 built against plans for 93,600.[12]

Much has been made of the way in which German industry managed to overcome its difficulties, and it is true that under its Armaments Minister, Albert Speer, a genius in maintaining production, herculean efforts were made to maintain and even increase production. Although careful selection of statistics will sometimes show production increasing, such massive raids, well targeted and repeated so that repair work was affected, created major problems which accumulated and could not be easily or quickly overcome. It is sometimes forgotten that in addition to their own factories, and others given over to war production, the Germans also had the use of factories in the occupied territories.

There were other successes during the Battle of the Ruhr, in addition to much-improved accuracy. Not the least of these was the improvement in the standard of air gunnery. Previously, many bomber gunners had not fired at night-fighters, believing that this gave their position away, and many also failed to appreciate the importance of giving their pilot a running commentary on the movements of night-fighters, reducing their ability to take avoiding action, recommended as being a steep diving turn and corkscrew. During the Battle of the Ruhr, this changed, and gunners were given strict orders to shoot as soon as they saw a night-fighter, as long as they didn't hit other bombers.

Three technical devices were produced to help: Boozer, Monica and Serrate. Boozer, available from spring 1943, picked up enemy radar, a yellow lamp flashing if it detected the FuG 202/212 aerial radar of a night-fighter, and a red lamp if it detected a Würzburg ground radar. Unfortunately, the device picked up transmissions over such a wide area that over enemy territory the lights flashed on and stayed on. Monica, which appeared in late June, was an active device in the tailplane of the bomber, producing a clicking sound if it detected another aircraft, but it reacted even when Allied bombers were flying in a concentrated stream. Serrate was intended to be superior to both these, giving a bearing on an enemy night-fighter's position.

All in all, growing experience and improved professionalism had made the bomber a truly formidable weapon.

The Daily Round

Throughout this period, major operations were mixed with smaller ones, keeping relentless pressure on the Germans. The 'Gardening' mine-laying operations were maintained, still often using crews in the later stages of their training. Daylight raids continued, with No. 2 Group mainly targeting Luftwaffe bases in France and the Low Countries, using fast medium bombers such as the Lockheed Ventura, Mitchells and Bostons. The more difficult operations against railways were usually conducted by de Havilland Mosquitos, used on precision attacks, as well as many night-time 'hit and run' raids on Berlin. Amid this abundance of modern aircraft, Bomber Command even found time to allow some of its elderly Whitleys to operate anti-submarine patrols on loan to Coastal Command.

Typical of the daily round of operations was 19 May 1943. During the day, 12 Lockheed Venturas attacked the airfield at Ploujean, near Morlaix, while the Whitleys of No. 91 Group mounted five anti-submarine sorties. A Mosquito of No. 8 Group undertook a meteorological reconnaissance. After dark, 6 Mosquitos raided Berlin, and 5 Wellingtons dropped leaflets over France. There were no losses on what was, for Bomber Command, a quiet day.

THE 'DAMBUSTERS' RAID ON THE RUHR DAMS, 16/17 MAY 1943

The raid on the Ruhr Dams, OPERATION CHASTISE, was one of the RAF's most famous raids of the Second World War, having seized the public

Meanwhile, the British and American commanders met in Canada. Here is Gen 'Hap' Arnold (left), commander of the USAAF, with his British opposite number, ACM Sir Charles (later Lord) Portal. (IWM HU54920)

imagination ever since. Even before the outbreak of war, as early as 1937, the significance of the dams to the German war effort had been recognized. The difficulty lay in finding a suitable means of attack and suitable weaponry, since the dams were extremely heavily built, and the huge reservoirs of water which they contained also helped to protect them from conventional bombing. In this case, the driving force for an attack on the dams came not from within the RAF or even the War Cabinet, but from outside, from an inventor called Barnes Wallis, the designer of the Wellington bomber, who with hindsight can be regarded as probably the most inventive and fertile mind in the history of British aviation in the twentieth century.

Wallis had been interested in the destruction of the dams since before the war, not because he had any knowledge of the RAF's interest in them, but because he saw the destruction of Germany's energy supplies as the key to Allied victory with the minimum impact on civilian lives. After experiments and tests, he became convinced that a 'bouncing bomb' would be the answer, and he planned two different versions, a small version known as Highball, which could be used by aircraft such as the Mosquito bomber against ships, and a larger version, Upkeep, to be delivered by a Lancaster bomber against the dams. Although often described as a 'bouncing bomb', the weapon was more usually described as a mine within the RAF. Initially, the Air Ministry was doubtful, the Admiralty showing greater interest in Highball, but eventually the project began to be taken seriously, even though 'Bomber' Harris himself thought that the idea was 'tripe of the wildest description . . . there is not the smallest chance of its working.'[13] To be fair to Harris, apart from the daily pressures of running Bomber Command, he was constantly being bombarded with ideas on how to win the war by people with scant technical or tactical knowledge or experience. He was also desperate to see as many Lancasters in operational service as possible, and as quickly as possible, and the 'bouncing bomb' concept meant that a number of aircraft would have to be specially modified, and therefore taken out of the mainstream of operations. Nevertheless, his superior, the Chief of the Air Staff, Marshal of the Royal Air Force Lord Portal, was convinced, and Harris was told in March 1943 that the operation was to proceed. The irony was that Highball, which was received with so much more enthusiasm by the Admiralty, largely with an attack on the German battleship *Tirpitz* in mind, failed its trials.

The operation was to involve 20 Lancasters being modified to take the large Upkeep 'bouncing bomb', in a new squadron within No. 5 Group, initially known as 'Squadron X', but soon re-designated as the now famous 617 Sqn. Wg Cdr Guy Gibson was selected as commanding officer of the new squadron. Gibson was a regular RAF officer from pre-war days. He had flown Handley Page Hampdens, winning the Distinguished Flying Cross (DFC), and had then switched to one of the new night-fighter

RAF armourers prepare to load sixteen 250 lb bombs into a Short Stirling of No. 1651 Heavy Conversion Unit at RAF Waterbeach. (IWM TR8)

A Handley Page Halifax MkII of 35 Sqn, RAF Linton-on-Ouse, flown by Flt Lt Reginald Lane (later Lt Gen, Canadian Armed Forces), in June 1942. This was the first squadron to use the aircraft operationally. Note the Rolls-Royce Merlin engines of this early version, rather than the Bristol Hercules radials of later marks. (IWM COL185)

The most potent bomber in the European theatre was the Avro Lancaster – these are three Lancaster MkIs of No. 44 Sqn in flight. (IWM TR206)

Ground crew maintaining a Lancaster's Rolls-Royce Merlin engines. (IWM TR20)

Battle damage on a Lancaster of 619 Sqn which was forced to land at Rinkaby, in neutral Sweden, where the aircraft was interned, in January 1945. (RAFM P014267)

The controls of a Boeing B-17G Fortress – contrast this with the Handley Page Hampden shown earlier in this book. (RAFM P017917)

A rare air-to-air colour shot of a de Havilland Mosquito B.MkIV in flight. This aircraft belonged to 105 Sqn which operated the aircraft from September 1942, to May 1943, flying twenty-three sorties. (British Aerospace)

Infra-red reconnaissance of a V-1 flying bomb launch site. (IWM COL33)

A Hawker Siddeley Vulcan of 44 Sqn, one of the aircraft flown from Ascension Island to the Falklands. (RAFM P016446)

By the time of the Falklands campaign, 57 Sqn was still operating bombers, except that these had been converted to the tanker role. Handley Page Victor tankers of 57 Sqn are pictured at Ascension Island. (IWM FKD1169)

The Falklands Campaign would not have been won without the British Aerospace Sea Harrier, which could act as a fighter or carry four 1,000 lb bombs. This aircraft belonged to 800 NAS. (IWM FKD475)

The RAF placed great faith in its JP233 runway denial weapons, shown here being deployed from a Tornado GR1, but the need for the aircraft to maintain a steady course while the munitions were dispersed posed great risks to the aircraft and its crew. (IWM GLF1306)

The Gulf War saw the American carriers in action. Aboard USS Saratoga, a Grumman A-6 Intruder waits in the background, wings folded. Flight deck crew functions can be identified by different colour shirts, with yellow for the plane director (centre), red for ordnance men, or armourers (left), and green for the catapult crew (right). (IWM GLF993)

Ordnance men aboard Saratoga hurry a Phoenix air-to-air missile. The F/A-18 Hornets in the background proved their worth on fighter and bomber sorties. (IWM GLF992)

F/A-18 Hornets and A-6 Intruders share the flight deck of another American carrier, Independence, *during the Gulf War. (IWM GLF1004)*

Originally renowned for the novelty of its VTOL (vertical take-off and landing) capability, the Harrier has also proved itself to be a versatile and effective aircraft using short take-off and vertical landing. Here, RAF Harriers of 1 Sqn taxi out ready for take off at Gioia del Colle in southern Italy during the Kosovo crisis. (© British Crown Copyright/MoD)

Designed to carry nuclear weapons during the Cold War, the Boeing B-52G Stratofortress saw action in Vietnam, effectively carpet bombing Viet Cong positions and supply routes, and then gained a new lease of life with the advent of the cruise missile, being used to fire these during the Gulf War and in 1999's Balkan conflict. (RAFM P050707)

squadrons (almost the equivalent of poacher turning gamekeeper), had gained a bar to his DFC, and had then returned to bombers, commanding 106 Sqn, which had been equipped with the notoriously unreliable Avro Manchester, and which, at the time of his selection for 617 Sqn, was starting to re-equip with the Lancaster. He had been awarded the Distinguished Service Order for his leadership, and had 71 operational sorties on bombers. In theory, he had earned a good rest, with even the possibility of being stood down from operations for the rest of the war, but this was a man who was never happy unless he was flying. For him, and many others, a staff job – or 'flying a desk' in RAF slang – was something to be avoided at all costs. In his introduction to Gibson's book, *Enemy Coast Ahead*, Harris recalled the time when, in order to give him a rest, Gibson had been transferred to a staff job at Group, and: 'he was found in his office with – literally – tears in his eyes at being separated from his beloved crews and unable to go on operations . . .'.[14]

The Aircraft
Once again, the RAF's beloved and sturdy Lancaster heavy bombers were selected for this role, but a number of modifications had to be made, including the removal of the bomb bay doors to accommodate the 'bouncing bomb' each aircraft would carry.

The Action
The new squadron was supposed to be comprised of volunteers nearing the end of their second tour of duty, but in fact this proved to be impossible to achieve, so apart from Gibson and his two experienced flight commanders, the other eighteen pilots included one who had completed two tours, another 10 who had completed one tour, and the remainder were still on their first tour. Intensive special training was given, including

Guy Gibson's 617 Sqn Lancaster, ready for the famous raid on the Ruhr Dams, with its 'bouncing bomb' slung under the fuselage. The bomb bays of the squadron's aircraft had to be modified for this operation. (IWM HU69915)

An aerial reconnaissance photograph of the Mohne Dam, clearly showing the breach through which the reservoir's contents flooded. Water is continuing to pour through, and the foam covers the spot where, before the raid, the power station stood. (IWM CH9687)

low flying and mock attacks on a dam in a remote part of Wales – not always to the delight of the locals, who had no idea what was going on.

It was essential to the success of the operation that the 'bouncing bombs' be dropped from an altitude of precisely 60 ft on to flat calm water. Obtaining such a precise altitude caused some problems at first, until the idea was adopted of equipping each aircraft with two spotlights, one forward and the other towards the tail, which were angled so that the two spots merged into one at exactly the required height.

To obtain the maximum benefit from the operation, the dams had to be full of water, and for this reason a date in the middle of May was chosen. The raid was to be in three waves. The first was to consist of nine aircraft led by Gibson himself, and was to attack the Mohne Dam, and then the aircraft which still had bombs were to attack the Eder, and if all went well and some aircraft still carried their bombs, these were to proceed to the Sorpe. The second wave would head direct for the Sorpe. The third wave would be held in reserve, in case the first and second waves' bombs were not sufficient to breach the dams. The aircraft would fly out and back at a height of just 60 ft to avoid radar detection.

Several diversionary aids were also to be mounted that night, drawing German night-fighters away from 617 Sqn's aircraft. Mosquito sorties

Survivors of 617 Sqn's raid on the dams, pictured outside the Officers' Mess at RAF Scampton. Guy Gibson is in the middle, while the American Flt Lt J.C. McCarthy is third from the left in the back row. Shannon is fourth from the right in the front row. (IWM HU63354)

were flown against Berlin, Cologne, Düsseldorf and Münster, and although these entailed just 9 aircraft, it would be enough to stimulate the defensive system into action. No fewer than 54 'Gardening' mine-laying sorties were to be mounted off the Friesian Islands, and a handful of Wellingtons undertook leaflet-dropping.

The aircraft took off on the raid on the night of 16/17 May, with Harris, Cochrane (the Group Leader) and Wallis all present to see them go. On the outward flight, each wave lost an aircraft to AA fire, while the second wave also lost an aircraft which hit a high-tension cable and exploded, and another aircraft from the third wave crashed into trees while trying to evade AA fire at low altitude. A sixth aircraft also failed to reach the target, being forced to return early after hitting the surface of the sea and losing its bomb. Another second-wave aircraft had to return after its intercom was put out of action by AA fire.

On this operation the leader, Guy Gibson, took the outward flight over the Dutch coast, which they reached after being in the air for some 70 minutes, at low level, initially approaching at around 100 feet. It was a bright moonlit night. To get lower, the spotlights were switched on and the aircraft descended to 60 feet. As they closed on the coast, the gunner in the front turret began to swing his weapons either way, ready to deal with any flak ships which might be watching for mine-layers off the coast, while the rear gunner took off his Mae West so that he could squeeze himself into the rear turret. Gibson warned the front gunner to stand by as the aircraft crossed the coast, and then switched the lights off. On this occasion, as they roared over the Western Wall, skirting the defences and turning this way and that to present a difficult target, no shots were fired.

King George VI, wearing the uniform of a Marshal of the Royal Air Force, inspects ground crew members of 617 Sqn during a visit to RAF Scampton on 27 May 1943 – a good indication of the importance attached to the operation. The aircraft, named Frederick III, *carries a caricature of the commanding officer of 57 Sqn, which shared Scampton with 617! (IWM TR1000)*

On they flew. Gibson's wave found the Mohne Dam:

As we came over the hill, we saw the Mohne Lake. Then we saw the dam itself. In that light it looked squat and heavy and unconquerable . . . A structure like a battleship was showering out flak all along its length . . . There were no searchlights. It was light flak, mostly green, yellow and red, and the colours of the tracer reflected upon the face of the water in the lake. The reflections on the dead calm of the black water made it seem there was twice as much as there really was . . .

Down below the Mohne Lake was silent and black and deep.[15]

There were many unusual features on this raid. Normally, aircraft would attack as close together as possible, and several years of wartime experience had shown that it was unwise to hang around, although master bombers had to do this. Experience had also shown that it was asking for trouble to make more than one run at a target. These unwritten rules of successful bomber warfare, and indeed of bomber survival, now had to be ignored completely.

While Gibson prepared for his bombing run, the other aircraft dispersed to the prearranged hiding spots in the hills, so that they should not be seen either from the ground or from the air. Gibson flew his aircraft in a wide

circle and came around down moon, over the high hills at the eastern end of the lake. On straightening up he began to dive towards the flat water 2 miles away. Over the front turret, the dam was silhouetted against the haze of the Ruhr Valley, and those aboard could see the towers and the sluices clearly in the bright moonlight, to the delight of Spam, the bomb-aimer. Gibson recalls:

> Of the next few seconds I remember only a series of kaleidoscopic incidents.
>
> The chatter from Joe's front guns pushing out tracers which bounced off the left-hand flak tower.
>
> Pulford crouching beside me.
>
> The smell of burnt cordite.
>
> The cold sweat underneath my oxygen mask.
>
> The tracers flashing past the windows – they all seemed the same colour now – and the inaccuracy of the gun positions near the power station; they were firing in the wrong direction.
>
> The closeness of the dam wall.
>
> Spam's exultant, 'Mine gone.'
>
> Hutch's red Very lights to blind the flak gunners.
>
> The speed of the whole thing.
>
> Someone saying over the RT, 'Good show, leader. Nice work.'[16]

After the aircraft passed over the dam, the tail gunner sprayed the dam with bullets until the aircraft was out of range. The aircraft circled, and

Gibson, Martin, Shannon and McCarthy are among this happy group of 617 Sqn members standing outside Buckingham Palace after their investiture for the Dams raid. (IWM HU62923)

the crew could see a thousand-foot high column of white water where the mine had exploded, having been placed accurately by the bomb-aimer. They could see that the surface of the lake had been agitated by the explosion, as if it were storm-tossed. Water was slopping over the dam, almost as if it had been breached. This impressive start nevertheless made difficulties for the crews who followed. The mines could only be dropped in calm water, and there was a ten-minute delay, which seemed like hours to Gibson's crew, before the next aircraft could make its bombing run. Above them, the night fighters had gathered, waiting to attack, but unable to do so while the squadron's aircraft remained at low altitude.

Gibson then called for the next aircraft to attack: Flt Lt 'Hoppy' Hopgood in 'M'-Mother. They watched as he made his approach, seeing his spotlights closing together as he flew low over the water, then saw a long jet of flame streaming out of one of his inboard fuel tanks as the aircraft was hit by the flak. Despite all of this, the mine was dropped, although Gibson supposed that the bomb-aimer had been wounded, because it missed the dam and fell on the power house. Then the aircraft started to climb as the pilot struggled for altitude to give his crew a chance to bale out, but, at about 500 ft, there was a sudden bright flash and a wing dropped off, then the aircraft disintegrated. Despite this, Gibson accompanied the next aircraft as it ran in to the attack, and saw another successful attempt, even though the aircraft was badly damaged and lost an entire wing tank of fuel. The fourth aircraft, Sqn Ldr Melvyn 'Dinghy' Young in 'D'-Dog, followed. Again, the aiming was spot on, and again water flooded over the dam, giving Young the idea that the dam had finally burst, but Gibson, circling, could see that hadn't. Again, another long wait, before the fifth aircraft could attack, escorted on its bombing run by Gibson's aircraft and that of Sqn Ldr 'Micky' Martin, their gunners firing at the AA defences. This looked like a repeat of the earlier attacks, with the dam resisting, and at first Gibson couldn't see because of the spray on his windscreen. He ordered the sixth aircraft to come in to attack, before he saw that the dam had finally been breached by Flt Lt David Maltby's aircraft. He warned the sixth aircraft to turn away, and went to take a closer look. The dam had a breach about 100 yd wide. Water, 'looking like stirred porridge in the moonlight', was gushing out and rolling down the valley.

The bomber crews watched as the AA gunners ran for safety from the crumbling dam, except one, who remained at his post firing at the aircraft until one of them silenced his gun with a burst of tracer.

Apart from the lengthy time, the best part of an hour, spent over the target, the other unusual feature of this raid was that Gibson's aircraft remained in constant touch with the base at Scampton, where their AOC had been joined by both 'Bomber' Harris and Barnes Wallis. One of his crew was asked to tap out the morse message 'Nigger', the name of Gibson's faithful black labrador who had been killed by a car on the afternoon before the raid, to tell Scampton of their success. As this was being done, the crews could see the headlights of cars fleeing the torrent of water, and the lights changing colour from light blue to green and then to purple as the waters overcame them: 'We knew, as we watched, that this flood water would not win the war; it would not do anything like that, but it was a catastrophe for Germany.'[17]

They then pressed on to the Eder Dam. This was more difficult to locate, as fog was settling in the valleys, and once they had located it, it was also difficult to tell one valley filled with water from another filled with fog. Gibson's aircraft fired a red Very light over the dam to identify it for the crews who were following. The bombing approach to the Eder was far steeper, and the aircraft had to dive steeply over a Gothic castle overlooking the dam, dropping from 1,000 ft to 60 ft before levelling out and dropping the mine, then having to climb steeply to avoid a mountain a mile away on the other side. On the other hand, there was no AA flak as the bombers approached. The first aircraft, flown by Dave Shannon, went in but could not get into position for a successful drop and had to struggle to get away over the mountain while still carrying its load. He tried four more times, before Gibson called in the next aircraft, flown by Sqn Ldr Henry Maudsley, who made two attempts before making what the pilot described as his final run, running in then pulling away before turning quickly and 'literally flinging his aircraft into the valley'. Those watching could see his spotlights together, indicating that he was at 60 ft, and then the red Very light being fired to indicate that the mine had been dropped. Then they saw that he had dropped his mine too late. It bounced, exploded on the parapet of the dam, lighting up the valley as if it were day for a couple of seconds, while the blast sent the aircraft out of control. Gibson was able to speak to the pilot, and he thought that he heard a faint reply, then nothing.

The first aircraft now returned, and after a dummy run, hit the target accurately with its mine, but without breaching the walls. The third aircraft, flown by Plt Off Les Knight, was ordered in, and after a dummy run, dropped its mine on the next run. Those watching saw the earthquake effect as it exploded at the base of the dam, then the dam collapsed. The water gushed out, and the bombers were able to follow its progress, 'swirling and slopping in a thirty-foot wall as it tore round the steep bends of the countryside . . . saw it extinguish all the lights in the neighbourhood as though a great black shadow had been drawn across the earth . . . we knew that a few miles further on lay some of the Luftwaffe's largest training bases . . . a modern airfield with every convenience, including underground hangars and underground sleeping quarters . . . We turned for home.'[18]

An American serving with the RAF, Sqn Ldr J.C. McCarthy, led the second wave and his was the only aircraft in that wave to survive to attack the Sorpe Dam, which he breached. One of the third-wave aircraft managed to widen the breach, although even so, the damage to the dam was far short of the full breach anticipated. Both the second- and third-wave leaders were shot down on the return trip, marking a total of 8 aircraft lost out of the 19 which had set out, as well as 2 forced to return.

Comment

Unfortunately, the impact of the raid on German war production was far less than had been anticipated, but it is generally credited with giving the RAF and many elsewhere a considerable boost to morale, showing that specialized precision raids were possible, even when fighting against the odds.

The main impact of the destruction of the Mohne and Eder Dams lay not in the damage to the hydro-electric stations swept away as the two dams burst, nor even the flood damage to other industry and communications, as the British saw it, but according to German accounts after the war, the loss of water, needed for so many industrial applications. According to the German Minister for Armaments Production, Albert Speer, the loss of hydro-electric stations in themselves mattered little, since Germany's main power source lay in the coal-fired stations, which were linked through a grid system, but:

> the harm to us was the water for the coking plants for gas, which was a key to our industrial processes . . . and water for the cooling processes in steel production and other industry. We needed a lot of water and the Ruhr wells could not possibly supply sufficent water. If the Sorpe could have been breached as well it would have been a complete disaster. But it was a disaster for us anyway . . . My fear was that you would bomb the reconstruction work from high level and prevent us from storing the water so urgently needed . . . because the situation was already a disaster for us for a number of months.[19]

There was a large price to pay for a one-off operation, taking into account not only the heavy losses, but the amount of time a proficient bomber squadron was unavailable for other operations. Had there been follow-up raids to attack and disrupt repair work, the operation would have been far more worthwhile, and it would have been a testament to the considerable skill and courage of those involved.

As it was, the big surprise is that the losses were not even higher, given the relatively small force against which the Luftwaffe could concentrate its resources, and the number of runs which had to be made over the target. Gibson's own great courage and skill in hanging around, effectively acting as the 'master bomber', and ensuring that his men could do their best, can only be marvelled at.

OPERATION GOMORRAH: THE BATTLE OF HAMBURG – THE FIRST RAID, 24/25 JULY 1943

Germany's second largest city, the northern city of Hamburg on the Baltic, was a major industrial centre and port as well as a naval base. It was a tempting target of immense strategic value and, being on the coast, was ideally suited to H2S location and targeting. On 27 May 1943 the operational order for the city's destruction was circulated to the Bomber Command groups. Given the title OPERATION GOMORRAH, it was emphasized that the destruction of the city would be of significant value in shortening the war, but that it would take more than 'a single night'. The raid was scheduled for the night of 22/23 July, allowing the first use of a new device, 'Window', to disrupt the enemy radar at a minute past midnight. Unfortunately, the weather was too bad on the set night, and remained bad for the following night, so the first raid had to be postponed to the night of 24/25 July.

Window was one of the most successful aids used by Bomber Command in the ceaseless battle against German AA defences. Early experiments in dropping aluminium strips to confuse enemy radar had seemed to have little effect, but experiments at the Telecommunications Research Establishment (TRE), found that oblong aluminium strips were effective.

A Handley Page Halifax of 427 Sqn silhouetted against the evening sky as it waits to take off for Hamburg. (IWM HU67607)

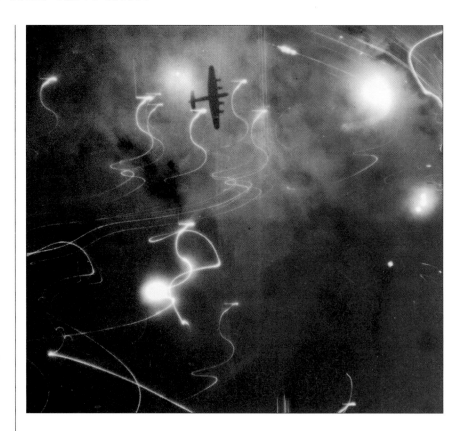

Hamburg was a major port and an important manufacturing centre. Here an Avro Lancaster is silhouetted against fire and flak in January 1943. (IWM C3371)

Oil refineries on fire at Hamburg. (IWM MH7979)

Around major targets the Germans built these potent 'flak towers', effectively flak fortresses, to provide concentrated heavy fire against Allied bombers. This example at Hamburg was designed by Albert Speer. (IWM HU71323)

This was known as early as April 1942, but the project was shelved after Fighter Command objected, pointing out that Window had interfered with the radar on the RAF's night-fighters, and if Bomber Command started to use it, the Luftwaffe's bombers could be expected to do so as well.

Fighter Command continued to object even later in the year, when Air Scientific Intelligence reported that the Germans were aware of the principles behind Window and were expecting it to be used. Fighter Command wished the introduction to be delayed until they had effective counters to it. By April 1943, with losses beginning to mount again, Harris pressed hard for its introduction, but on this occasion he was overruled by the Allied Chiefs of Staff, who wished its introduction to be delayed until after the invasion of Sicily, set for 10 July. Even then, it took Churchill's personal intervention before Window could be introduced.

The irony of the situation was that despite secrecy and wartime censorship, the device had been known outside the RAF for some time, even featuring in a *Daily Mirror* cartoon as early as July 1942.

The Aircraft

As was usually the case on a major operation, Bomber Command deployed the full range of aircraft available to it.

The Action

On the chosen night, diversionary raids were mounted to distract German attention for as long as possible. Thirty-three Lancasters were sent to attack Leghorn, the major port close to Pisa in Tuscany, while six

Wellingtons undertook a 'Gardening' mine-laying operation, small numbers of Mosquitos mounted raids on Bremen, Duisburg, Kiel and Lübeck, and even at this late stage in the war, some aircraft were sent on a 'Nickel' leaflet raid over France.

A mixed force of 791 Lancasters, Halifaxes, Stirlings and Wellingtons was assigned to the Hamburg raid, each aircraft having its own supply of Window. The bomber streams, with up to 200 from each group, would converge into one stream, about 10,000 ft deep, 5 miles wide and 50 miles long, all heading in the same direction. The crews were instructed to drop a bundle of Window at one-minute intervals, starting at 60 miles from the target, and continuing until they were 60 miles from the target again on their homeward run. One wireless operator recalled that the foil strips being unloaded into the night sky were like 'a shoal of fish darting along in the murky water.'[20] The Pathfinder aircraft were fitted with H2S, and used yellow, green and red target incendiaries, while the main attack force dropped a mixture of high explosives and incendiaries. It took just 50 minutes for 728 aircraft to drop 2,400 tons of high explosive, 40 per cent of it within 3 miles of the target. Coming after a spell of hot, dry summer weather, the high explosive soon fanned the incendiaries into a firestorm.

Meanwhile, Window had caused much confusion. One of those flying on the operation recalled:

We heard one German controller get fixed on a packet of this stuff which obviously was not an aircraft and telling it to waggle its wings and so forth, without any success. When another controller saw extra aircraft appearing where only one had been before, he burst into indignation over the radio, 'The English bombers are propagating themselves', and then we heard a quite different voice taking command and I wondered whether it might be Göring himself and it turned out it was.[21]

Only 12 aircraft failed to return.

In accordance with the POINT BLANK directive, daylight saw a raid by 234 USAAF Fortresses operating over the same area, 68 attacking Hamburg itself.

Just three Mosquitos raided Hamburg that night, enough to unnerve those living there and to agitate the air defences. There were also Mosquito raids on Cologne and Gelsenkirchen. The main target for the night of 25/26 July was Essen, using Oboe for navigation and aiming, and Window against the defences. The maximum effort against Essen was not far short of that on Hamburg, with 705 aircraft used, and of these, 604 attacked. One of the most successful raids against a German city at the time, a staggering 60 per cent of the bombs fell into the target area, leaving fires which were still burning two days later, and causing considerable damage to the Krupp works. Despite this, and Essen's fearsome reputation for heavy AA defences, only 26 aircraft were lost.

Daytime saw another visit to Hamburg by the USAAF, with 54 Fortresses, of which 2 were shot down. That night, most of the RAF Bomber Command crews were stood down, taking a much-needed break after two nights on operations, but five Mosquitos maintained the pressure on the city and its inhabitants by night.

The second major night raid on Hamburg came on 27/28 July, with 787 bombers deployed. Once again Window was used, but the Germans now recognized it for what it was, and the controllers had adapted their technique, so that instead of giving guidance onto individual bomber targets, they gave a running commentary on the position of the bomber stream. Casualties were higher than on the first raid, but at 17 aircraft, just over 2 per cent, were lower than would have been likely without Window. The five Mosquitos sent over Hamburg on the night of 28/29 July were able to report that the fires were still burning.

The third raid on Hamburg took place during the night of 29/30 July, and the 777 bombers deployed included Mosquitos for the first time. On this occasion, accuracy fell off, with about a third of the bombers hitting the target area. Losses were also much heavier, at 28 aircraft, showing that the Germans had managed to adjust completely to Window.

As before, Hamburg was left alone for the following night, while a raid was conducted on Remscheid in the Ruhr with 273 aircraft. Again, this was successful, with Oboe guiding Pathfinder Mosquitos so that 191 aircraft hit the target area. More convincing still, post-raid reconnaissance photographs showed the centre of the town had been flattened. Losses were heavy, however, at more than 5 per cent, but of the fifteen aircraft shot down, 8 were Stirlings, out of just 87 of these aircraft. The problem was that these aircraft were slower than the later 'heavies', and tended to be picked off by the night-fighters, so from this time on, the type began to be progressively withdrawn from offensive operations.

The fourth and final raid on Hamburg was on 2/3 August. The weather was poor, with dense cloud. Again, a large force was mustered, 740 aircraft, although only 425 claimed to have attacked the target, and because they couldn't see the markers, most aimed blind. Losses were heavy, at 30 aircraft, with another 51 badly damaged.

Comment

The best comment on the success of these raids must come from the Germans themselves, including the German propaganda chief, Joseph Goebbels. Goebbels was as keen an observer of the raids on Hamburg as he had been on Essen, and after the third raid, on the night of 28/29 July 1943, he noted:

Kaufmann, in a first report, spoke of a catastrophe the extent of which simply staggers the imagination. A city of a million inhabitants has been destroyed in a manner unparalleled in history. We are faced with problems that are almost impossible of solution. Food must be found for this population of a million. Shelter must be secured. The people must be evacuated as far as possible. They must be given clothing. He [Kaufmann] spoke of about 800,000 homeless people wandering up and down the streets not knowing what to do.[22]

Albert Speer took up the same refrain:

The devastation of this series of air raids could be compared only with the effects of a major earthquake. Gauleiter Kaufmann teletyped Hitler repeatedly, begging him to visit the stricken city. When these pleas proved fruitless, he asked Hitler at least to receive a delegation of some of the more heroic rescue crews. But Hitler refused even that . . . Hamburg had suffered the fate Göring and Hitler had conceived for London in 1940.

Hamburg put the fear of God in me. At the meeting of Central Planning on July 29 I pointed out: 'If the air raids continue on the present scale, within three months we shall be relieved of a number of questions we are at present discussing. We shall simply be coasting downhill, smoothly and relatively swiftly . . . We might just as well hold the final meeting of Central Planning in that case.' Three days later, I informed Hitler that armaments production was collapsing and threw in the further warning that a series of attacks of this sort, extended to six more major cities, would bring Germany's armaments production to a total halt.[23]

If further evidence of the success of the bomber campaign was needed, *Generalfeldmarschall* Erhard Milch spoke to a conference of gauleiters on 6 October 1943, and dealt specifically with the worsening armaments situation resulting from combined RAF and USAAF attacks:

Our supply position should be approximately 2,400 to 2,500 planes per month – the figures for various types fluctuate slightly. Unfortunately we had to suffer a decrease in the last two months due to the strong attacks of the enemy on our aircraft production centres. The greater part of our factories producing fighters have been attacked by day as well as by night. The enemy has attacked, in preference, the most important supply factories so that in September we constructed 200 fighter planes less than, for example, in July, when we achieved a peak production of 1,050 fighters. This month of September we should have reached 1,300 aircraft and we would have achieved this if the destruction had not taken place. Not only has the direct destruction of aircraft factories affected us, but so also has that of aircraft components. I assume Minister Speer, as the responsible person, has already reported in detail on this question. The worries we have in this field are extremely great . . . a total of 1,800 planes were produced in September. In the previous month, however, the number was 1,900 and in the month before that, more than 3,000. We hope, however, that we can make up for this loss providing there are no big attacks which inflict new damage . . . How severely our supply position can at times be affected by what seems minor things, can for instance be seen from the attacks on Hannover and on Hamburg. In both cases our metal variable-pitch propellers were badly hit. We produced during this month [he is referring to September] fifty-two of our most important types of planes, but . . . we were only able to deliver four to the front because propellers for the others were not available until ten days later . . . in Hamburg our production has suffered very severely; because of the loss . . . of 3,000 skilled workers who are still missing.[24]

The Russian leader Stalin repeatedly demanded that the US and UK open a second front to relieve the pressure on the Soviet Union, but according to Speer, the bombers were really doing this:

In Russia our 8.8 centimetre anti-aircraft gun with its precision sight had proved to be one of the most feared and effective anti-tank weapons. From 1941 to 1943 we produced 11,957 heavy anti-aircraft guns [8.8–12.8 cm] but most of them had to be deployed for anti-aircraft purposes within Germany or in rear positions . . . Fourteen million rounds of 8.8 or higher calibre flak ammunition were used for purposes other than anti-tank ammunition, for which only 12,900,000 rounds were provided.[25]

After the war, speaking in 1972, Speer enlarged upon this:

The Russians were wrong in complaining at the lack of a second front, because the second front was there by your air attacks, because if we had had at the Russian front all these anti-tank guns – the 8.8 would have been disastrous for them. The production of 8.8 to 12.8 centimetre anti-tank guns from 1942 to the end of 1944 was 19,713 guns, but only 3,172 of these went to the Army, the rest, 75 per cent, had to be diverted to anti-aircraft defence against your bombing. It is a most interesting point, because I think that the damage you did by bombing was very heavy, but the damage you did by weakening the German Army was much more. This applied also to the optical industry and the electronics industry which were working largely for defence needs at the expense of the urgent requirements of the Army. Admittedly, the production of 7.5 centimetre anti-tank guns was the greatest, but these guns were not so effective against the heavy armoured Russian tanks as the 8.8 centimetre gun which was highly effective.[26]

Speer also believed that had the ball-bearing industry received concentrated attacks, the armaments programme could have been seriously weakened after two months, and at a standstill after four months, although Harris, reflecting on the heavy losses encountered by the Americans over Schweinfurt, suggested there would have been no US Eighth Air Force left after a few weeks.

The destruction of Hamburg was not merely psychological: in destroying the city the RAF also cut German submarine production by 40 per cent, and delayed submarine production elsewhere through a shortage of components.

THE OIL WAR: PLOESTI, 1 AUGUST 1943

There were many significant targets which were either simply too far out of range for an attack from the British Isles, or which were sufficiently far to prevent the bombers carrying a worthwhile load. One of these was Ploesti, the oil production centre in Romania. The success of the Allied campaign in North Africa now meant that airfields were available for a strike at the underbelly of the Reich. The date was dictated by the weather, since the Allies had succeeded in breaking the German weather codes, but as these were changed every month, the first day of each month was the last on which they could be certain of an accurate decode.

The oil industry was one of what 'Bomber' Harris described as 'panacea' targets. Nevertheless, the success of any war effort is dependent

An essential part of the Allied bombing campaign was the need to destroy Germany's oil supplies – this US Ninth Air Force B-24 Liberator is shown over the oil plants at Ploesti in Romania. (IWM ZZZ11980F)

upon oil, rubber and ball-bearings, and one cannot criticize the Allies for wishing to inflict the maximum damage on such a target. However, for all the intelligence available to them, they had not realized that Ploesti was one of the most strongly defended areas in the European theatre.

The Aircraft
On this occasion the USAAF was using the Consolidated B-24 Liberator, because of its long range.

The Action
The US Ninth Air Force sent 178 B-24 Liberator bombers to Ploesti, taking off from their North African bases at dawn on 1 August. The round trip of 2,100 miles required them to carry 9 tons of fuel each, so that their bombload was limited to 2 tons per aircraft. The Germans in turn had decoded Allied communications, and had intercepted a message warning Allied air commanders not to attack the bomber force.

In any operation good fortune is important. The Ploesti raid was dogged with bad luck. The Germans knew that a large bomber force was on its way within an hour of it taking off. North African bases were never as secure as those in the UK – a legacy of the earlier German and Italian

Once bases were secured in North Africa, the Allies put these to good use. This is a B-24D of the US Ninth Air Force's 1st Provisional Group at one such base. (RAFM P008495)

presence was a network of spies. On the three-hour flight across the Mediterranean, ten aircraft crashed or had to return because of mechanical difficulties. Worse was to follow when, just before the formation crossed the Albanian coast, the aircraft carrying the chief navigator suddenly spun out of control and crashed into the sea. The aircraft carrying the deputy navigator left the formation and wasted time looking for survivors, lost contact with the rest of the formation as a consequence, and had to return to base, leaving the whole operation in less experienced hands.

Then the weather intervened. The formation ran into dense cloud over Yugoslavia, and the two leading formations opted to climb above the cloud, while the other three flew below it at an altitude just high enough to take them over the mountains, the logic probably being that since their attack was to be at low altitude, it would be better to stay low than have to descend through cloud closer to the target. The formation was not separated by altitude alone – the two leading formations flying above the clouds encountered a strong tailwind, so they were soon well head of the rest of the formation. As they approached the target, the formation was supposed to use three cities as navigational points. The trouble was, these looked much the same from the air, and low-lying mist contributed to the confusion. As a result, the two leading groups ended up on the wrong course, and headed for Bucharest, the Romanian capital, some 30 miles from Ploesti, where they aroused the AA gunners. Although they had realized their mistake, the Romanians also realized that the bombers' true destination was Ploesti, and alerted the defences. Meanwhile, the two leading formations had turned to make their low-level run towards the target, but from the wrong direction.

Meanwhile, the remaining three formations were approaching Ploesti from the right direction, only to find the leaders crossing their path, and the defences alerted. One of the leaders' aircraft cut through a barrage balloon cable, was hit at least five times by flak, and caught fire, but still managed to lead its formation over the target before crashing into a refinery. Confusion reigned as aircraft struggled to find their targets, tried to avoid being caught in AA fire, took evasive action to avoid hitting balloon cables, and then had to look out for oncoming aircraft from the two leading formations, trying desperately to avoid a collision. Added to this, German and Romanian fighters appeared.

Many aircraft were shot down, or fell out of the sky owing to collision with another aircraft or a barrage balloon cable, crashing to the ground, in one case on to a women's prison, killing many of the inmates. Others crashed into buildings or into the streets, or into the oil refinery.

One pilot said later that: 'We were pulled through the gates of hell.'[27] Hell lasted for twenty-seven minutes, leaving many aircraft damaged and many with wounded crew members. They struggled to shake off the fighters and make their way back to base. Seven aircraft landed in neutral Turkey. Some headed for friendly Mediterranean islands – one aircraft landed on a road in Cyprus. The pilot recalled: 'We landed on a highway in the mountains of Cyprus. I pulled over looking for a place to park, and there was a truck crashing into us.'[28] Another reached Sicily, almost out of fuel, and crashed into seven P-40 fighters. 'No one was hurt, but our crew got a very cool reception.'[29]

Others were less lucky, crashing into the sea, while two collided over Bulgaria. Just eleven aircraft reached their base at Benghasi in Libya, the last having been in the air for 16 hours. The airmen were too tired for debriefing. Of the other 178, 57 had been shot down, and others had crashed. More than 500 airmen had been lost. Nevertheless, oil production at Ploesti was cut by 40 per cent for the following two months.

Comment

What damage could have been inflicted to German oil production if Ploesti had been subjected to repeated visits over several days, with occasional follow-up attacks to prevent production restarting! The raid was effective, but at too high a price. The accident to the lead navigator's aircraft was pure bad luck, but for the deputy lead navigator's aircraft to pull out of the formation to look for survivors was, no matter how well-intentioned, poor judgement. Other aircraft could have been deployed to this role rather than abandoning the main bomber force to less experienced hands, and possibly the loss rate would have been much less as a result.

Nevertheless, the USAAF's war on oil production was eventually to be one of the undisputed successes of the bombing campaign, which later led directly to the breakdown of the offensive in the Ardennes at the end of 1944. Even the most cynical critic of bombing accepts that the bombing of oil supplies must have shortened the war by several weeks. The attack on railway and water transport, mainly by the RAF, was suffocating German industry by the end of 1944. By September 1944 the USAAF, with assistance from the RAF, especially during the closing stages of the war, had cut aviation spirit production, which fell steadily to 156,000 tons in May, 54,000 in June, 34,700 in July, 17,000 in August and 10,000 tons in September, and the effect of this can be best judged from the fact that the Luftwaffe had needed 165,000 tons during April. Taking fuel overall, production had fallen by two-thirds. Battlefield mobility was almost non-existent. Speer, the Armaments Minister, could still produce aircraft, but the Luftwaffe could not fly them, and its ability to do so for the future was finally undermined by the virtual cessation of pilot training. The USAAF dropped 131,000 tons of bombs on oil targets, while the RAF dropped another 94,000 tons.

But, as in any bombing campaign, it is persistence which brings victory. In the winter months, as bad weather reduced the frequency of bomber operations, plant was returned to production, and aviation spirit rose to 21,000 tons in October, 39,500 tons in November and 24,500 tons in December, before collapsing almost completely by the end of January. The Ardennes offensive took place, timed to coincide with weather which would keep much of the Allies' air power on the ground.

The problem was that 'Bomber' Harris repeatedly resisted the efforts of his superiors to maximize the RAF's contribution to the attack on oil production. Albert Speer maintains that the larger British bombs did far more damage than those of the USAAF: 'The most successful operation of the entire Allied strategic air warfare was against Germany's fuel supply. Looking back, it is difficult to understand why the Allies started this undertaking so late . . .'.[30]

Another problem was that the main raids on the oil production system came in March and April 1944 and Albert Speer, who knew the true picture of the industrial effort, believed that had the raids continued throughout the summer at the same intensity, Germany 'would quickly have been at our last gasp'.[31]

GERMANY STRIKES BACK: IBEX, 1943–5

The growing pressure on Germany by the end of 1943 led to a plan for what became known as OPERATION STEINBOCK (IBEX), a desperate attempt to bring Germany's bomber forces to bear upon key targets in Britain – in effect, retaliatory attacks for the damage inflicted by the RAF and US Eighth Air Force on major German cities. The Allied bombers were by this time inflicting serious damage on German cities, disrupting production and creating a massive problem of homelessness among the civilian populations. In contrast to the period of the Blitz, for the first time the Luftwaffe would be able to deploy heavy bombers over targets in England, with the arrival of the new Heinkel He177 four-engined bombers.

In addition to heavier aircraft and heavier bombs, the Luftwaffe also had new navigational aids, including *Egon* (similar to the British Oboe) – relying on transmissions from two *Freya* stations 100 miles apart, the first providing a signal for the aircraft to fly around the circumference of a circle whose radius was the distance between the radar station and the bomb-release point, while the second station provided the instruction to release the bombs. Up to a distance of 170 miles from the transmitter, the system was accurate to about 220 yd.

The crews could also use *Truhe*, an airborne receiver which enabled the Luftwaffe formations to make use of the British Gee navigational system, but this was restricted to a select band of pathfinder aircraft within I/KG66. To keep the new systems secret for as long as possible, *Y-Gerät* and *Knickebein* were also used to enable aircraft to navigate as far as the coast of England.

The Aircraft

The new Heinkel He177 heavy bombers were each able to carry two 5,500 lb bombs. Another new weapon was the IB1000 container, capable of carrying 620 small incendiary bombs placed in layers which would be released at intervals as the container fell, providing an even spread of incendiaries over a wide area.

Developed in haste to meet the Luftwaffe's need for a truly heavy bomber, the He177 had four engines mounted in pairs to drive two propellers, with each 'double' Daimler-Benz DB610A unit providing 2,950 hp. Unfortunately, these units were prone to overheating, and were so unreliable that the aircraft was unpopular with ground and aircrew like, eventually earning the unwelcome sobriquet 'The Flaming Coffin'. Based on a 1938 design, the aircraft entered service in 1942, but was plagued by design faults as much as technical difficulties. For example, the aircraft was heavier than necessary because of the stipulation that despite its large size it should be capable of dive-bombing. The mid-wing also limited the size of the bomb bay. Early plans to provide remote-controlled machine-guns for defence had to be abandoned, and conventional weapons with gunners were provided instead.

The Action

The whole effort was to be under the control of *Generalmajor* Dietrich Peltz, who later described the effect of the raids:

> The attacks on the cities were like a few drops of water on a hot stone: a bit of commotion for a short time, then the whole thing was forgotten and people carried on much as before . . . Of course, there would have been losses if we had tried to attack the power stations. But it was clear that however I employed my force against England in 1944, there would have been serious losses.[32]

In common with his US counterparts, Peltz believed in attacks on energy targets, and especially power stations, but Hitler and Goering wanted the cities attacked.

The British night-fighter system was by this time formidable, depending on the highly manoeuvrable de Havilland Mosquito, although there were sometimes unexpected risks for the crews.

Luftwaffe losses were mounting, compounded by the growing inexperience of the bomber crews, with the élite veterans, many of whom had been active in Spain and elsewhere before the onset of the attacks against targets in the UK, dead or PoWs.

Typical of the raids at this time was that on 14 May 1944, when 91 bombers were sent to raid Bristol. *Gefreiter* Rudi Prasse was an observer in one of *II/KG2*'s Ju188s, which had taken off from its base at Vannes at 00.30, carrying two 2,200 lb and two 110 lb bombs, being routed over German-occupied Guernsey, marked by four searchlights. They flew over the English coast at 23,000 ft, at 310 mph. As they arrived over the city they were coned by two searchlights, and were forced to dive through 1,000 ft while making a steep left turn to escape. Then heavy flak started. *Gefreiter* Rudi Prasse recalled:

> To the left and below us a flaming red torch goes down. I note in my log: 'Aircraft shot down at 01.42 hours, south-west of Bristol.' . . . One short glance at the map – that must be the target there. I nudge Hans and point to the right: 'We will attack'.

Bomb-doors open, switches on!

There is a small jerk as our bombs fall away.

Bomb-doors close!

Our *Dora*, lighter by more than two tons, obeys its pilot and sweeps round in a steep left turn, on to a south-easterly course away from the target. Soon we are clear.[33]

The aircraft landed safely at Vannes at 03.50. Others were less fortunate, as 6 out of the 91 aircraft were lost. While the Luftwaffe recorded dropping 83 tons of bombs, British records indicate that just 3 tons landed on Bristol itself.

Comment

This was an example of just how inexperienced the German heavy bomber crews were, causing little damage, although the loss rate of just 6.5 per cent could have been far worse, and on many of the early RAF raids, often was. Overall, there were far too few German heavy bombers, and they were in squadron service too late to have a significant impact on the outcome of the war.

SCHWEINFURT-REGENSBURG, 17 AUGUST 1943

After Hamburg, during the first half of August 1943, the RAF switched its attention to raids on Nuremberg and Mannheim, and to northern Italy. The USAAF continued with its systematic attacks on the key war industries, including ball-bearing production – the key component of any mechanical equipment – and aircraft production. The twin targets of Schweinfurt and Regensburg fitted neatly into this strategy.

The Aircraft

This was another raid for the Boeing B-17 (see p. 124).

The Action

Set for 17 August, the US Eighth Air Force made its first raid on Schweinfurt and Regensburg, which, despite the distances, were attractive to the Americans because they fitted neatly into their list of strategic industries, ball-bearings being manufactured in Schweinfurt, and the Messerschmitt Me109 being manufactured at Regensburg (although, as with most major Second World War aircraft, production took place in a number of sites). The US 4th Bombardment Wing was assigned to Regensburg, RAF Spitfires and USAAF P-47s providing fighter cover as far as the German border, the maximum for the P-47 (the Spitfire's range was even shorter), and after the raid the Fortresses would continue to North Africa, in what the RAF termed a 'shuttle' raid. The US 1st Bombardment Wing would attack Schweinfurt, and would also have an escort outwards, a similar escort waiting for it as it left Germany on its homeward leg back to its base in England.

Meanwhile, the USAAF also planned raids on the Me109 factory at Wiener Neustadt, which was assigned to the US Ninth Air Force, based in North Africa.

The bombers would be on their own for 300 miles, showing touching faith in their ability to defend themselves, even though their later raids on Hamburg and other targets in the north of Germany had resulted in a heavy loss rate of almost 7 per cent. The raids were preceded by attacks on German airfields in northern France, in an attempt to reduce the number of fighters operational against daylight raids. A total of 376 bombers were sent against the two targets, and of these 60 were shot down, a loss rate of 17 per cent. The bombing at Schweinfurt was scattered and inaccurate, and although Regensburg's aircraft factory appeared to have been badly damaged, the suspicion was that damage to the roof and structures was superficial, leaving machinery and production lines intact.

The heavy losses made some of the Americans question the wisdom of continuing with the daylight raids. Brig Gen Anderson, commanding VIII Bomber Command, had secretly flown on two RAF night raids, and in September ordered one of his squadrons, the 422nd, to fly with the RAF so that tactics could be compared. Nevertheless, the Americans persevered with day raids. Commentators are divided over this. Some believe that the Americans did not want to play 'second fiddle' to the British, others feel that the impact on the combined targets would have been weakened if night and day raids did not follow one another, maintaining intense pressure on

Many raids, such as that on Regensburg, were at extreme range for UK-based aircraft, and so the concept of shuttle-bombing was conceived, with aircraft flying on to bases in North Africa once they had dropped their bombs. Here, the crew of one of the Regensburg B-17s, Torchy, *pose with the red fezes and Arabian knives bought as souvenirs of their visit to North Africa. (IWM HU66283)*

German defences and the population over a period of a week or more. Another view is that there could have been congestion over the targets and even over English airfields had both air forces been operating at night.

What did become apparent shortly after the combined bomber effort started was that the USAAF were finding accurate daylight bombing difficult over targets visited by the RAF during the preceding hours of darkness because of the huge pall of smoke from the fires, and it was decided that the order would be reversed, future operations having the USAAF bomb a target in daylight, to be followed by the RAF after darkness fell. In fact, Bomber Command had been expected to follow the USAAF raid on Schweinfurt, but had been diverted to another more pressing objective, the missile sites at Peenemünde. Harris was in any case dismissive of what he viewed as the Americans' 'panacea' targets.

USAAF bomber losses were not to be stemmed until the arrival of true long-range escort fighters, starting with the P-51 Mustang in early 1944, and then followed by the Lockheed Lightning.

Comment

The relatively heavy losses suffered at this stage were a result of a lack of adequate long-range escort fighters – something which would soon be

An attack by Boeing B-17 Fortresses on the ball-bearing factories at Schweinfurt, 17 August 1943. (IWM US157)

Re-arming B-17s at a base in Britain. The boxes of ammunition contain 46,000 rounds, sufficient for seven aircraft. (IWM HU66788)

remedied. The relative lack of success was a reflection of another problem, which is that industrial targets have to be selected carefully.

Two types of industrial target were difficult, the first being those which had heavy industrial installations, such as steel furnaces or heavy presses, which could withstand blast damage. The second was industries such as aircraft manufacture, in which jigs and other equipment, while easily damaged, could also be easily replaced. For all the air forces involved in the Second World War bombing campaigns, there were many false victories in which buildings were damaged, but their contents left relatively unscathed.

OPERATION HYDRA: PEENEMÜNDE, 17/18 AUGUST 1943

The notorious German 'V-weapons', which were to be targeted on British towns and cities in the closing stages of the Second World War, have sometimes been represented as a surprise to the British War Cabinet and to the military, but in fact German work on rockets had been known to the British as early as November 1939, two months after the outbreak of war. The early reports of a secret German test installation at Peenemünde, on the Baltic Coast of northern Germany, were at first regarded as either propaganda or a German false trail. It was not until the winter of 1942/43 that reports began to be taken seriously, and by April 1943, the British were finally convinced that rockets were being developed at Peenemünde.

The Aircraft

This was an operation requiring the largest bombs available, and Lancasters predominated (see p. 115), but there were also Stirlings and

B-17s drop their bombs over a target somewhere in Europe. (IWM HU71933)

Halifaxes (see pp. 114–15), while Mosquitos flew on diversionary raids (see p. 146).

The Action

The raid on the missile sites required both accuracy and a heavy bombload capable of penetrating the launch sites and manufacturing facilities. An attack earlier in the summer was rejected because of the need for longer hours of darkness for the bombers. There was also concern over the means of achieving accuracy in a large-scale raid. 'Bomber' Harris by now favoured using Pathfinders, led by Air Cdre Donald Bennett, but there was also the 'master bomber' technique favoured by Guy Gibson on the Ruhr dams. Other techniques included 'offset marking', where an obscured target was indicated by markers set at a distance from the target, while 'time and distance' used visible reference points in line with the target, as had happened in a number of raids on the Ruhr, where yellow incendiaries had preceded the red and green incendiaries at the target.

AVM Ralph Cochrane, the Air Officer Commanding No. 5 Group, was consulted by Harris, who was aware of the combination of techniques used at Freidrichshafen. As for a leader, Gp Capt John Searby was chosen. After tests of the combination of techniques on a raid on Turin on 7/8 August, Searby realized that accuracy was still far short of requirements. Harris felt this was so important that he opted for a moonlit night, even though this would make the bombers easy prey for night-fighters.

The plan was to send the bombers over German-occupied Denmark rather than over Germany itself, flying across the Baltic before turning towards the target, while, as usual when a major raid was in progress, there would be a diversionary raid by Mosquitos on Berlin. There were a number of unusual features on this occasion, the first being that the Mosquito raids would start several nights before the attack, raiding Berlin in three out of the four nights, and reaching the German capital by flying over or close to Peenemünde, while the diversionary raid would accompany the main bomber force, but continue towards Berlin. This would convince the Germans that the RAF was planning to mount an intensive campaign on Berlin, similar to that upon Hamburg.

The night of 17/18 August was chosen for the raid, by now code-named OPERATION HYDRA. A total of 596 aircraft were deployed in three waves, although this figure would have been higher but for the fact that some 60 Stirlings, intended to fly with the first wave so that they would be less likely to be vulnerable stragglers on the homeward journey, were out of position, having found their own home airfields fogbound on arriving back from a raid the previous night. The eight Mosquitos on the Berlin diversionary raid dropped markers to persuade the Germans that the heavy bomber force was indeed headed for the city. They also used Window, alerting the fighter controllers, who expected a major raid. The ruse worked, and 150 night-fighters were scrambled.

At Peenemünde 16 Pathfinder aircraft aimed for Rügen Island, 7 miles north-west of the target, dropping the new 'red spot fires', impregnated cotton wool which was ignited at 3,000 ft and then burnt on the ground for ten minutes. For the time and distance element of the marking, red target incendiaries were dropped on three points, with yellow target incendiaries for the target itself. Incendiary colours were changed from raid to raid to make it more difficult for the Germans to lay decoy markers. The Pathfinders had used H2S, supposedly at its best when dealing with coastal or estuarial targets, but it failed to work as well as expected, possibly due to marshy conditions which could blur the distinction between land and water, so the red spot fires were dropped late, and in turn the red markers were some distance south of their intended location. As a result, the first wave of Stirlings from No. 4 Group bombed the wrong target, but Searby, as Master Bomber, was able to correct this, supported by a reserve force of Pathfinders. The second wave of Lancasters from No. 1 and No. 3 groups found that the wind had changed, so that the target incendiaries started to drift out over the sea, but again Searby intervened. The third wave of aircraft from No. 5 and No. 6 groups had been warned that, although using time and distance, they were to bomb automatically at the end of their timed run only if they failed to see any markers, otherwise they were to aim for the markers and disregard their own calculations. This would have been fine, but Searby had failed to notice that the markers on the third aiming point had not been placed correctly.

There was relatively little AA fire, most of what there was being suppressed by the first wave, and the first two waves had little contact with night-fighters, which had been successfully drawn away by the Berlin diversionary raid, so that No. 1, No. 3 and No. 4 Groups lost just three aircraft each. By the time the third wave arrived over the target, those night-fighters which had not been forced to land for refuelling knew exactly what was happening, and No. 5 Group lost 17 out of 117 Lancasters, while No. 6 lost twelve of its mixed force of 61 Lancasters and Halifaxes. Nevertheless, despite the difficulties in marking the target, considerable damage was done, and production of the V-2 rocket was delayed. Altogether, 3.5 million lb of high explosive and almost 600,000 lb of incendiaries had been dropped, although not all of them on the target.

Comment

This operation simply had to take place. The importance of destroying the V-weapons can be judged from the fact that between 12 June 1944 and 28 March 1945, 8,564 flying bombs of both the V-1 and V-2 types were launched against England. Of these, 1,006 crashed shortly after launching, and while just 2,400 reached England, they were enough to kill 6,184 civilians and seriously injure another 17,981. The V-1 raids ended early in September, and were followed by the V-2, with 1,190 launched, killing 2,855 people and seriously injuring 6,268.

The total damage of the flying bombs, with a 1 ton warhead, and of the rockets, with a 0.75 ton warhead, was less than three concentrated and well-targeted bomber raids on Germany. Nevertheless, the V-2 in particular, which could not be detected or countered, had a serious impact on morale.

BATTLE OF BERLIN,
18 NOVEMBER 1943–25 MARCH 1944

After the successes of the 'Thousand Bomber Raids' and the Combined Bomber Offensive, including the Battle of the Ruhr and the 'Dambusters', as well as the many operations against Hamburg, it was time to take the battle to the German capital, Berlin. The idea was that striking at the heart of the German empire would seriously undermine morale, especially during the build-up to the Allied invasion of Normandy, 'D-Day'. Nevertheless, the raids on Berlin – which totalled 16 – were to be difficult, operating over long distances in the middle of winter to a heavily defended target. Worse still, Churchill's pronouncements meant that any element of surprise was lost.

The founder and leader of the RAF's Pathfinder Force, Gp Capt (later AVM) Donald Bennett, recalled:

. . . the losses of Pathfinders overall for the whole war were no worse, in fact slightly less than for the main force. You had to have an element of surprise to do that, with the great exception, when we really did suffer was during the Battle of Berlin, which was a scandalous thing.

It was a Churchillian doing. They told the Hun we were coming to Berlin every night without exception and of course we had a terrible time because we could not adopt any tactical surprise.[34]

The bodies of German air raid victims laid out in a hall in Berlin, shortly before Christmas 1943 – note the Christmas trees around the side. (IWM HU12143)

The Aircraft

The aircraft were mainly Lancaster and Halifax heavy bombers (see pp. 114–15), plus Mosquitos (see p. 146), which mainly acted in the Pathfinder role.

The Action

The Battle of Berlin consisted of 14 raids by Bomber Command, with the first on the night of 18/19 November 1943, and the last on the night of 24/25 March 1944. Winter brought its own problems, but the long nights were essential for the long journey to and from the target. To fool the enemy, Berlin was attacked from unexpected angles, even flying past the city and then turning to attack it from the east, while the German night-fighters would have been ordered to patrol over Leipzig and Stettin.

As with the Battle of the Ruhr, this was a campaign in which the Pathfinders were to be invaluable. The Pathfinders were supposed to be volunteers, but in practice, this wasn't always the case. Air Cdre John Searby tells of his time as CO of 83 Sqn, when as a Wing Commander he interviewed all new members of the squadron:

'Why did you volunteer for Pathfinder work?'

The captain, a young Pilot Officer, answered for his crew, 'We didn't Sir; we were told to pack our bags and get down here as soon as possible.'

'Do you know the terms of service in the Pathfinder Force – sixty sorties straight through?'

'Yes we do know that Sir – but it's OK now that we've got here.' As a crew they had around ten sorties to date; which meant – if all went well – they would be required to fly a further fifty with the Pathfinders. They seemed undaunted by the prospect.[35]

On the first raid losses were relatively light, with just 9 out of the 444 Lancasters and Mosquitos deployed failing to return. This was while there was still an element of surprise. Operations in the depths of winter meant

An Avro Lancaster Mk I of 149 Sqn in flight, 1943. The bulge under the fuselage is for the H2S radar. (RAFM P014545)

that the bomber crews had more to worry about than just night-fighters and heavy AA fire. In one case a wireless operator is supposed to have used his elbows to tap out messages on his morse key because both hands were frozen.

WO Randolph Rhodes was in a Halifax of 35 Sqn, part of the Pathfinder Force, on the night of 28/29 January 1944:

Icing began shortly after we crossed the enemy coast and due to the rapid build-up the Skipper decided to lose height in an attempt to reach the warmer air below. From the mid-upper turret I could see the heavy ice layers and realized that this might well be my third and last operational

Getting battle-damaged aircraft back over friendly territory was one thing, landing safely was another. This Lancaster Mk III reputedly of 100 Sqn crashed on landing at RAF Waltham after a raid on Cologne on the night of 16/17 June 1943. (RAFM P014344)

A Handley Page Halifax Mk III of 462 Sqn, Royal Australian Air Force, preparing to take off for a daylight raid over the Ruhr in 1944 – the inscription on the tail shows that it was the crew's last flight in a tour of operations. (IWM MH6838)

flight. Down we went and soon became a target for what appeared to be every flak battery on the Continent of Europe. Searchlights illuminated the cloud through which we were flying and the stuff came up thick and heavy from the batteries below. Such was the weight of ice we carried that our journey downwards was no longer a matter of choice and we jettisoned the bombload and returned to base.[36]

It was the bitter cold on these operations that many crew members recall. On the second night of the offensive, temperatures dropped to around –40°F. Although there was heating in the cockpit, the rear gunners had nothing. Heated clothing was not widely available for RAF bomber aircrew at this time.

One gunner recalls:

On our squadron, 90 per cent of the rear gunners were out of action after the second night – they'd all got frost-bite where the oxygen mask fitted, and the fingers and toes. To replace them we had to go to the OTUs and grab all people there – some had just started training – some had never been airborne . . . Some had never fired a gun . . . They were only a pair of eyes. They couldn't do much with .303s . . .[37]

Whether the air-to-air gunnery was effective or not, the night-fighters were persistent, and they knew each bomber's blind spot. The German night-fighters approached from below or from the side of the bombers, and positioned themselves firing upwards. The preferred method was to rake a Lancaster from the nose to the tail with the cannon. An alternative which was also highly effective was to shoot at the wings, hoping that there would still be fuel in the tanks:

Once you'd got a twenty-ml shell in the tanks, that was it . . .

Flying to Berlin some pilots took the view that they should get in and out of the target as quickly as possible. Be the first one home, that way there'd be less chance of getting hit. They'd charge into the target,

Another aircraft from the same squadron in the air on the way to the target. (IWM MH6839)

getting all they could out of the engines and to hell with whoever used the aircraft after them . . . We always knew who they were because they'd be home about an hour before anyone else.

Sensible and reasonable pilots, and I regarded myself as one, would be careful how they used the engines and would take indirect routes, so they arrived back later. I always tried to fly so that there would be about two hours of petrol left when I got back to England. I flew around for about twenty minutes and then came in. An experienced pilot would bide his time . . .[38]

An air gunner, Plt Off Beale, recalled the routine of the Berlin raids, having flown on nine of them. Before each operation the crews would attend a briefing, after which his first task was to check his equipment, which included his heated flying clothes, which were being introduced at this time, before visiting his aircraft at dispersal to check the guns. There was just time after this for him to join the rest of the crew for a meal, which included large slices of fried bread, chosen to provide heat and energy. Once aboard the aircraft, getting ready for take-off, he would conduct his turret checks, which included speaking over the intercom to the pilot so that he would recognize his voice during the flight:

I settle down in my rear turret to let the pilot know everything I see – it's pretty lonely in the rear turret, but the pilot calls up every five or ten minutes to make sure that you're OK. I like to check up with the other

A Halifax of 578 Sqn in the air over Germany. (IWM MH9936)

gunner too, but any attempt at conversation is strictly taboo. When you are over the target, it may well be ablaze – it very often is these nights. But you can't stare at anything bright to avoid destroying your night vision.[39]

A Mosquito pilot, John Hudson, whom we met earlier with his recollections of the Halifax, recalls:

I hadn't flown a Mosquito by night. Quite a sensation taking off with a four-thousand cookie – it made the aircraft pendulous . . .

After we'd bombed I headed north for Hamburg, the quickest way, dropped down to two or three thousand feet intending to come back fairly stately . . . when the Germans picked me up with one of their master searchlights . . . first thing I knew was this damn great blue searchlight got me, with about twenty others. My natural reaction like we used to do in the dear old Lancaster was an absolutely steep diving turn . . . On the Mozzie which is fingertip control, we actually rolled! . . . the cockpit was full of paper and maps and the avigator standing on his head . . . I was a bit more careful from then on![40]

The raids on Berlin were increasingly costly for Bomber Command, with 456 aircraft lost on the 5,000 sorties. This was a reflection of the distance which the aircraft had to fly over first enemy-occupied territory and then over the Reich itself, a long distance there and back again, and of the

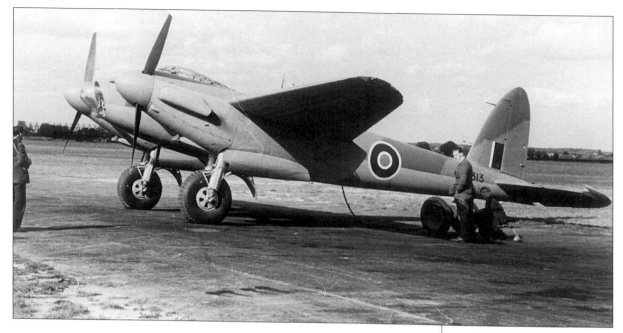

massive defences surrounding the capital. Nevertheless, these losses were far higher than they might have been, due to German awareness of the target each night.

Comment

Berlin was too obvious a target to ignore, although losses might have been lower if, after the initial raids, the target had been visited on a less regular basis, with other cities attacked in between raids on Berlin to keep the Luftwaffe guessing about Bomber Command's intentions. By this stage of the war, 'hit and run' precision raids by fast Mosquitos might also have been more cost-effective.

The de Havilland Mosquito was the best light bomber of the Second World War, possessing speed and range, and it could carry a 4,000-lb bomb. This was a B.MkIV at the de Havilland factory at Hatfield in 1942. (British Aerospace)

The versatile Mosquito was also in use as a fighter-bomber, and typical of the role was this FB. MkVI, seen here with underwing bombs and bomb bay doors open. (British Aerospace)

KNOCKING DOWN THE WALLS OF JERICHO:
THE MOSQUITO RAID ON AMIENS PRISON,
18 FEBRUARY 1944

The prison at Amiens held about 700 French men and women, of whom about 250 were political prisoners. The idea of an attack on the prison came from Dominique Ponchardier, leader of a Resistance group known as the 'Sosies', which worked closely with British intelligence. It was prompted both by humanitarian concerns and because of the success the Germans had enjoyed in their battle against the French Resistance in the Somme area. After many initial doubts, the RAF agreed to press ahead with the raid.

The Aircraft

This was an operation for the de Havilland Mosquito (see p. 146), since it required great precision and speed. One of the pilots on the raid was Sqn Ldr Duncan Taylor, at that time commanding a flight on 21 Sqn, who had happy memories of the Mosquito:

> It could be skittish on the ground – on take-offs and landings it could swing quite badly. You had to be on the ball, but, having said all that, it was incredibly manoeuvrable, it was faster at low level than anything the Germans had, even the Fw190, and on one occasion I was able to destroy an Fw190 without firing anything. He came on my tail and I was about 500 feet over France, and I went into a spiral and he was so intent in getting me in his sights – he was so young and inexperienced – he flew into the ground. He didn't realize I was going downhill!
>
> We all felt secure and masters of our own destinies in that aircraft.[41]

The Action

The RAF decided to use the Mosquitos of No. 140 Wing, which included 21, 464 (Australian) and 487 (New Zealand) Sqns. Six crews were

One of the most audacious operations of the war was the raid on Amiens prison to liberate French Resistance leaders – this is one of the aircraft which carried out the raid, a de Havilland Mosquito of 464 Sqn, RAAF. The photograph was taken some time after the raid, hence the invasion stripes. (IWM HU56290)

assigned to the operation from each of the three squadrons, with three Hawker Typhoon squadrons providing an escort. The objective was to knock down the walls, more than 20 ft high, which meant flying at 10 or 15 ft if the bombs were not to sail over the wall and destroy the prison buildings. Timing was as essential as pinpoint accuracy if the aircraft were not to blow each other up with their bombs. Taylor recalled:

It was quite well planned – possibly we used too much force – we really didn't need to use so much, but there was an air of urgency about it because we were told there were going to be mass executions in the next few days so we hadn't much time and when we did it we had to be pretty certain about achieving the aim. A model was made of the gaol and the three squadrons who were to take part all studied it and then coins were tossed as to . . . because they decided to use two squadrons for the direct operation itself and one squadron in reserve which would be there hanging about to finish off if the others didn't achieve their objective. It was an attempt to limit the amount of power that was being used as the gaol was on the edge of a very built up area of Amiens and also there were inmates who had nothing to do with the war, so the objective was to breach the walls in two places and they were chosen to go diagonally at corners . . . this had to be done very low level, you had to toss the bombs in. We had developed a technique of 'skip bombing' just letting the bombs hit the ground and we knew, depending on the type of surface they hit, just how far they would go and how high.

Four aircraft were to strike one corner, and four aircraft the corner diagonally opposite and endeavour to breach the walls. The gaol was a compact building of about five storeys high and oblong. At each end there was a lean-to structure about three storeys high; one held the gendarmerie, the prison warders, the other was messing quarters for the Gestapo and German authorities. So, another eight aircraft, four a side, were to attack these two end bits and if any of these fail, the third squadron, having already divided itself into fours, would be prepared to have another go at any one of these objectives. And it was a toss of the coin, and unfortunately my squadron commander couldn't toss a coin to save his . . . so we got the reserve job.[42]

The first six aircraft were from 487 Sqn, flying in two sections of three, charged with breaching the walls, and the second six were from 464 Sqn, again flying in two sections of three, with the task of placing their bombs against the prison walls, attacking the two annexes on either side of the main prison used as quarters for the guards, with the intention of shaking every door off its hinges and every lock out of its hasp, as well as destroying the prison walls.

Using 11-second-delay bombs, the first wave of aircraft was to be over the target at 12.03, with the second wave at 12.06. The third wave of aircraft from 21 Sqn was to hold off until 12.16, and then attack any of the objectives which had not been achieved by the first two waves. If the first two waves were sucessful, 21 Sqn was to return without dropping its bombs. Two additional aircraft were assigned to the raid, one carrying film equipment to record the success or otherwise, and the other carrying the wing's CO,

Gp Capt Charles Pickard, who was acting as an observer rather than leading the raid because most of his experience had been in high-level night bombing.

The operation had been delayed because of bad weather, heavy snow and low cloud. Although all the Mosquitos took off safely from their base at Hunsden, near Ware in Hertfordshire, four became separated from the rest of the formation in ten-tenths low cloud and blinding snowstorms on their way to Littlehampton, where they were due to rendezvous with the escorting Typhoons flying from Westhampnett and Manston. Just 8 out of 12 Typhoons managed to reach the rendezvous.

The weather improved as they crossed the Channel, flying just above the surface. They climbed to 5,000 ft to cross the French coast 10 miles north-east of Dieppe, then dropped down again to fly low and fast across the snow-covered countryside. The Typhoons raced alongside them on the outside of the formation. Navigation at low level with many landmarks and roads indistinguishable because of the snow was difficult, and the leading aircraft missed Amiens and had to orbit twice to find the road. Duncan Taylor again:

Unfortunately, when we got over there on this day there had been a big snowstorm and the countryside was white and we didn't really know how far a bomb might skip on snow- it might even go right over the jail into the town, so a rapid redecision was made on the spot that what we would try and do would be to chuck them into the wall straight in. It almost took us back to the days of the anti-shipping strikes – it was a very similar operation, really.

. . . some of the pilots, not very many, and some of the flight commanders, had actually been on shipping strikes way back, so it all came home to roost.[43]

The first formation was down to five aircraft, with three in the first section and two in the second.

The first three aircraft dropped their bombs, which fell through or over the eastern wall, two of them shooting across the prison courtyard to explode after hitting the western wall, while the third struck the main prison building. The two remaining aircraft of the second wave attacked the end of the north wall where it joined the west wall, knocking it down, and yet again, one bomb slipped through to hit the main prison building.

The second wave of aircraft now consisted of just four aircraft, two in each section. The leader of the wave, Wg Cdr Bob Iredale, thought at first that he would have to attack the eastern wall, but as he approached he saw the delayed-action bombs destroy the western wall, and then the northern wall. Both sections successfully attacked the two annexes, demolishing both buildings.

Although disappointed at not being directly involved, Taylor had by now a bird's eye view of the action as it developed:

The raid went fairly well, the walls were breached. One set of bombs went astray, hit the middle of the gaol building itself, the roof, which caused some deaths, but had another effect in that where there were tight locks the percussion shattered the bolts and in many cases [prisoners] just had to push the doors open and go out. There were a lot

A line up of 464 Sqn's Mosquitos after the raid on Amiens prison. (British Aerospace)

of wounded, I'm afraid, but nevertheless about 200 or so got out and the most important ones . . . but there were two very key people who had been taken in, without the Germans knowing quite how key they were – senior officials in the Pas de Calais area [who] were party to the invasion plans, or at least part of them.

The Germans suffered very badly in their wing, including the Gestapo chief of the area, and his mistress, who had been visiting the gaol, they copped it.

I suppose you would describe it as an 80 per cent success – a few people were killed by a couple of bombs which landed in the town itself.

We saw the general uproar . . . we saw people breaking out and running . . . it being white they showed up starkly . . . the underground group who knew about this were hiding in the woods and copses and they had trucks to take them away . . . one hid in an undertaker's coffin.[44]

Scores of prisoners died in the attack, and many more were injured. Some abandoned their chance of escape to help the injured. Not all of the cell doors had been blown open, and one prisoner grabbed the cell keys from the Gestapo offices and ran down a corridor unlocking the doors. Others were so stunned by the explosions that their escape was a matter of duty and discipline rather than desire. Nevertheless, more than 400 prisoners escaped, aided by the Resistance forces led by Ponchardier into the prison, and all of those determined to escape were clear of the prison by 12.15. A number of prisoners were either recaptured or gave themselves up to safeguard their families from reprisals, but overall, 250 retained their freedom, including 12 who were due to be shot the following day. During the attack, 102 prisoners were killed, along with about 50 guards, and 74 prisoners were wounded, many by small arms fire from the guards. A small number of prisoners who had helped those wounded in the raid, including some guards and Gestapo members, were pardoned by the Germans.

Many of the guards recovered quickly enough to chase after the prisoners, but the latter managed to make good their escape after the photographic Mosquito swept down low over the prison – the prisoners kept on running, while the guards spreadeagled themselves on the ground! Meanwhile, the Typhoons were locked in battle with a force of Fw190s which had arrived on the scene.

The disappointed members of 21 Sqn turned for home, while the rest of the formation started to return to base. Sqn Ldr McRitchie's aircraft, leader of the second Australian section, was hit by flak, and although he managed to nurse his ailing aircraft for some distance, the starboard wing dipped and it crashed – McRitchie survived and became a PoW, but his navigator, Flt Lt Sampson, a New Zealander, was killed.

As he turned for home, Pickard's aircraft was caught by a lone Fw190, which shot off part of its tail, after which the aircraft dived out of control, killing both Pickard and his navigator, Bill Broadley. Of the Typhoons, one was shot down near the target, although its pilot managed to bale out, and another was lost in bad weather after returning over the English coast.

Comment

This was one of the most spectacular operations ever, but the Mosquito squadrons became expert at attacking specific targets, even on one occasion attacking a Gestapo headquarters at the Hague in an operation timed to coincide with lunchtime for children in the adjoining school.

Whether or not too much force was used is an impossible question to answer. The Mosquito pilots had to succeed, and too little force would have been useless, since there could be no second chance. Even today, such accuracy would be praiseworthy, but given the techniques of the day and the change in the weather, which affected their estimates of how accurately they could place their bombs, the operation was little short of miraculous.

D-DAY AND AFTER

The RAF's preparations for the Allied invasion of northern France in June 1944 had started a year earlier. On 1 June 1943 the 2nd Tactical Air Force (2nd TAF) was formed to support both the invasion and the long advance towards Germany. Tailored to meet the anticipated demands of ground commanders, elements were drawn from the several different commands of the RAF. Bomber Command provided No. 2 Group, Fighter Command Nos 83 and 84 Groups, and the newly-formed Transport Command provided Nos 38 and 46 Groups. The USAAF equivalent was the formation of the US Ninth Air Force. Together, these two major commands were integrated into the Allied Expeditionary Air Force, under the command of ACM Sir Trafford Leigh-Mallory, RAF, who had considerable fighter experience, and had been responsible for the fighter cover for the ill-fated Dieppe operation of 1942.

Nevertheless, despite the invasion force being given what was in effect its own air force, debate started over whether the USAAF and RAF strategic bombing forces should also support the invasion force. Opinion polarized between those who thought that this should be so, and those who believed (as did both Harris and his US counterpart) that the bombers' best

The RAF also conducted shuttle-bombing raids – this is the Australian Flt Lt (later AM) Harold Martin of 617 Sqn with his crew and their Lancaster at RAF Blida in Algeria, after a raid on the Antheor Viaduct in the south of France. For the photograph they were joined by some army officers. (IWM HU55719)

contribution to the success of the invasion would be to cripple the overall German war effort and undermine morale in Germany itself.

In an attempt to find a compromise, Marshal of the Royal Air Force Lord Portal advised Churchill that he felt that the UK-based element of Bomber Command should not be used until 14 days before the invasion date, D-Day, and then half their effort, as well as all of that of the Allied forces in the Mediterranean, should be switched to support the invasion. While the landings were taking place, Bomber Command would provide 100 per cent effort, rapidly being reduced to 75 per cent for the three weeks following, and then back to 50 per cent for the following four weeks.

In the case of Bomber Command, the conflict was between hitting German fighter production to reduce the number of aircraft ready to attack the invasion force, and hitting communications, especially railways, so hard that the Germans could not move troops and supplies quickly to the battlefront. Harris pointed out to his superiors that Bomber Command was not suited to 'fleeting' targets because of the need for preparation, and that it would be ill-suited to daytime operations. One thorn in Harris's side at this time was the leading British Government adviser on science, Solly Zuckerman (later Lord Zuckerman) who had been appointed to advise Leigh-Mallory. Zuckerman believed that attacks on railways were vital, and that, from his post-invasion analysis of OPERATION HUSKY, the Allied invasion of Sicily, the targets to go for were major junctions and marshalling yards, rather than bridges or tunnels, largely because the former were bigger targets and easier to hit, while the latter required greater precision. Spaatz objected to the plan because they wanted to resume raids on Germany, and especially to seek to interrupt the production of oil. Harris objected to both Zuckerman's and Spaatz's proposals, preferring instead to concentrate on destroying the offensive capabilities of the Luftwaffe, and also believing that the oil plan would require too much precision bombing.

In the run-up to the invasion, a series of attacks started, aimed at destroying aircraft factories in France, using 617 Sqn and the 12,000 lb 'Tallboy' bomb. The squadron had by this time perfected its low level marking procedures. The raids were assigned to nights when Anglo-American POINT BLANK operations were not possible. The first raid took place on the night of 6/7 March, at the railway junction at Trappes, and was highly successful, leaving few French civilian casualties, and the railway yards were out of action for a month. There were five similar raids, many of them carried out by Halifaxes of Nos 4 and 6 Groups. No. 1 Group attacked the marshalling yards at Aulnoye on the night of 10/11 April, using a modified version of Oboe in which the equipment was used to drop green target incendiaries onto the target, and two master bombers followed this up by dropping more accurate red target incendiaries, before ordering the remaining crews to aim at them.

In mid-April 1944 Harris isolated No. 5 Group from the main force of Bomber Command. The group was redesignated as No. 54 Base, and included three Pathfinder squadrons, Nos 83 and 97 with Lancasters, and No. 627 with Mosquitos, as well as 106 and 617 Sqns, both of which had been commanded by Guy Gibson.

During May, as raids on France intensified, so did German night-fighter activity. On raids against targets in France on 3 May, 42 out of 362 bombers were lost, and the following week, out of 89 bombers sent to attack the marshalling yards at Lille in northern France, 12 failed to return. Hitherto, operations over France and Belgium had counted as 'one-third' of an operation when calculating the end of a tour of duty for bomber crews, but as the pressure intensified, crews were given a full one-operation credit on each occasion, regardless of the location of the target.

On the day of the invasion Bomber Command operations included three squadrons of No. 100 Group, of which one was from the USAAF, flying jamming missions over the invasion fleet, while 111 aircraft dropped Window off the Pas de Calais to create the impression of an invasion around Boulogne, and another force of bombers flew along the course of the River Seine to create the impression of a landing near Le Havre. A large force of more than 1,100 Halifaxes, Lancasters and Mosquitos attacked German coastal batteries.

Meanwhile, the USAAF had been attacking oil targets in Romania, with aircraft from the US Fifteenth Air Force in Italy raiding Ploesti on three occasions during April, while two attacks were made on oil installations inside Germany on 12 May. In the latter operation, which had originally been planned for April, but was delayed due to poor weather, a secondary consideration was to force the Germans to divide their fighter defences. The RAF also conducted four raids against oil installations in Germany, mainly in the Ruhr, during June, but these proved to be costly, with 93 aircraft lost from the total of 832 sorties mounted. Worse still, only one of the four operations, that at the Nordstern plant at Gelsenkirchen on the night of 12/13 June, was successful. Better results came with a further five raids in July, mixed with area bombing of Hamburg, Kiel and Stuttgart, 132 aircraft being lost on 3,419 sorties.

Once the Allied troops were ashore, Bomber Command continued to operate against railway targets, also being tasked with operations against other targets, such as troop concentrations. On the night of 7/8 June, while 212 aircraft attacked troops massing in the Forêt de Cerisy, 617 Sqn made a successful attack using 12,000 lb 'Tallboy' bombs against a railway tunnel at Saumur, and succeeded in demolishing it.

Daylight operations were also mounted, including attacks against shipping in the port at Le Havre on 14 June, and at Boulogne the following day. Both raids were executed without incurring a single casualty from the 234 aircraft at Le Havre and the 297 at Boulogne.

The raid on Le Havre was needed because the port was strongly occupied by German troops, and there were heavy coastal batteries which were proving to be an embarrassment to the coastal monitor *Erebos*: the ship could not bombard the coastal fortifications because it was outranged by the German guns. AVM Donald Bennett recalls:

> I was asked if I could deal with some batteries up on the coast because the batteries were going to fire at the good ship *Erebos* . . . So I said yes, of course we'd lay it on. So we laid on a hundred training aircraft, each one carrying, I think it was twelve or fourteen . . . 1,000 lb HE. And they went in on a Sunday afternoon. I watched it all myself. I went over in a Mosquito. And they plastered these batteries with high explosive and the batteries were duly silenced. The good ship *Erebos* then came within range . . . and shelled Le Havre.
>
> The next morning, the good British press, true to form to the end, had banner headlines right across the front page – 'Royal Navy shells Le Havre' and at the bottom right hand corner, there was a little piece about one inch, that said 'Heavy bombers also attacked Le Havre'.[45]

After this, a major daylight effort over France, with strong fighter escorts, became part of Bomber Command's operations during the second half of June and throughout July, almost 10,000 sorties being flown for fewer than 40 aircraft lost. By this time the Germans were showing signs of having suffered heavy losses in fighters, especially day-fighters, and were obviously having difficulties in replacing them. Suitably encouraged, Bomber Command carried the offensive to Germany in daylight for the first time on 27 August, when 216 Halifaxes from No. 4 Group, preceded by 27 Pathfinder Lancasters and Mosquitos, carried out a successful raid against the oil refinery at Homberg in the Ruhr. Another four such raids followed over a period of three weeks, with 803 sorties mounted, for the cost of just ten aircraft. Throughout this period, a third of Bomber Command's aircraft were operating against the V-1 launch sites, reducing the force of such weapons which the Germans could deploy against England.

The attacks on German troop concentrations were described by an Army officer serving with an armoured unit who was a witness of the raid on 7 July:

> Then, just as the evening shadows are beginning to dim the skies of a lovely evening, there is a great droning in the air and out of the haze from the north a few tiny specks appear – our bombers . . . The first Lancasters are over the target, only a mile or two from where we are, and masses of red glittering flames are put down to guide the others. Now, literally as far as the range of my binoculars, the sky is filled with bombers, coming on in a slow relentless stream like something out of a Wellsian dream, or one of the early war films of the sky filled with the Luftwaffe, but now there is not a single German plane in sight. High

above our bombers, Spitfires and Lightnings are weaving about like little silver minnows in a great inverted fish bowl. Still the stream of bombers comes on and great vibrations shake the ground as their loads of bombs crash down. A vast red glow shows that fires have been started, and one by one they wheel over and stream northwards for England again.

Then a second wave comes in, this time at a higher altitude. By this time the flak has almost faded out, but there are still occasional puffs of black smoke quite close to our planes, but they fly steadily on and once again there is the crump-crump of heavy bombs going down. One only of this massive air fleet is shot down, and as the darkness closes in, the last attackers become tiny specks in the sky. This is the greatest morale booster we have experienced, and it shows our complete mastery of the air to perfection.[46]

The Allied invasion of northern France on D-Day, 6 June 1944, soon called for close support from the RAF. Much of the action lay with the close support fighter units of the RAF and USAAF, operating on what might now be called ground attack duties. Nevertheless, there were many targets which called for the use of heavy bombers, and aircraft were moved from the now round-the-clock bombing of major industrial and military targets in Germany to help ease the pressure on the invading forces, as they fought to move out from their Normandy beachheads. For 57 Sqn, one of the units transferred to this task, these tactical operations were a reminder of the squadron's earlier history during the First World War, although on this occasion the operations were on a far grander scale, and there was little comparison between the DH4s and the mighty Lancasters.

For a raid on the Orne bridges during the night of 13/14 June, the squadron had an extra member, flying in 'G-George', the aircraft of A Flight's commander, Sqn Ldr D.I. Fairburn. This was Ronald Walker, Air Correspondent of the *News Chronicle*, who was given the identity of second engineer on the flight, in case the aircraft was shot down and he was taken prisoner:

It was still light when we gathered at the dispersal point for Lancaster G for George. The bomb doors yawned to reveal a maximum load of 1,000-pounders.

Engines were run up and equipment checked. With three-quarters of an hour to wait we stood around 'nattering'. The last cigarette smoked, a word from the pilot and we boarded the Lanc . . . following the order to the flight engineer, 'Full power', came that always exciting moment. Almost 30 tons of aeroplane, carrying within its structure tons of petrol and many more tons of bombs, gathers itself and races past the runway lights at ever-increasing speed until the whole thing lifts away from the earth with an ease that can never cease to be rather surprising.

G for George ploughed smoothly through the night. Crossing the south coast our navigation lights went out, and we approached enemy France on a course which would avoid the assault area. After two or three changes of course we crossed the French coast. As we neared the target gun flashes and flak bursts in the surrounding sky increased. Except for one burst which came near but missed, the war avoided us.

Suddenly the glow of the coloured markers dropped by the Pathfinders became visible. Heavy flak was bursting far above us and lines of red balls came sailing up in a rather leisurely fashion to burst into stars. A bunch of searchlights illuminated the cloud base.

As G for George ran up to bomb cloud got in the way and we had to have another shot at it. 'Bomb doors open' came the call and we ran up to bomb with the markers clearly visible through drifting cloud. Quietly from the bomb-aimer, 'Steady, steady, steady. Hold it.' Finally, 'Bombs gone'. The job was done.

To the north, slight hell was breaking loose. Apparently Allied guns in the assault area. As we neared the French coast enemy fighters laid a trail of brilliant flares behind us on the cloud layer, beneath a half moon deeply tinged with red. Through and above cloud, G for George flew home to land in first light of a new day.[47]

Not all operations went so well. When things became really desperate, the crew of a stricken aircraft would attempt to bale out, the pilot being the last to leave, unless he was badly injured, in which case this doubtful privilege belonged to the navigator, who usually had some basic flying training so that he could get the aircraft home if the pilot were to be incapacitated, allowing the RAF to man its heavy bombers with just one pilot. Even if everyone did get out, a safe landing was not always guaranteed, since parachutes might not open, or people could be injured badly or even killed while getting out, and then into a hostile sky with AA munitions flying past, and aircraft, often of both sides, milling around.

In December 1944 another Lancaster, 'J-Jig' of 57 Sqn, flown by Lt P. Becker, South African Air Force, was shot down, and the sole survivor was Sgt Vic Tomei, the aircraft's bomb-aimer:

Turning for home, we were attacked. Our port wing and engines caught fire, the flames could not be extinguished and orders were given to bale out. I jettisoned the hatch but the aircraft started to spin. We straightened out and I was thrown out feet first, catching the back edge of the hatch before I fell. My parachute opened but I began to spin, being held by one clip only. I corrected this and landed in a farmyard where I was captured by a group of armed villagers.[48]

OPERATIONS AGAINST THE V-WEAPON SITES

Germany's V-weapons – the revenge weapons – posed a significant threat to the security of Britain's towns and cities, especially London and the south-east of England. Individual V-1 flying bombs and V-2 ballistic missiles did cause serious casualties, but they also had a serious impact on morale. While less damaging than the bomber raids of the Blitz, it was important to destroy as many of the weapons themselves at their launch sites. Several different techniques were used against the V-weapon sites, including high-level heavy bombing and low-level precision attacks.

Both the USAAF and the RAF had to divert their attention to attacking the V-1 and V-2 weapon launch sites – this was an attack at Crècy on 6 July 1944, by the USAAF's 34th Bombardment Group (Heavy). The RAF's Lancasters and Mosquitos were also given these tasks. (IWM HU59900)

The Aircraft

In this instance, this was an operation for the Mosquito light bomber (see p. 146).

The Action

Against the V-1 sites in particular, low-level attacks were found to be the most effective, but not before a variety of methods had been used, including what almost amounted to dive-bombing, although none of the RAF's bombers really possessed this capability.

Sqn Ldr Duncan Taylor was involved in raids against the V-weapon launch sites in 1943. Most of these were located in the Pas de Calais area, and had been attacked from high altitude, but this proved to have little effect. A change of tactics was required, with the RAF switching to low-level attacks, a practice which required highly skilled map reading at very high speed by the navigators if the targets were to be found and then attacked with accuracy. Taylor's navigator used quarter-inch maps, which were precise, although bulky and difficult to handle in the cockpit. Taylor recalls:

Even when I couldn't see the target, he would say: 'In two miles, it's dead ahead of you.'

It was difficult. They were very well defended . . . that was why it was desirable to approach them at very low level to give them as little warning

A 1944 photograph of Bomber Command's chief, ACM Sir Arthur 'Bomber' Harris, in the Bombing Interpretation Room at Bomber Command HQ. (IWM HU44269)

as possible and as little time to bring their guns to bear. The only trouble was they were often very well hidden in woods and very difficult to pick out so all sorts of techniques were tried, including one idiotic one of flying at around 5,000 feet and dive-bombing them or semi dive-bombing them, but that really gave the German gunners the time of their lives because it was the perfect height at which to shoot at anything . . . I had two sergeant pilots in my flight and they were the salt of the earth, they never got to lead anything because they were sergeant pilots, and they just put up with all the flak that was going, and I thought 'Why shouldn't they? They're very experienced.' I said to one of them: 'You're going to lead the flight. It was one of these 5,000 footer jobs, and I just went along as a number eight or something. We had a turning point onto our target . . . We could see the squadron ahead of us, which was aiming for a similar target close by the one we had, in the distance being surrounded by anti-aircraft fire along the route it was going, they were popping all over, and I thought to myself, 'I wonder what the sergeant's going to do for they'll have got our height by now and they'll have us.' They've had plenty of warning and he solemnly turned onto course and followed the other squadron about three miles behind it, heading straight for the nonsense and out of self preservation if nothing else, I said to Phillip, 'We're taking over, get navigating', roared up to the front, just roared over the intercom that I was taking over and turning port and they all came with me back to the turning point . . . down on the deck, flew along at low level, with Phillip map reading like crazy and the squadron in front and ahead being shot at all the way – nobody touched us . . . because we only had bombs on for this operation that exploded instantaneously, there was no point in trying to drop them, we would only have blown ourselves up and so Phillip had to get it right, and he did, telling me when to pull up and we went into a very steep climb the whole squadron, wing over and there was the target in front of us, we dived at it and away.[49]

On his squadron's raids, Taylor liked to avoid German AA fire. It was impossible for the Germans to provide AA cover for the entire French coastline, even before they occupied Vichy territory. Instead, they concentrated their fixed AA defences on major targets, such as the submarine pens, and for the open coastline depended on mobile AA batteries which would be located at different points in the hope of catching bombers on their way to a target. Rapidly relocated AA batteries were a menace, and there was insufficient time for the Resistance or reconnaissance to pass a warning to the bomber crews.

Taylor recalls one French farmer who had a solution:

This French farmer used to plough with white horses to warn the RAF that there was a German mobile 40mm AA battery in the area, so we'd go off somewhere else. I wondered if he ever got found out because he used to plough at the wrong time of the year sometimes, and the

After the invasion of Normandy, the Allied air forces were tasked with helping the ground forces. This was the result of American bombing by the 34th Bombardment Group (Heavy) some 4 miles from St Lô in preparation for the break-out from the Normandy bridgehead. (IWM HU59907)

Germans weren't that thick, not to get the message, but he did it for months. He was our own private early warning system . . .[50]

Comment

As with many bomber operations during the Second World War, there was an element of trial and error on the attacks on the V-weapon launch sites. Heavier bombs proved effective, especially with the V-2 silos, which were far more resilient than the launch rails of the V-1s. Nevertheless, precision was an important factor, regardless of which type of bomb was used. By this stage of the war, however, bombing either had to be low-level, with the added element of surprise, or very high-level area bombing, to make life difficult for defending fighters and AA gunners.

THE ADVANCE ON GERMANY

By the time the Allies had broken out of the Normandy beachhead, the Luftwaffe was no longer viewed as the major threat, and in September 1944, fresh objectives were drawn up for the bombers, both British and American. Portal, Head of the RAF, and his USAAF counterpart, Arnold, issued a joint directive on 14 September requiring the strategic bomber forces to ensure the 'progressive destruction and dislocation of the German military, industrial and economic systems and the direct support of land and naval forces'.[51] In practice, this meant that oil was once again to be given top priority, followed by transport, tank production and ordnance depots, then other motor transport production. This did not preclude attacks on industrial areas, but these were to be confined to those periods when weather or other tactical considerations meant that raids on the primary objectives were impractical. If necessary, raids against industrial targets could be conducted 'blind'.

These objectives were translated into action, with Mosquitos operating against a wide variety of targets, not least oil and transport. On 3 October heavy bombers were used against the Westkapelle Dyke, a target identified by the armies as essential, and on 4 October Mosquitos and Lancasters raided U-boat pens at Bergen, in Norway. Then, on the night of 4/5 October, 551 bombers were sent against Saarbrucken, and a third of them concentrated on the railway marshalling yards. On 6 October the synthetic oil plants at Sterkrade and Gelsenkirchen were attacked, followed by a raid on Dortmund that night, with 523 aircraft deployed. Cleve and Bochum were other targets attacked in force at the time. Army support operations covered Walcheren on 11 October, and the following day there was a heavy raid on the Wanne-Eickel oil refinery.

Many of the operations used large numbers of aircraft, often between 400 and 600, but on 14 October 1944 RAF Bomber Command mounted a major 'Thousand Bomber Raid', the first since mid-1942. This time there was a difference: this was a major British daylight raid. No fewer than 1,063 aircraft from Nos 1, 3, 4, 6 and 8 Groups were sent to Duisburg, with 50 of the aircraft, from No. 1 Group, specifically allocated raids on the blast furnaces and rolling mills. There was more to come, because after darkness, 1,008 bombers returned to Duisburg, while 240 aircraft of No. 5 Group attacked Brunswick, while smaller forces of Mosquitos were

A Boeing B-17 Fortress with bomb bay doors open as it prepares for a raid on the German port of Swinemunde. (IWM EA57087)

attacking Berlin, Düsseldorf and Mannheim. This massive effort was supported by 120 radio countermeasures sorties by No. 100 Group, and another 141 sorties, some of which used operational training unit aircraft and crews, were mounted as diversions. No. 3 Group had eight aircraft dropping supplies to Resistance units in enemy-occupied territory. All this came from an operational force of 1,317 aircraft and crews, most of whom had been active during the day over Duisburg. An indication of the success of the countermeasures and the even greater strain on Luftwaffe night-fighter units was that losses were light, 15 aircraft failing to return from the

A Junkers Ju188 at the airfield at Melsbroek in Germany. (IWM HU71227)

Duisburg day raid, another 6 lost during the night raid, a Lancaster lost over Brunswick and a Mosquito over Berlin.

The pressure was relentless. On 15 October, 9 Sqn was sent to make a daylight raid on the Sorpe Dam using 'Tallboys', and then that night, 506 aircraft raided Wilhelmshaven.

Obviously, such pressure could only be maintained for short periods. On 18 October, 128 Lancasters from No. 3 Group made a daylight raid on Bonn, and on the night of 19/20 October a dual operation saw 583 Lancasters and Mosquitos attack Stuttgart, while another 270 aircraft struck at Nuremberg. On 21/22 October 263 aircraft were sent to Hannover. Another 'Thousand Bomber Raid' followed on the night of 23/24 October against Essen, with 1,055 aircraft sent for the loss of just 8 against this once notorious target. On 25/26 October, there was another busy night, 771 bombers raiding Essen, 243 aircraft bombing an oil refinery at Homberg, and 327 aircraft bombing Walcheren in support of ground forces. Bergen was bombed the following night by 244 aircraft of No. 5 Group.

On 26 October aircraft from the famous 617 Sqn and from 9 Sqn made an unsuccessful attack on the German battleship *Tirpitz* as she lay at anchor, although 617 Sqn succeeded in capsizing the vessel when it returned again on 12 November.

At this point in the war, Harris's view that bombing German industry was to be credited for the growing Allied aerial supremacy seemed to be confirmed by an Ultra intercept of a message from the Japanese Military Attaché in Berlin to Tokyo, which stated that Germany's main priority for the coming battle within its own borders was to regain aerial supremacy.

November started with oil once again being emphasized as the main priority for the bomber forces, with transport again second. In fact, Bomber Command stepped up its attacks on the oil industry, which accounted for 20 per cent of sorties in November, compared with 5 per cent in October. Harris was not going to let the German cities off the hook quite so easily, however, and major raids on Bochum, Düsseldorf, Gelsenkirchen and Oberhausen started the month, with that on Düsseldorf almost a 'Thousand Bomber Raid', at 992 aircraft. Significant raids were also made on other German cities, although generally with bomber forces of 200–400 aircraft deployed.

Another major operation required by the Allied ground forces arose on 16 November, when 1,188 bombers were sent against military targets at Daren, Heinsburg and Jülich during the day to support the US First and Ninth Armies as they mounted OPERATION QUEEN, their thrust towards the Rhineland. On the way was the River Roer, with seven dams, which if breached by the Germans once the Allied advance had progressed that far could inflict heavy casualties and impede Allied operations as far away as the Netherlands. The US solution to this was to breach the dams first, impeding the German defence and allowing the floods to recede before the Allies advanced. The commander of the US First Army, Gen Courtney Hodges, wanted two of the dams breached by the bombers, and at Supreme Headquarters Allied Expeditionary Forces (SHAEF), staff recalled 617 Sqn's success against the Mohne and the Eder dams, and passed the request to 'Bomber' Harris. Realistic about the chances of a successful attack, Harris pointed out that there were difficulties, not the least being that 617's attempts on the Sorpe with Tallboy bombs had been unsuccessful, and it

Despite being above ground, this was a German air raid shelter in Düsseldorf. Many German houses had cellars, which acted as improvised shelters, although they could also be death traps if the family had hoarded fuel! (IWM HU67607)

was unlikely that an attack on the Urft and Schwammenauel Dams, being of similar construction, would be any more successful. He also knew that once the first raid was mounted, the Germans would be able to manipulate the water levels in the dams to ensure that any further attack, no matter how successful in breaching the dams, would be of little more than nuisance value. There was also another important factor in any operations in support of ground forces: as they advanced, accuracy was vital to ensure that bombs did not land among friendly forces, so blind bombing was out of the question – the '3 miles from the centre of the target' standard so sought after earlier in the bombing campaign was simply unacceptable in such circumstances.

Raids were mounted against the two dams, but it was not until 3 December that visibility was good enough. Even so, on that occasion 200 Lancasters from No. 1 Group with the aid of Pathfinder Mosquitos were unable to identify the target. Low-level attack was impossible because of the strong AA defences around the dams, and there was no time to manufacture more of the specialized 'bouncing bombs' which had contributed to 617 Sqn's success. The following day, 30 Lancasters and Mosquitos from No. 8 Group were sent against the Urft, and succeeded in bombing both ends of it, but without breaching the dam. On the next day, 5 December, Lancasters from No. 3 Group failed to identify the Schwammenauel. Yet again, 205 Lancasters from No. 5 Group were sent to the Urft on 8 December, 129 aircraft attacking the dam, but failing to breach it. Then, on the night of 9/10 December, 230 Lancasters, again from No. 5 Group, were despatched to the Urft, with a searchlight at Aachen to provide illumination and guidance, but returned to base without dropping their bombs. They tried again on 11 December in daylight, and succeeded in dropping their bombs, but still without breaching the dam. Harris suggested bombing the spillways in the hope of eroding the hillside and weakening the dams, assuming that the hill itself was not solid rock, but Lord Tedder felt that enough was enough, and vetoed requests from the Americans for any further attempts.

The bombers returned to the oil offensive, although discouraged by estimates that it would take 9,000 sorties per month to keep the 42 synthetic oil and benzol plants in western Germany out of action, and a further 6,400 sorties to suppress the 15 plants in central Germany. Worse, winter weather meant that operations could only be mounted on three or four nights per month. By December, 30 per cent of Bomber Command's sorties were area attacks, 25 per cent were on transport, mainly railways, and fewer than 8 per cent on oil. It may have appear that orders were being disobeyed, but the targets were not easy and the weather often meant that alternative targets had to be sought. In fact, despite their commitment to the elimination of the oil industry, the US Eighth Air Force had attacked just 40 per cent of the oil targets attacked by Bomber Command, and dropped half the bomb tonnage.

DRESDEN, 13/14 FEBRUARY 1945

The year 1945 started badly, for despite the belief that the Luftwaffe was a spent force, on New Year's Day 800 German fighters mounted a surprise attack on Allied airfields in France and Belgium, destroying and damaging 465 aircraft, although losing 400 of their own – as much a reflection of the loss of experienced Luftwaffe pilots as of Allied aerial supremacy.

The war was still far from won. The Allied armies were making slow progress in the West, and the Russians had achieved relatively little since the previous summer. A renewed Russian offensive in the East started in earnest on 12 January. While some believed that an all-out raid on Berlin or another major city might end the war, the more widely held view was that this was unlikely, and that the best that could be hoped for would be that such a raid would help the Russian advance. The Allied chiefs of staff favoured a raid on Berlin, spread over four days and nights, dropping more than 25,000 tons of bombs, with the intention of driving people out of Berlin, who might then clash with the stream of refugees from the east, causing confusion. This was known as OPERATION THUNDERCLAP, and the desire to help the Russian advance was to a great degree stimulated by political considerations, proving to the Russian leader, Stalin, that the Western powers were doing everything they could to support the Russian advance. Indeed, at the Yalta Conference of Allied heads of government, the Russians sought bomber raids, and listed Berlin and Leipzig as their preferred targets.

The US Eighth Air Force made heavy raids on both Berlin and Magdeburg, but the RAF could not find the right conditions. Throughout February, the main force of RAF operations was against oil and communications targets. The exception was on the night of 13/14 February, when a massive raid was mounted against Dresden, an important

Boeing B-17Gs of the 91st Bombardment Group in formation. (RAFM P017494).

A huge pall of smoke rises over Dresden after the Allied raids. This photograph was taken from the suburbs. (IWM HU3316)

communications centre and relatively unscathed, having received just one minor raid, by the Americans in October 1944. The city was also known to be crowded with refugees from the East, which is the main reason for the controversy which has surrounded this operation to the present day.

The Aircraft

A mixed force of Lancasters, Halifaxes and Mosquitos (see pp. 114–15 and 146) was sent on this operation, followed by USAAF B-17s and B-24s (see pp. 124 and 126).

The Action

The attack was to be in the spirit of the combined bomber offensive, with US and British raids alternating, day and night. The US Eighth Air Force was supposed to mount the first raid, in daylight on 13 February, but bad weather over Dresden meant that they were diverted to Münster, Brux and Pilsen. This meant that the RAF had the first shot, 805 Lancasters and Mosquitos being drawn from most of Bomber Command, with the exception of No. 8 Group, and the raid was mounted in two waves, directed by master bombers in Mosquitos. The first-wave Pathfinders arrived over the target with their master bomber at 22.05, descending through heavy cloud to lay red target incendiaries accurately on the centre of the town, with Pathfinders from No. 5 Group adding their contribution. Then the first wave of bombers arrived with more than two hundred aircraft.

The second wave was not scheduled to arrive until 01.30 on 14 February, so that maximum disruption would be caused to the fire-fighting and rescue operation. One German woman, then a small child, recalled

The devastated centre of Dresden. (IWM HU3321)

many years after in a television interview that when they saw the target incendiaries being dropped, 'they thought that someone was mounting a fireworks display, and didn't seek shelter immediately'. Many left the air raid shelters and were in the open when the second wave arrived.

Most of the bombers were with the second wave, which had 529 aircraft. One member of the second wave's aircrew recalled:

> We could see the light on the clouds. We didn't come into clear air until over the target. So there was first a glow through cloud, and then clarity over the target. Then a cry from the crew: 'Bloody hell, look at that!'
>
> Below us was a town well ablaze, giving the impression of flying over a town in peacetime – lights all over the place. But there was only a quick, snatched glimpse for gunners – then you had to go back on sky search . . .
>
> The master bomber was on the air, calling instructions where to bomb. The bomb aimer made his usual run-up. 'Bomb doors open – left – left – steady – bombs away.' Having delivered the bombs, we had only one thought in mind: 'Let's go home and get the hell out of it.'
>
> We knew the town had really taken a pounding, but I can't remember flak over the target . . .
>
> The glare followed us back 100 miles or more . . .[52]

No fewer than 772 aircraft claimed to have attacked the target, and this was borne out by raid and post-raid photography, which showed that this was one of the RAF's most successful missions of the war. The bad weather had kept most of the night-fighters grounded, and the heavy AA artillery had been sent to the front, while the 20 mm guns left in the city were only effective against low-level attack.

Shortly before noon that day, 400 USAAF aircraft attacked, repeating this performance on the following day, and returning again on 2 March. The old city included many wooden buildings, so fires were difficult to contain. No one will ever know how many people were killed at Dresden, and estimates have been put as high as 100,000 or more, since the city's peacetime population had been swollen by the arrival of refugees fleeing the advancing Red Army. Generally, the casualty roll is accepted as being in the region of 50,000.

Dresden had not been Bomber Command's only operation on the night of 13/14 February: a further 368 aircraft were deployed against the oil refinery at Bohlen, while Mosquitos from No. 8 Group were deployed against Bonn, Dortmund and Misburg. These operations were supported by 117 aircraft from No. 100 Group, using a variety of techniques, including Window and radio countermeasures, but heavy cloud over the target meant that results were not on a par with Dresden.

Comment

The attack on Dresden was one of the most controversial of the Second World War, with many arguing that so close to Germany's defeat, the raid was unnecessary, while there have also been stories that the raid was designed to demonstrate the power of the RAF and the USAAF to the Soviet Union. The opposing argument was that German troops were pouring into and through Dresden, slowing the advance of the Red Army. The Russians had been calling for heavy bombing attacks, favouring a number of German cities, and at the time lacked a heavy bomber force of their own, having followed a similar doctrine to the Luftwaffe in having large numbers of light and medium bombers operating in support of ground forces. In addition to the large number of troops being moved through Dresden to the front, many government departments had been evacuated to the city, which had become an important administrative centre. What also contributed to the disaster which befell the city was the lack of substantial air raid precautions, including shelters, combined with the bulk of the buildings being constructed of wood.

In terms of the way in which the raid was conducted Bomber Command had performed well, and the follow-up raid by the USAAF during the day fitted into the pattern of the combined bomber offensive. Meanwhile the war in Europe still had almost three months to run.

THE END: THE FINAL RAID ON KIEL, 2/3 MAY 1945

The port and naval base of Kiel remained an important target for Bomber Command right to the end of the war, although the early fears of causing civilian casualties which had inhibited raids during the first winter of war had by this time long gone.

The Aircraft

On the night of 2/3 May a force of 299 Mosquitos and Halifaxes (see pp. 114 and 146) was sent against Kiel, and while we are familiar with these aircraft, the Halifaxes were modified to provide electronic countermeasures to protect the bomber force. These aircraft belonged to a specialized unit, No. 100 Group.

The Action

On the night of 2/3 May 128 Mosquitos attacked Kiel. With a raid by 16 Mosquitos on Weggebeck and Husam airfields, this marked Bomber Command's last offensive operation of the war. On this occasion No. 100 Group flew 155 sorties to help protect the bombers, and three of this unit's Halifaxes were the last casualties in Bomber Command. One squadron commander in No. 100 Group remembered the night well, because he nearly joined the casualty list:

Knowing that this was to be the more than likely the last operation of the war I took an entirely new crew with me, except for Flying Officer Bates, my navigator. I thought that it would be nice for newly trained aircrew who hadn't done an operation to have the experience and excitement of a raid for the last time. Thank God in many ways that I did this, for it probably saved my life! We were attacked over Kiel by a Ju88 and I had great difficulty in shaking him off. Twice he attacked and twice I weaved out of his cannon fire but this was a tough fighter pilot and he wasn't put off. Trust my luck, I thought, to get shot down and killed within sight of VE Day! I eventually managed to get out of range of the searchlights and the next time the Ju88 attacked he hadn't the advantage of seeing me brightly coned in the sky and missed us by miles . . .

We eventually shook him off and set course for home having dropped our 'window' and bombload over Kiel. At last I felt relaxed and the fear whilst being attacked was gone . . . I put 'George' [automatic pilot] in and was happily sipping my coffee, when the rear gunner screamed at the top of his voice 'enemy fighter coming in astern'. I dropped my thermos flask, spilling coffee everywhere in panic, pulled out the automatic plot and thrust the control column forward in a sudden dive. As luck would have it, his first burst of cannon fire went over the top of us along the fuselage and holes were punched in my old Halifax. I was virtually panic-stricken at being caught napping and loathed the thought of being shot down into the North Sea miles from land, so I flung the Halifax about desperately and dived down to sea level in an attempt to shake the Ju88 off. We eventually lost him and all breathed again.[53]

Comment

The importance of an alert crew was highlighted by this action, where the new boys were on the look-out for enemy fighters, and yet sufficiently well trained to realize the importance of passing on information to the pilot. Maintaining the pressure on the Germans right to the end was important, for not everyone favoured surrender.

TAKING THE WAR TO JAPAN

The biggest problem facing the USA on entry into the Second World War was the vast distance across the Pacific, which meant that it was to be some time before the war could be carried to the Japanese mainland. In Europe, whenever the weather permitted, enemy-occupied territory could be bombed by the RAF and, from 1942 onwards, the USAAF. Because of the nature of the Japanese attack on Pearl Harbor, many Americans, in the armed forces and in political life, felt that the priority was to make war on Japan, leaving Germany to the British until after Japan's defeat. In the end, this debate settled effectively on a policy of engaging all three of the Axis powers in war at the same time. The decision to commit vast resources to the combined bomber offensive in Europe was no doubt driven by the knowledge that it would be some time before large land-based bombers would be able to range freely over Japan.

The destruction of the Imperial Japanese Navy was an essential preliminary to an attack on Japan itself. In the Pacific as in the Atlantic, naval superiority was as important as air superiority, and in the Pacific even more than in the Atlantic, air and naval superiority were for some time one and the same, since for two years this was a war between opposing carrier fleets, albeit augmented by land-based aircraft whenever this was practical, and with a considerable US submarine campaign.

Nevertheless, if land-based bombers couldn't reach the Japanese home islands, they could operate elsewhere, usually on the fringes of the vast Pacific empire which Japan had so quickly occupied during the first few months of the war in the Pacific.

Meanwhile, there was one attempt to combine the range and warload of the land-based bomber with the flexibility and ability to approach the target of the aircraft carrier in the so-called 'Doolittle' raid on Japan in 1942.

OPERATION SHANGRI-LA: THE 'DOOLITTLE' RAID, 18 APRIL 1942

The Japanese attack on Pearl Harbor had been a serious blow to US morale, but not necessarily to US confidence. Striking back at the Japanese was difficult given the overwhelming might of the Imperial Japanese Navy and,

Operations in the Far East saw the USAAF operating at extreme ranges over terrain which was naturally hostile. The long range of the B-24 was a useful asset until the war moved closer to Japan. (RAFM P011423)

of course, the distances involved. Even the US Navy's carrier force in the Pacific was heavily outnumbered by the Japanese at this stage of the war.

Generally regarded as the brainchild of Lt Col James 'Jimmy' Doolittle of the USAAF, the idea of using land-based bombers for a raid on Japanese cities was in fact the idea of a US Navy officer, Capt Francis Low, who in January 1942 proposed using a carrier to take a small force of Army bombers to raid targets on the Japanese home islands. The idea was evaluated by a naval pilot, Capt Donald Duncan, who felt that it could work, using the B-25 Mitchell medium bomber. Once Ernest King, the naval commander, and his USAAF counterpart, 'Hap' Arnold, had accepted the idea and obtained presidential approval, Doolittle was selected as leader for the operation. He was well qualified. A natural pilot with flair and leadership, he was also an aeronautical engineer.

Doolittle quickly verified Duncan's belief that the B-25 was the right aircraft.

Ships and Aircraft

Two aircraft carriers were selected for the attack, USS *Hornet* and the *Enterprise*. These were two sister ships, belonging to the Yorktown class. Both ships displaced 19,800 tons, and were of classic aircraft carrier design with a starboard island and a maximum speed of a worthwhile 33 kt. Both ships could accommodate up to 80 aircraft, and had three lifts and two catapults forward. Unusually, there was an additional set of arrester wires located forward, so that aircraft could land over the bows in a strong wind, but this feature had little practical use, and it was later removed, as were the additional catapults in the hangars angled to allow aircraft to be flown off to port or starboard through the hangar deck apertures.

A twin-engined, high-wing, medium bomber, the North American B-25 Mitchell was powered by two 1,700 hp Wright R-2600-29 radial engines which gave a top speed of 275 mph, a range of 1,350 miles and a warload of 4,000 lb. The 16 aircraft allocated to the operation were stripped of almost everything to reduce their weight and increase their range. The much-prized Norden bombsights, ventral gun turrets and radios were all dispensed with, while additional fuel tanks provided an additional 1,141 US gallons (950 Imperial gallons/4,319 litres). The aircraft did receive a primitive bombsight, plus auto-pilots as well as dummy guns in the tail to discourage Japanese fighter pilots. Pilots were drawn from the 17th Bomber Group and 89th Reconnaissance Sqn, and were given training in making short take-offs, but only Doolittle actually performed a take-off from a carrier, and then only to prove the feasibility of the idea.

The Action

The aircraft were loaded aboard the *Hornet*, which left port in San Francisco on 1 April 1942, looking as if she was ferrying the aircraft to Hawaii or the Philippines. The ship was to launch the aircraft while within 400 miles of the Japanese islands. The aircraft would carry out the attacks on their targets, and then continue to airfields in that part of China not occupied by Japan, to refuel before taking off again to rendezvous at Chungking. This gave rise to the name SHANGRI-LA for the operation, after the fictitious land beyond the clouds.

The Japanese became aware of the approach of a task force by 10 April, based on information from the radio intelligence unit of the Japanese Combined Fleet at Hagashishima, and assumed that it included at least two and possibly three carriers. The Americans had had to use the radio to ensure the rendezvous of the two carriers. The Japanese were not too concerned with the approach of the US ships since they had a network of picket ships some 700 miles offshore. They believed that the ships would be carrying standard USN carrier-borne aircraft, which would have to move within 300 miles of their target before launching an attack, so they believed that they would have 15 hours' warning of any attack.

The Japanese would have had to rely on land-based fighters to counter the attack, since their main carrier force was still returning from a series of raids on Ceylon, with another three ships covering the assault on Port Moresby. Only one carrier, the *Kaga*, was in Japan, but she was undergoing a refit, and was not operational.

After the rendezvous, the Americans maintained radio silence, giving the Japanese no further clues about their position or their intentions. Early in the morning of 18 April, the carriers crossed the picket line, and the force commander, Vice Adm (later Adm) William 'Bull' Halsey assumed that the Japanese would know their position. He was correct: the force was discovered by a Japanese naval vessel, and it was decided to advance the operation while still some 550 miles off Japan. With Doolittle leading, the aircraft took off from the carrier without any mishaps, and headed at low level over the Pacific to their assigned targets.

The aircraft were spotted by a Japanese patrol aircraft, but its report was rejected by the Japanese because their intelligence sources knew that the Americans did not have twin-engined carrier-borne aircraft. Nevertheless, the Japanese did have fighter aircraft on patrol, but these were flying at 10,000 ft and missed the bombers as they flew in at just 150 ft. The bombers attacked Tokyo, Yokosuka and Nagoya, among a number of locations, and caused relatively little damage. Flying over Tokyo, they also strafed, accidentally machine-gunning two grammar school students, whose deaths formed the basis for the prosecution of the captured members of Doolittle's raiding party.

After the attacks, the first problems arose. The promised radio guidance to their Chinese airfields failed to materialize, and struggling without any guidance, two of the aircraft crash-landed in Japanese-occupied territory, or ditched in the sea. The crew of one aircraft which flew on to land in 'friendly' Russian territory was arrested. The two aircraft which crash-landed in Japanese-occupied territory landed near Hankow. The Japanese commander in Shanghai informed Tokyo of their capture, and they were taken to Japan and prosecuted for the deaths of the schoolchildren, three crew members suffering the death penalty. It was only when they heard of the two bombers that the Japanese realized that the raid was a true one-way attack, but the presence of prisoners also meant that their propaganda machine was able to claim that nine aircraft had been shot down.

The returning Japanese carriers were ordered to intercept the US warships, but failed to find them.

Comment

The raid was not uncontroversial in the USA, being criticized by many as meaningless bravado, while others were even more vehement, judging it a waste of experienced aircrew and much-needed aircraft. Certainly, little damage had been done, partly because of the curious decision to divide the small force between a number of targets, which can only be justified as an attempt to alarm as many Japanese as possible. A concerted raid on one specific target, such as the Imperial Palace compound, could have had a dramatic impact on Japanese political and military thinking. As it was, concern for the future well-being of the Emperor caused Adm Yamamoto to adopt a less confident and increasingly defensive strategy, inhibiting the Imperial Japanese Navy's operations for the rest of the war. Without an attack, there might not have been a Japanese plan to take Midway Island, and hence no battle, denying the US Navy an early strategic victory.

Yet the raid was a disaster for the USA's Chinese nationalist allies, whose leader, Gen Chiang Kai-Shek, had objected to the plan, stressing that the Japanese would carry out reprisals against the Chinese. He was right. On 21 April, the planned advance of the China Expeditionary Army was brought forward, and OPERATION CHE-KIANG was launched against Chekiang and Kiangsi provinces. Chiang Kai-Shek was later to report to the US Government: 'Japanese troops slaughtered every man, woman and child in those areas . . .'.[1] In all, a quarter of a million Chinese were killed.

BOMBING THE 'BRIDGE OVER THE RIVER KWAI', 1944–5

The so-called 'bridge over the River Kwai' is famous among the British mainly because of a popular book and film about the British PoWs who were forced by the Japanese to work as slave labour building the bridge. In fact there was no river of this name, but the work of fiction is generally accepted as having been based on fact, even to the extent that the US 10th Air Force destroyed the bridge.

The Aircraft

The aircraft used for the operations against bridges in southern Thailand was the Consolidated B-24 Liberator (see p. 126). For these operations, the long distances meant that the front bomb bays were converted into additional fuel tanks, while the rear bomb bays carried four 1,000 lb bombs.

The Action

The USAAF's Liberator squadrons were initially based in India, flying fuel over the 'hump' – the Himalayas – to China, and for a period some squadrons were based in China itself. Among these were 492, 493 and 496 Sqns, which were later moved back to India for a campaign of 'bridge-busting' against targets in southern Thailand. They also bombed the docks at Bangkok. Each squadron had 18 aircraft, although usually just 9 from each squadron were sent on a raid, possibly because of the

A B-24J above the clouds. (RAFM P011428)

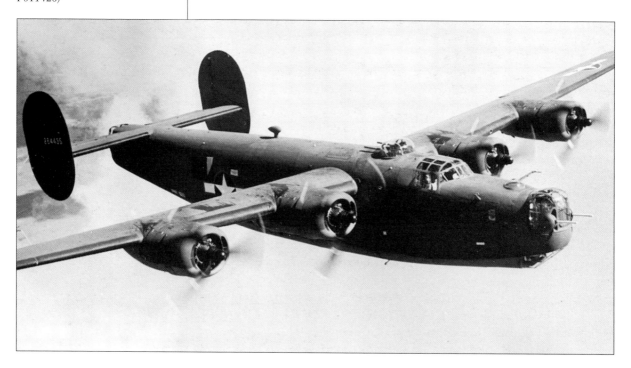

number of hours which had to be spent in the air – sorties had a duration of 15–18 hours. This was a demanding schedule, flying 1,500 miles each way, most of it at an altitude of just 50 ft above the sea, and allowing little margin for error or a lapse of concentration.

Carl H. Fritsche was a pilot with the US 10th Air Force's 492 Sqn. His initial raids were against Mandalay in Japanese-occupied Burma, but he later made 19 'bridge-busting' sorties into southern Thailand, as well as a number of raids on Bangkok Docks. He recalled:

I flew over the bridge many times on decoy work or flak suppression. We were well aware, and were briefed before we left, of the dire situation of the prisoners and so we were instructed not to strafe or bomb in any way that might endanger the men on the ground . . . Now in order to do this we had decoys at 2–3,000 feet while other aircraft came up the river very low to do the bombing.

The American Air Force listed every bridge . . . Kwai bridge was 277, and this is what we called it.[2]

The raids continued until the Japanese surrender, although Fritsche himself left India in July 1945. He initially went to the USA for conversion training so that he could be posted to Okinawa as commander of one of the new Boeing B-29 Superfortresses, to take part in the final attacks on Japan – he was on a troopship en route to Okinawa when he heard the news of Japan's surrender.

As the war in the Far East developed, the USAAF received larger aircraft, the high-flying Boeing B-29 Superfortress, seen here with its smaller cousin, the B-17 Fortress. (IWM NXF27991)

Larger still was the Convair B-36, dwarfing the Superfortress in this shot. The B-36 was developed in case bases in the United Kingdom became untenable, and had transatlantic range. (RAFM P11435)

Comment

This was the routine of war – regular strikes against communications targets in enemy-occupied territory, hoping to cause the maximum damage and disruption with the least cost to innocent civilians and, in this case, PoWs. Generally, the Germans made less use of Allied PoWs than did the Japanese, although this may have been largely because so many of the prisoners held in Germany were aircrew officers, and the Geneva Convention prohibited the use of officers as slave labour (a rule the Japanese ignored).

The combination of strategic bombing, augmented by tactical operations by the RAF against Japanese forces in Burma and the unconventional (for the time) but successful war waged by the British Chindits in the Burmese jungle, meant that the Japanese advance across Asia ground to a halt in Burma. Increasingly, shortages of men and materials, and the disruption of the communications links between the occupied territories and the home islands, meant that the Japanese forces were under great pressure.

ATTACKING STRATEGIC TARGETS IN THE FAR EAST, 5 JUNE AND 10/11 AUGUST 1944

As bases closer to Japan became available in 1944, it was possible for the USAAF to consider taking the war to Japan itself, which had remained unscathed since the 'Doolittle' raid in 1942. At first, there was a difference between the war in Europe, where Germany had been bombed increasingly heavily, as had Italy to a lesser extent, and that in the Far East, where the Japanese military had gone away to fight, leaving the civilian population to continue production. Japanese industry and industrial workers had continued as normal, although as the fortunes of war swung against Japan, shortages of fuel, raw materials and food started to emerge.

The US effort against Japan was helped not just by the availability of landbases within striking distance of the home islands, but by the introduction of a new high-altitude heavy bomber, the Boeing B-29 Superfortress. This aircraft's high-altitude operations meant that defending fighter pilots could not reach it, until, using *kamikaze* pilots, they stripped their aircraft of everything, including cannon, and started their 'ramming' attacks (see p. 102).

As with the war in Europe, mine-laying was to become of major significance in the closing stages of the war against Japan. The impact on the Japanese can be judged by the fact that monthly shipping through the Shimonoseki Straits was reduced from more than half a million tons in March 1944 to just 5,000 tons by August 1945. By then, the daily number of calories available on ration was 1,400, and some Japanese experts believed that had the war continued for another year, at least seven million would have died from malnutrition.

The first raid by the B-29s was by the 58th Bomber Wing, part of the USAAF's 20th Bomber Command, based in India. The 58th was the only bomber wing to have four squadrons in each of its four groups. Based in

The rapid advance of US forces across the Pacific meant that airfields had to be hastily constructed, with priority given to runways and hard standing for the B-29 Superfortresses, so that this airfield has an improvised air to it. (IWM NYP69366)

India, the 58th had 120 aircraft by May 1944, and its commander, Brig Gen 'Blondie' Saunders, was anxious to take the war to the enemy. A second wing, the 73rd, was working-up in the USA, and would be posted to Saipan once the island was occupied by US forces, ready to raid Japan itself. Meanwhile, the 58th was well situated to attack Japanese forces in South-East Asia.

The Aircraft

The largest bomber of any nation during the Second World War, the Boeing B-29 Superfortress saw relatively little action in Europe when it entered service in 1943 because the aircraft was intended to strike at Japanese industry. With a more streamlined fuselage than the earlier B-17 Flying Fortress, the B-29 had four 2,500 hp Wright radial engines to provide a maximum speed well in excess of 300 mph and a bombload of as much as 20,000 lb. Among the new features of this high-flying aircraft were remote-control gun turrets.

The Action

The first target for the B-29s had been the Makesan Railway Yard at Bangkok. On 5 June 1944 Saunders led 112 aircraft to Bangkok, taking off from their base, specially adopted for the larger aircraft, on the Ganges Plains in southern Bengal, at Kharagpur (other bases, also ex-RAF, were at Chakulia, Piardoba and Dudkhundi). For the raid, the aircraft each had a crew of 11 men: aircraft commander, pilot, bombardier, navigator and flight engineer (all officers), and central fire control gunner, left and right gunners, tail gunner, radio operator and radar operator (all enlisted men). The B-29s took off before daylight for their 2,681 mile round trip, ready to mount their raid in daylight from 23,000 ft. It took 90 minutes for the entire force to become airborne. Out of 112 aircraft, 98 were able to head for the target area after take-off, while another 5 were lost because of mechanical problems. Just 77 reached the target area, but of these, just 48 were able to hit the target. No aircraft were lost to enemy action.

Another significant early operation by B-29s took place on the night of 10/11 August 1944, when 14 aircraft from the 462nd Bomber Group, led by Col Richard Carmichael, were sent to lay mines in the Moesi River at Palembang, the huge oil refinery complex in Sumatra. This was part of an operation involving 56 aircraft from the 58th Bomber Wing, and 39 were sent to bomb the Pladjoe Oil Refinery complex, with the loss of one aircraft.

Although all the mine-laying aircraft returned safely, just eight mine-laying aircraft reached their target, and each dropped two mines from altitudes of 100–1,000 feet. This was the longest mission mounted by aircraft in the China-Burma-India theatre, 4,200 miles non-stop, with aircraft in the air for 19 hours, and it had to be staged from the British base at Trincomalee in Ceylon (now Sri Lanka).

Ed Perry was Group Navigator for 462nd Group, which had 14 crews, all well experienced. He recalls:

The plan had called for release of the mines in the river using radar if necessary. However . . . we could see that conditions were very good for visual release. There was a bright, full moon at about 11 o'clock, which reflected off the river surface. Tall trees along the river really highlighted the water surface, with the trees being quite dark and the river surface shimmering from the rays of the moon. Our release points were the furthest down river, therefore, the one closest to the aiming points being attacked by the bombers. Before our release, we could see bombs going off at about 2 o'clock. We could see anti-aircraft fire and searchlights across the area. 'Red', our bombardier, and the gunners did some low level strafing as we went upstream to our release points. Since we were the first low-level aircraft along the river, we had the element of surprise in our favour.

As we approached the scheduled release for our two mines, we saw a large ship, presumably a tanker, in the channel. Red released our mine before we reached the ship, strafed the ship as we passed overhead, at not more than 350 feet altitude, and released the second mine just beyond the ship. The tail gunner reported that both mines entered the channel. At this point, we broke away . . . and started our climb out.[3]

The B-29s looked invulnerable, but bad weather and mechanical problems often combined to cause the loss of an aircraft. This was especially true once aircraft were based at forward bases in China, which entailed flying over the 'hump' from India to China over the Himalayas. Stubbs Roberts was a flight engineer on one of 468th Bomber Group's B-29s:

Twice, I had to hit the silk because of mechanical trouble. Each time with a different crew, my bales took place on both sides of the Hump. Our first two attempts to fly safely over the world's tallest mountains with my regular crew ended in a bale-out when two engines failed just as we entered the crest of the mountains. We turned around to return to our base in India, but when another engine failed, Sims gave the bale-out signal. We all were lucky enough to make it out of the plane and eventually make it back to our base at Kharagpur.

My second encounter at looking up at a silk canopy of a parachute came on a supply run to Pengshan. Fate had placed me in the flight engineer's seat flying with another crew. Jim Patillo's flight engineer reported to sick call the morning of this particular flight, so operations assigned me to fill in for him. This time the flight went well until we started our descent into A-17, our destination at Pengshan, China. Suddenly, during the descent, propellers on two engines ran away, and the pilot could hardly control the plane. He finally passed the bale-out word, now becoming a familiar word to me. The entire crew made it out of the plane, but we lost the co-pilot and one of the gunners.[4]

They were eventually picked up by friendly Chinese civilians, and were treated like heroes. After spending a couple of nights in a small village, they were escorted by Chinese soldiers, who took them by boat and cart to Pengshan.

Comment

The reduction in shipping brought about by the use of mine-laying aircraft proved the worth of this form of aerial warfare. Not only does mine-laying inflict damage on the enemy's lines of communication, it also forces them to devote resources to mine clearance, itself a hazardous and difficult operation. Better still, the Japanese proved themselves time and again to be extremely poor at taking defensive measures. They failed to protect their merchant shipping through a properly organized convoy system, which, along with escort carriers, could well have made life more difficult for the mine-laying aircraft.

Other weaknesses of the Japanese war effort also became apparent, including the failure to introduce new technology, so that as the Americans made new advances, the Japanese could not keep pace. Later in the war, as USAAF bombers started to fly over the Japanese home islands, the lack of suitable fighters meant that the Japanse had to resort to the use of suicide aircraft to 'ram' the bombers – a wasteful practice which cost the lives of experienced pilots, by this stage of the war in short supply.

FIRE RAID ON TOKYO, 9/10 MARCH 1945

Throughout the war, the Americans had been reluctant to attack civilian targets. This policy changed during the long and hard-fought struggle across the Pacific towards Japan itself. The commander of the USAAF in the Pacific, Gen Curtis LeMay, decided on the controversial policy of using incendiary bombs against Japanese cities. Like 'Bomber' Harris in the RAF, he saw this as one means of forcing the Japanese leadership to seek surrender. The change in policy was controversial, and in fact originated in Washington. Many, including Adm Chester Nimitz, the US Navy's commander in the Pacific, were opposed to the idea, believing that the war could only be won by attacking industrial and military targets

LeMay was anxious to make the new policy work. He was responsible for the tactics, if not the strategy. These included the decision to abandon high-level bombing and instead attack at altitudes of 5,000–8,000 ft.

The Aircraft

The aircraft were the new Boeing B-29 Superfortress (see p. 216). For the raid on Tokyo, the aircraft were to leave their gunners behind, with the exception of the tail-gunner, who would act as an observer only, because all the guns were to be removed. This would save 3,000 lb per aircraft, enabling a heavier bombload to be carried.

The Action

In a further break with the USAAF's normal strategy of day-bombing, the attack was made at night, with take-off at 18.00, reaching the target around midnight. On reaching the target, they would find that it had been marked by a force of twelve Pathfinder B-29s, which would have dropped flares around it, leaving the main force to bomb within this 'ring of fire'.

Taken together, such radical changes dismayed the bomber crews. They had been accustomed to flying with the heavy defensive armaments of the US bombers, and often with long-range escort fighters as well. The Pathfinders were also seen as alerting the enemy defences to the forthcoming raid. Some protested that casualties could reach 75 per cent. But LeMay and his staff officers were unsympathetic, giving out the not altogether reassuring message that if these predictions were correct, they would have to send for replacement crews from the USA.

By this time the USAAF had no fewer than three B-29 wings in the Marianas – the 73rd, 313th and 314th. This gave LeMay 325 B-29s for the first Tokyo raid. The force was carefully routed, with each wave given precise directions, since the aircraft would have just enough fuel for the round trip, with nothing to spare for diversions. The gamble of removing the guns from the aircraft was based on an intelligence report that the four main Japanese home islands had just two night-fighter squadrons between them. The threat from AA guns was also discounted, because the Japanese, unlike the Germans, did not use radar-controlled AA guns, depending instead on searchlights for direction. The USAAF believed that this far into the war in the Pacific, only two B-29s had been lost to ground fire. The combination of speed and low-level attack would give the AA artillery little time to focus on the aircraft.

Using island groups as navigating points, the radar operators were instructed to aid the navigators. Late in the afternoon of 9 March the B-29s were ready at their bases in Guam, Saipan and Tinian Island. The preparations were watched by LeMay, while the operation was led by Gen Power, flying with the 314th Bomber Wing. Power's aircraft was to be one of the Pathfinders, carrying M-47 incendiaries, while the main force bombers carried M-69 incendiaries filled with napalm.

Chester Marshall flew on this raid, taking off from Isley Field on Saipan, and noting with apprehension the long taxi from the aircraft's hard standing to the end of the runway, using precious fuel which might be desperately needed on the homeward leg. The aircraft flew out to Tokyo, close to Iwo Jima, where heavy fighting was continuing on the ground.

Marshall recalls that an hour or so after passing Iwo Jima, they entered a weather front which was often to be found between Iwo Jima and Japan. Flying at about 2,000 ft, the bomber force descended to reduce the chances of mid-air collisions. As the target area drew closer, the bombers began to climb to their bombing altitude. They climbed through zero visibility, relying on the radar operator to warn of other aircraft before breaking out of the clouds at 5,000 feet:

We . . . looked upon one of the most horrifying scenes we had ever witnessed. We were still 50 miles or so from landfall, and we could see the fires in Tokyo. Scanning searchlights filled the sky, trying to pick up approaching B-29s. We saw our first B-29 as we came closer to the searchlights . . . you could tell they were being fired on because of the tracer bullets going up to them. We knew that several hundred B-29s should be all around us . . . How had we missed hitting a plane while climbing in that weather front? . . . We donned our dark glasses to try to avoid being blinded if caught in the searchlights. We noticed two B-29s were caught in the lights. When one light would get locked on, other lights would scan over to also lock on, and then they sent up barrages of flak. A B-29 caught in four or five searchlights is a beautiful but horrifying sight. You knew that its crew could be shot out of the sky any minute . . .

. . . Finally, we were caught in a fast-moving beam which, after scanning past us, switched back and caught us. It was brighter than daylight. We finally escaped the lights, but a much tougher chore lay ahead . . . Looking down into the streets of Tokyo, you could see the flames coming from house windows, and the smell of burning debris was bad, but as we moved on further and opened our bomb bays, we were sickened by the sweet smell of burning human flesh. It was nauseating, I missed at least two meals before I could eat anything again.[5]

They dropped their bombs and started to turn to get out of the smoke and flames which were reaching up to more than 10,000 ft before hitting wind shear. The strong updraft generated by the heat lifted the heavy bomber, pinning the crew to their seats, unable to control the aircraft. Unpleasant and frightening though it was, the updraft had pulled the aircraft up by 5,000 ft, luckily without flipping it onto its back, as happened to many aircraft on incendiary raids, leaving the crew struggling to right the aircraft before it crashed out of control.

The raid lasted two hours, and aided by a 75 mph gale, destroyed more than 16 square miles of the city, demolishing some 25 per cent of all buildings, some 267,000 in all. The Japanese officials running the city estimated that 83,783 people were killed, and another 50,000 or more seriously injured, with more than a million homeless. This was despite earlier attempts to minimize the destruction from such an attack by creating fire breaks, bulldozing thousands of homes in the hope of preventing still greater destruction.

Comment

The change of policy was understandable, but over-optimistic. The US Army and US Marines, fighting island-by-island across the Pacific, had already experienced not just Japanese tenacity in attempting to hold on to territory, but an attitude which saw anyone, civilians included, who attempted to surrender being shot in the back. The incendiary raids were nevertheless a step-by-step escalation of the war against the Japanese home islands, and while it would take the use of nuclear weapons to bring Japan to surrender, the Americans had to try something else before committing themselves to weapons of such massive destruction.

As it was, the raid on Tokyo was followed by an incendiary raid on Nagoya the following night, and by a similar raid on Osaka the night after that, then Kobe and a return visit to Nagoya, before the USAAF ran out of incendiaries.

THE ATOMIC BOMB: HIROSHIMA AND NAGASAKI, 6 AND 9 AUGUST 1945

After the initial incendiary raids, the USAAF stepped up its bombing attacks on Japanese cities, so that there were 60 major raids between June and August 1945, destroying some 60 square miles of Japanese cities, and concentrating on the 65 Japanese towns and cities with more than 100,000 inhabitants. In all, in this short bombing campaign, the USAAF dropped 154,000 tons of bombs on Japan.

This intense rate of bombing had little impact on the country's military leadership, even though it forced more than eight million Japanese to flee the urban areas and seek what refuge they could in the countryside. Rations were at starvation levels, 1,400 calories per day per person. Fuel was scarce, and the little that remained was reserved exclusively for the military, and especially for the final *kamikaze* onslaught of 5,000 aircraft, many of them unsuitable second-line training or communications types.

The Allies put in hand preparations for the invasion of Japan, with the RAF, now that the war in Europe had ended, planning to send a substantial force of its new Avro Lincoln heavy bombers, the successor to the Lancaster. This would have been the greatest invasion of all time, with the US Navy assembling a force of 26 aircraft carriers and light carriers, as well as 64 escort carriers, while the Royal Navy prepared to commit 4 aircraft carriers and light carriers, and another 18 escort carriers. All of this was done with a sense of great foreboding, expecting massive loss of life amongst both the invaders and the defenders, and with a grim outlook for the many PoWs held in Japanese prison camps, and for the populations of the occupied territories, for despite the massive gains made by the Americans as they fought across the Pacific, all of South-East Asia remained in Japanese hands, as did China and Hong Kong, Malaya, Singapore and the Indonesian Archipelago.

Col Paul Tibbets, USAAF, at Tinian Airfield in the Marianas with his Boeing B-29 Superfortress, named Enola Gay *after his mother. This aircraft dropped the first atomic bomb on Hiroshima. (IWM HU44878)*

Against this desperate situation, the only option was something final and devastating, and it existed in the form of the atomic bomb. This new means of warfare had been developed during the war years under the title of the 'Manhattan Project', and tests had shown it to be of such tremendous power that even some of the scientists involved feared to use it. The new US President, Truman, was briefed about the bomb, and accepted the advice of his military advisers that it should be used. When the Japanese rejected the demand for unconditional surrender from the USA and the UK at the Potsdam Conference, the stage was set for the use of the atomic bomb.

The Aircraft

Once again, the aircraft used on both atomic bombing missions was the B-29 (see p. 216).

The Action

The USAAF's 509th Composite Group had been formed as early as 1944 in view of the possibility that nuclear weapons might have to be used against Germany. Once German defeat was seen as inevitable without recourse to the nuclear option, the force was moved to Tinian Airfield in the Marianas in May 1945, and was ready to use nuclear weapons by 1 August.

On 6 August, at 02.45, the Group's CO Col Paul Tibbets took off in his Boeing B-29 Superfortress, named *Enola Gay*, followed by two observation aircraft. Weather conditions were important, to ensure that

The aftermath of the first use of an atomic bomb, at Hiroshima, 6 August 1945. (IWM SC278262)

An aerial view of Hiroshima, showing the city centre. (IWM HU66801)

the bomb would fall on the right target, and as he took off, Tibbets did not know which of three Japanese cities would be his target. Shortly after 07.00, he was directed to Hiroshima. A little more than an hour later, at 08.15, while flying at 31,600 ft, the U-235 atomic bomb, known as 'Little Boy', was released, exploding at an altitude of 1,000 ft. Within seconds, 78,000 people were dead and another 51,000 were injured, while 176,000 were homeless. More than 70,000 buildings had been destroyed.

Office buildings at Hiroshima, 300 yards from the hypocentre. (IWM HU66803)

Three days later, on 9 August, a second Boeing B-29, named *Bock's Car* after its captain, dropped another atomic bomb, this time on the city of Nagasaki, while Japan's leaders still debated Truman's call of 6 August to surrender or face complete ruin from repeated attacks by the new weapon. Nagasaki was a major industrial centre with more than a quarter of million inhabitants, many of whom worked in the Mitsubishi factories. The bomb dropped on Nagasaki was more powerful than that used at Hiroshima, and was known as 'Fat Man', due to its shape, which resulted from a different fission mechanism. It killed 50,000 people and injured 10,000 more, a lower figure than that at Hiroshima since Nagasaki had many buildings in valleys, which protected them from the burst.

The RAF had an observer flying in *Bock's Car*, Gp Capt Leonard Cheshire, a former commander of the famous 617 Sqn. In contrast to his earlier experiences flying in the RAF's bombers, the B-29 was a revelation to Cheshire, with relatively little internal noise, in shirt-sleeve order and without an oxygen mask, flying at 39,000 ft at almost 400 mph. Weather conditions were perfect, with a bright clear blue sky:

He put on his welder's glasses and looked out towards the unsuspecting city that seemed to drowse unwarily in the sun's fresh warmth. He looked out and wondered what would happen below them.

And below them, as the two silvery, ephemeral aircraft droned lazily towards Nagasaki, the not very efficient Japanese Air Raid Service issued an alert and later, almost immediately, relaxed it. In the two valleys that forked into the heart of the city about 100,000 people lived poorly and worked stolidly, in their

Gp Capt Leonard Cheshire, VC, a former commanding officer of 617 Sqn, was a British observer of the dropping of the second atomic bomb flying in the B-29 Bock's Car, named after its captain, at Nagasaki on 9 August 1945. (IWM CH12667)

national fashion. On the other side of the city another 160,000 dwelt and worked. The whole town was about as big as Portsmouth.

Then suddenly the faint rhythmic droning of American engines, so different from the erratic harshness of their own aircraft, was heard . . . and three parachutes dropped lazily . . . and men and women looked upwards curiously.

There came a bright flash in the sky and many shut their eyes at its brilliance. Others kept them opened . . . the bright flash built up within itself a heat so incredibly radiant and vicious that their eyeballs were savagely seared into blindness.[6]

Preceded by a pillar of purple fire 10,000 ft high, with perfect symmetry, unlike a conventional explosive fireball, it seemed to say to Cheshire: 'Against me, you cannot fight.'[7]

Cheshire recalled later:

. . . this bomb was obviously a very big one and the more bombs dropped on Japan in the shorter time, the sooner the war would end and save many more lives, both Allied and Japanese, than any mere air raids could destroy . . . I may as well

This was what Tibbets saw – the 20,000 ft high mushroom cloud which shot up after the explosion. (IWM MH2629)

A school building 50 yards from the blast at Nagasaki. The building appears to have been only slightly damaged, but in fact the entire interior was destroyed by fire, which did not spread through the building as would a conventional fire, but instead started simultaneously on each floor. (IWM MW82)

confess that we were so keen on dropping this bomb on Nagasaki, and would have been so disappointed if the war had ended without our doing so, that some of us jokingly suggested, if Japan *did* surrender before we flew to Nagasaki, that we might even fly there and drop the bomb just the same![8]

Japan accepted the Allied surrender terms on 20 August, but the formal date for surrender was set for 2 September. The surrender only came after much debate, and even an attempt at a *coup d'état* by those military leaders opposed to it.

Comment

The use of the atomic bomb was a matter of cruel necessity. Some Japanese have complained about the short interval between the dropping of the two bombs, but this ignores the fact that it took another eleven days before the signing of the surrender.

Many have questioned why Hiroshima and Nagasaki, important military and industrial targets as they were, were chosen rather than Tokyo. The answer lies partly in the devastation which had already been visited upon the capital, and partly because of the need to leave both the government and the Emperor alive to surrender and enforce the surrender on the Japanese commanders in the field.

Opposite: This was the effect on Nagasaki, the city's Matsuyami-machi district. (IWM HU66808)

AN UNEASY PEACE

The ending of hostilities in both Europe and the Pacific did not
lead to the peace for which the world had been waiting. The
Soviet Union quickly showed its determination to hang on to the
territories through which it had advanced towards Berlin and
the final downfall of the Third Reich. In the Far East, many nationalist
groups were determined to wrest independence from their former colonial
masters, most especially in the case of the former French and Dutch
colonies, since these countries had been seriously weakened by their own
years of occupation, and had difficulty in asserting their authority.

After the war, the military situation could be taken as fitting one of five
different patterns. The first of these was the major stand-off between the
democratic Western powers and the communist Eastern dictatorships – the
so-called 'Cold War', in which the Western powers formed themselves into
the North Atlantic Treaty Organisation (NATO) for mutual protection,
while those in the East became part of the Warsaw Pact. There were
significant differences between NATO and the Warsaw Pact, apart from the
fact that NATO members viewed the alliance as being purely defensive, and
believed, with considerable justification, that the Warsaw Pact had an
offensive role. NATO was led by the Americans, but not dominated by
them, each member nation having complete control of its own armed
forces, and combined forces often operating under commanders who were
not Americans. The Warsaw Pact forces were always commanded by a
Russian officer, and the entire organization was completely dominated by
the Soviet Union. Nowhere was this more so than in East Germany, whose
armed forces were commanded by Russian officers. The Warsaw Pact also
had economic and political functions, in addition to the purely military.

The spread of communism and the emergence of Communist China as a
significant military power led to the creation of other regional alliances
modelled on NATO. The South-East Asia Treaty Organization (SEATO)
included both the USA and UK, as well as regional states, such as
Australia and New Zealand, but lacked NATO's integrated command and
communications structure and was eventually disbanded. Before this, the
Baghdad Pact, formed to combat the threat of communism to the Middle
East, had to change its name to the Central Treaty Organization after Iraq
became an aggressive dictatorship, and the organization did not survive
long. Ideas for a South Atlantic Treaty Organization failed to develop.

NATO saw UK and US heavy bombers kept at a high state of readiness
to launch first a nuclear and then later a thermo-nuclear deterrent to a

surprise Warsaw Pact attack. Initially, these were updated versions of the Second World War aircraft, with the B-29 replaced by the B-50, and the Lancaster by the Lincoln. The newly formed US Air Force soon acquired Boeing B-47 Stratojets and then the large Boeing B-52 Stratofortress heavy bombers, while in the mid-1950s the RAF saw the first of its trio of V-bombers, the Vickers Valiant, enter service, to be followed by the Avro Vulcan and the Handley Page Victor.

These aircraft were superseded by ICBMs (inter-continental ballistic missiles), and the Soviet Union, USA, UK and France acquired missile-launching submarines, providing greater mobility and security from a pre-emptive strike than land-based missiles. The USAF alone kept the faith with the heavy bomber, finding that the B-52 made an excellent launching vehicle for cruise missiles. Elsewhere, the emphasis changed to what would have been regarded as a medium, or even light bomber in Second World War terms. These aircraft had smaller crews, usually just two men, and two engines, but could often carry a bombload in excess of a heavy bomber of the war years, the Hawker Siddeley Buccaneer having an internal and external maximum load of 16 1,000 lb bombs. More potent still, many of these aircraft could carry nuclear bombs or missiles with a nuclear warhead.

Fortunately, the Cold War did not become a hot war, but the second type of conflict did: battles for independence in the colonies, mainly in Africa and Asia. These often involved nationalist movements taken over by communists, so they were frequently seen as battles between the superpowers, but by proxy. The UK, having granted independence to Australia, New Zealand, Canada and South Africa, and having followed this with independence for India and Pakistan, found many nationalist groups in many other territories anxious to accelerate the timetable for independence. The nationalists often knew that their countries were not ready for independence, but used the opportunity of gaining it prematurely to impose a dictatorship. The bomber rarely found a role in these wars.

The third and fourth military situations once again saw bombers at work. The third military situation resulted from disagreements between the new states, and most notably between India and Pakistan, Israel and its Arab neighbours, between North and South Korea, and North and South Vietnam. The Korean and Vietnamese conflicts involved the forces of other countries.

The fourth military situation involved instances where dictatorships looked for what has been described as 'territorial aggrandisement' – in effect what the Axis Powers had done, but on a smaller scale. Argentina seized the Falkland Islands, Iraq seized neighbouring Kuwait.

Finally, there were civil wars, usually in states in which the fighter-bomber rather than the bomber was involved, as in Cuba in the 1950s.

THE KOREAN WAR, 25 JUNE 1950–27 JULY 1953

North Korea invaded neighbouring South Korea early on the morning of Sunday 25 June 1950. Catching US and South Korean forces alike unawares, the North Koreans made rapid advances, helped by the fact that the USA had withdrawn its ground forces the previous year, in the mistaken belief that North Korea would content itself with guerrilla warfare and terrorism against the South. A rapid response was only to be expected, with the US Fifth Air Force, the largest constituent part of the US Far East Air Forces (FEAF), based in Japan, just 500 miles to the east. The role of the FEAF, originally formed in Australia in September 1942, some nine months after Japan's surprise attack on Pearl Harbor, was to counter any threat from the Soviets, by this time far from being an ally. But, on that Sunday morning, the FEAF was not at the advanced state of readiness which might have been expected.

The first notification of the invasion did not reach the headquarters of the FEAF until 09.45, almost six hours after the start. The message was relayed to the component air forces, which, in addition to the FEAF, included the Twentieth in Okinawa and the Thirteenth in the Philippines. In the state of confusion which reigned at the outset, no decisions were taken and no orders given. The Soviet Union and its allies fully expected that there would be no response. Added to this, most of the personnel were away for the weekend, while the weather, with low cloud and heavy rain, was poor for operational flying.

The FEAF included bomber, fighter, reconnaissance and transport units. The mainstay of the defensive fighter squadrons was the Lockheed F-80C Shooting Star, which equipped one interceptor and two fighter-bomber

Good targets were difficult to find in Korea, with relatively little heavy industry and a basic infrastructure, so bridges were the obvious targets in an attempt to disrupt communications, which were as likely to be ox carts as motor vehicles. This bridge was destroyed by aircraft from the British light fleet carrier Theseus. *(FAAM Camp/23)*

Another bridge, again destroyed by aircraft from Theseus. *(FAAM Camp/167)*

squadrons. Two all-weather fighter squadrons of North American F-82 Twin Mustangs completed the defences. There was a single reconnaissance squadron of RF-80As. Offensive units included two squadrons of Martin B-26 Marauders. There were also two squadrons of troop-carrying aircraft, Douglas C-54s, the military variant of the DC-4 airliner. The Twentieth had two squadrons of B-29 Superfortresses, based in Guam, as well as a long-range photo-reconnaissance unit with RB-29s. As the war progressed, Guam became the main base for B-29 operations over Korea.

One of the 'Korean' generation of naval aircraft, a Fairey Firefly lands on a British carrier. The Firefly fighter-bomber had a brief operational career before the Admiralty opted for an all-jet Fleet Air Arm. (IWM32250)

Arming a Hawker Sea Fury fighter-bomber aboard the light fleet carrier Ocean. *(FAAM Camp/165)*

The Aircraft

The Korean War saw a substantial number of fighter-bomber sorties, many of them from aircraft carriers off the coast, but the USAF made good use of its Boeing B-29 Superfortresses (see p. 216) and the smaller Martin B-26 Marauders – like the B-29, a Second World War aircraft.

The B-26 had entered USAAF service in 1942 as a fast medium bomber. As with almost all combat aircraft, there were many versions, but typically a B-26B would have twin 1,920 hp Pratt & Whitney radial engines, and nose and tail .5 in guns. Early versions suffered from the high wing loading – the highest of any US combat aircraft during the Second World War – which made handling difficult, especially during landings, but attention to these problems, including an increase in wingspan and slotted flaps, meant that the aircraft eventually ended the war with the lowest loss rate per thousand sorties of any US-built medium bomber. The bombload was normally around 2,000 lb, and the aircraft could exceed 300 mph if not too heavily laden.

The Action

The realities of international relations during a period of high tension – the Soviet Union had exploded its first atomic device the previous year – meant

The small size of the British light fleet carriers can be seen from this photograph of Ocean, *with Hawker Sea Furies ranged on her deck. (IWM A32243)*

that the FEAF could not respond immediately, even if it had been at a higher state of readiness. They could assist with the evacuation of US nationals, if the US Ambassador in Seoul called upon it to do so, but only if the evacuation itself was attacked could it respond, providing that the US commander in South Korean, Gen Douglas MacArthur, gave the orders.

Many have been tempted to draw a parallel between events that morning and those almost nine years earlier, when Japan mounted the surprise attack on Pearl Harbor. There is something in this – the USA had no idea of the massive build-up of North Korean forces. The Supreme Commander Allied Powers, MacArthur, who had been in command when the Philippines fell to invading Japanese forces, must also have felt a strong sense of *déjà vu*.

Hasty plans were put into effect by the FEAF, so by that afternoon, units were available for an evacuation, and a preliminary starting time of 03.30 the following morning was advised to the FEAF's HQ by the squadron commander given the task of making the preparations. These plans would have involved the B-26s patrolling off the coast, ready to intervene if necessary.

South Korean ground forces soon began to slow the advance of the invaders, but North Korean aircraft started to appear, two Yakovlev Yak-9

By contrast, the American carrier Valley Forge *had a far larger number of aircraft, including Vought Corsair fighter-bombers. (United States Naval Institute)*

fighters circling the airfields at Kimpo and Seoul, without any attempt at interception. There couldn't be any – the ROK Air Force consisted of just 60 aircraft – all trainers. MacArthur had vetoed South Korean plans for a small air force of 99 aircraft, including 25 F-51 Mustang fighter-bombers on the grounds that it would increase tension in the area! By contrast, North Korea had 132 aircraft, including 62 Ilyushin Il-10 ground attack aircraft, and a number of fighter types, including the Yak-3, Yak-7B, Yak-9 and La-7.

The evacuation was eventually ordered just before midnight, with North Korean tanks just 17 miles north of Seoul. Most of the evacuees went by sea on 26 June, while FEAF F-82s patrolled overhead in flights of four. All seemed quiet, until at 13.30, a solitary Lavochin La-7 dived out of the clouds, cannon blazing, and flew straight through a formation of F-82s, which took evasive action while the La-7 disappeared back into the low cloud. The air evacuation started the following day, 27 June, using the C-54s. At midday five Yak-7s appeared over Seoul and began to dive towards Kimpo Airfield, but were immediately pounced upon by five F-82s of the 68 and 339 Fighter Sqns, which shot down three of the intruders.

That evening the UN Security Council adopted a resolution to provide support for South Korea. Initially, the USAF was instructed that the FEAF's

Both the USN and RN used Grumman Avengers to good effect in the Korean War, although this aircraft had first seen service during the closing years of the Second World War. (IWM A24250)

aircraft could attack North Korean forces between the front line and the 38th Parallel. The first attack was by 12 B-26s which bombed a railway complex at Munsan, near the 38th, taking off from their base at Ashiya at 07.30 on 28 June. After attacking the railway, the aircraft bombed troop concentrations and road transport, although they suffered the effects of heavy ground fire: one was so badly hit that it crashed on landing at Ashya with the loss of its entire crew, and another two aircraft were badly damaged and had to make emergency landings. Another nine B-26s attacked North Korean forces north of Seoul later that day, without loss.

On 29 June nine B-29s bombed Kimpo Airfield, now in North Korean hands, dropping a large load of 500 lb bombs. Three Yak-9s which tried to intercept were soon put to flight, with one shot down and another damaged.

After the UN invasion of Korea, the USAF mounted a strategic bombing campaign using aircraft based in Guam and Kimpo. One problem in using the heavy bomber in Korea was the relative shortage of major industrial targets. Even so, Strategic Air Command identified five major industrial centres for attention by the B-29s, including the railway yards and armaments factories at Pyongyang; the port of Wonsan, with its oil refineries; Hungnam, a centre for chemicals and metals production; the port and iron foundries at Chongjin; and the naval base at Rashin. Other significant targets were the harbour at Chinnampo, with extensive metals industries, and five

The United States Far East Air Forces made extensive use of infrared camouflage detection photography as the war progressed, showing up anything which did not contain chlorophyll as white against the red of vegetation. In this case, a convoy of military vehicles was detected. (IWM COL37)

east-coast hydro-electric power complexes, as well as another at Sui-Hoi, which exported half its output to China. With the exception of Pyongyang, these targets were grouped on the north-east coast of North Korea.

Operations were inhibited by the need to avoid drawing the Soviet Union into the conflict on the side of Communist China, at this stage still a Soviet ally. This precluded an effective strategic bomber campaign against fighter bases in China, and the lines of communication and supply from China into North Korea could not be attacked. In addition, the Korean War saw an intensive fighter-bomber campaign by the Royal Navy and US Navy. The RAF's other commitments meant that its bomber force did not play a part in the war.

Comment

The USA and its allies did the best they could in demanding circumstances, but the war showed both a disastrous failure of intelligence and a serious lack of military preparedness. These were lessons which were quickly learnt, and changes were implemented so that during the rest of the so-called Cold War, aircraft were kept at a high state of readiness in case of a surprise attack, while enemy troop movements and military signals traffic were constantly analysed.

While the heavy bomber operations were inevitable and necessary, battles against an enemy with a relatively light and primitive infrastructure do not offer heavy bombers the hard targets which enable them to make a significant contribution to the conflict. This was a war better suited to the fighter-bomber, and had they been available at the time, the combat helicopter.

VIETNAM, 1964–75

The end of the Korean War failed to bring peace and stability to the Far East. Even before the Korean War had ended, fighting flared up over the remains of the old French colonial empire. Vietnam, which had been part of the former French Indo-China, was divided into a northern zone and a southern zone in 1954, with the northern a Communist dictatorship and the southern pro-Western. The other component parts of French Indo-China, Cambodia and Laos, maintained a vague neutrality. From 1957 onwards, Communist-backed guerrillas started to attack villages, highways and then towns in South Vietnam, often using supply routes which ran through Cambodia and Laos, making attack by the South Vietnamese forces more difficult.

While North Vietnam was a Soviet Union client state, South Vietnam had only the remains of equipment donated by the departing French forces. Starting in 1955, the USA provided South Vietnam with equipment and training, including military advisers, to assist the South Vietnamese forces, which were numerically weaker than those in the north. The number of 'advisers' grew steadily, until in numbers and rank they were more akin to regular US troops. In 1963, the newly elected President John Kennedy committed US forces to counter the growing menace of Viet Cong guerrillas, and encouraged the USA's allies to help. For the most part, active support came from South Korea and, for a period, Australia. The USA was to be active in Vietnam from August 1964 to January 1973, although final withdrawal did not take place until 1975.

The Vietnam War saw both the USAF and the US Navy engaged in strike operations, while the USAF used its Boeing B-52 heavy bombers for what amounted to carpet bombing, designed to break up concentrations of Viet Cong troops. As the war progressed, so-called 'smart' weapons came into widespread use, and these guided weapons made a significant impact on the accuracy of USAF and US Navy attacks, while at the same time cutting losses sharply, as aircraft were able to launch the weapons while still clear of the most intense AA defences around significant targets.

ROLLING THUNDER OVER VIETNAM, 1968

There were two types of mission, 'Rolling Thunder' and 'Alpha' strikes, the latter often involving three attacks per day. Alpha strikes were determined by either the White House or the Pentagon, while Rolling Thunder raids were at the discretion of the commanders of the carrier air groups.

During the 1960s and 1970s a typical Alpha strike mission from an aircraft carrier would consist of four A-4s or F-8s (sometimes one of each) operating in two pairs on an 'Iron Hand' mission to suppress enemy

One of the most significant aircraft of the Vietnam War was the Douglas A-4 Skyhawk, a highly manoeuvrable attack aircraft. (United States Naval Institute)

surface-to-air missiles, followed by two waves each of four A-4 bombers and one of four F-8s operating as bombers. The three bomber waves would be flanked by two F-8s as flak suppressors on each side, while another four F-8s flew as combat air patrol (CAP).

There were moments of dark humour. One carrier pilot with a casual attitude to pre-flight checks, sometimes referred to as a 'kick the tires and light the fire' aviator, soon learned his lesson when he jumped into an F-8 Crusader only to find that the groundcrews had towed an engine-less aircraft from the hangar to the parking area.

The Aircraft

A number of aircraft were significant in the Vietnam War, which lasted long enough for some types which were at the forefront of operations during the early years to have been replaced by more sophisticated aircraft. Just as the Korean War had often been a fighter-bomber war, Vietnam saw the more intensive use of this type of aircraft, while the presence of the B-52 should not conceal the fact that a new generation of bombers entered service, typified by the USAF's General Dynamics F-111 and the US Navy's Grumman A-6 Intruder, which were smaller, faster, more manoeuvrable and needed just a two-man crew. The early years of the war also saw intensive use of the Douglas Skyraider, which was the ideal aircraft for strikes against enemy supply routes.

An A-4 Skyhawk takes off from a carrier during the Vietnam War. (United States Naval Institute)

In the operations mentioned here, three aircraft were regarded as significant: the Douglas A-4 Skyhawk, the LTV A-7 Corsair II, which saw service with both the US Navy and USAF, and the Grumman A-6 Intruder. The McDonnell Douglas F-4 Phantom II was another naval aircraft also adopted by the USAF, and although primarily a fighter, it operated as a fighter-bomber, using both conventional and 'smart' weapons.

The Douglas (later McDonnell Douglas) A-4 Skyhawk had the distinction of carrying out more raids over Vietnam than any other aircraft type. It was developed as a simple, lightweight and inexpensive replacement for the Douglas A-1 Skyraider, and was small enough to operate without folding wings from US aircraft carriers. Deliveries of the A-4A had started in 1956, and this version of the single-seat aircraft used a 7,700 lb thrust Wright engine – later versions had improved thrust, with an 8,500 lb Pratt & Whitney J52 on the A-4E of 1961, and A-4F had 9,300 lb thrust. With external fuel tanks, a ferry range of up to 3,000 miles was available, with a maximum speed of 680 mph, while a fuselage and four under-wing strongpoints could take missiles, rockets or up to 8,000 lb of bombs.

The Grumman A-6 Intruder was an all-weather strike aircraft which incorporated the lessons of the Korean War. Used by both the US Navy

and the United States Marine Corps (USMC), the aircraft, which was two-seat in attack variants and four-seat in USMC electronic reconnaissance versions, used two 8,500 lb thrust Pratt & Whitney J52-P-6 turbofans for a speed of up to mach 0.95. A high-wing aircraft, it could carry up to 18,000 lb of bombs in a semi-recessed bomb bay or on under-wing strongpoints. The first A-6s entered service in 1961, and a number of the EA-6 variant remain in USMC service today.

The third important aircraft in the later years of the war was the Ling-Temco-Vought A-7 Corsair II. A development of the F-8 Crusader fighter, the single-seat A-7 was intended to be a replacement for the Skyhawk. First flown in 1965, the aircraft used a wide variety of power plants. Early versions used the Pratt & Whitney TF30 series of turbofans of either 11,350 lb or 12,200 lb thrust, but later versions used the Allison TF-41 (a licence-built version of the Rolls-Royce Spey) of 14,240 lb or 15,000 lb thrust. Maximum ferry range was 3,600 miles, and the warload was 10,000 lb on two fuselage and six under-wing strongpoints.

The Action

As always, the problem of a major strike was one of co-ordination and maintaining some kind of formation so that aircraft arrived over the target in the right order. This became difficult when subjected to ground fire and the ever-present threat in Vietnam of surface-to-air missiles (SAMs). An A-4 Skyhawk pilot from the carrier USS *Oriskany* in 1968, Bob Arnold, recalls:

I led an Alpha strike to a target six miles outside Hanoi. We approached at 12,000 feet, plus or minus 500, with no AAA [anti-aircraft artillery] or SAMs until two minutes from our time over target. From that point we had thirty missiles and every goddamned gun that could fire. A

Opposite: Another significant naval aircraft which made its operational debut during the Vietnam War was the LTV A-7 Corsair II, a potent attack aircraft. (United States Navy)

Ranged forward on the flight deck of Independence *was another significant Vietnam-era aircraft, the Grumman A-6 Intruder, with Corsair IIs. (FAAM Ind/224)*

An aerial shot of the Hancock *at speed off Vietnam. Douglas Skyhawks are prominent on the flight deck. (United States Naval Institute)*

Skyhawks again on the flight deck of the Oriskany. *(United States Naval Institute)*

couple of planes got shot up, all of us were forced down. Only two of us – my wingman and myself – made it to the target. He missed but I laid a string of eight or ten Mark-82s on target. We exited the area at 500-plus knots (no centreline tank) at 50 feet or less, violently S-turning all the way because my ECM [electronic countermeasures] gear told me a SAM was tracking me. It turned out to be overly sensitive equipment, but at the time we only knew that the damn things were deadly.[1]

While preoccupied with evading SAMs, pilots were vulnerable to attack by MiG fighters. The CAP provided for the strike missions was always briefed on the most likely axis of approach for MiGs flying from nearby airfields. They were also warned to resist any temptation to chase after MiGs 40 or more miles away, leaving the strike unprotected. The warnings were timely, for at first the North Vietnamese AF would provide one or two MiGs as bait for the less experienced fighter pilots anxious to score their first kills. Sometimes the intention would be to entice fighters away from the strike aircraft, sometimes the MiG's role would be to lure the unwary over heavy AAA or SAM sites:

Each strike pilot's dive heading had been assigned at briefing. Properly executed, the attack came from three or more directions. This had the effect of splitting the defences. An interval of ten seconds allowed each pilot a view of the target sufficient to position his pipper for an accurate drop. In 45- to 60-degree dives the bombers – sporty little Skyhawks, F-8-lookalike Corsairs, or bulbous-nosed Intruders – slanted down through 5,000 feet. Like the flak suppressors, they held their drop to about 4,500, bottoming out no lower than 2,800 above ground level.

Then it was nose-up. Crusaders and Phantoms lit the afterburners and rocketed upwards at 60 degrees or better. Height was life insurance coming off-target. It got a pilot out of small arms and light-caliber flak quickly and gave him room to maneuver against SAMs. If worse came to worse, height afforded invaluable time to nurse a damaged aircraft to the water or toward a 'safe area' for ejection.

Doctrine called for egress by sections. Element leaders and wingmen reformed, pursuing an irregular, high speed course eastward to the coast. True, a straight line was the shortest course to the beach, but it was also the most predictable. Course changes of up to 60 degrees, coupled with frequent altitude variations, made it difficult to enemy gunners to work out their fire-control solutions and also provided the pilot with an all-round view of the possible threats.

By the time the last planes had left the target area, about three minutes – and one or two eternities – had elapsed . . . Eventually the beach passed below and behind. 'Feet wet' was the radio call. Each aircraft checked its partner closely, looking for visible damage, leaking fuel, hung ordnance. If all appeared normal it was a routine matter of hitting the tanker or making directly for Marshal – the entry to the landing pattern – and land aboard.

. . . the A-7 . . . wasn't terribly fast, but it was fast enough. Like the Phantom, it was also adopted by the Air Force. Probably the only noteworthy problem was the rash of losses in spin-related accidents that occurred shortly after the plane joined the fleet. Evaluation determined the Corsair II hadn't been fully spin-tested before entering production, perhaps because of the push to get the new bomber into combat. But the gremlins were exorcized, and A-7 pilots still insist it's a gentleman's airplane.

The navy's round-the-clock bomber was the A-6 intruder . . . A two-seat, twin-engine, any-weather electronic marvel, the big Grumman had a lot going for it. Range, payload, and blind bombing were all in its corner; availability was not. A-6 sophistication translated to reduced serviceability rates, and in daylight the Intruder didn't deliver bombs significantly better than A-4s or A-7s, though it did deliver more of them.

On moonless nights and in grim weather (which was frequent) . . . the A-6 was the only game in town . . . A-6 crews have claimed . . . that their success in flying deep-penetration missions over rugged terrain prompted the air force to send the F-111 up north before it was ready. Although the 111 later became a good airplane, its early loss rate was prohibitive.[2]

Comment

The Americans did not start the war in Vietnam, but once they had intervened, the intensity of the conflict escalated. This was a classic example of the limitations of air power. Despite the heroism of many aircrew, the bomber and strike aircraft were wasteful when used against guerrilla fighters on the ground, especially when these were hidden in dense jungle. There was also a political reluctance to sanction repeated heavy raids against Hanoi, which could have limited the volume of supplies entering North Vietnam.

This was a war in which porters and mules on jungle trails on Laos and Vietnam had to be ambushed. There were few bridges, metalled highways or railway lines against which bombers could be sent. This was jungle warfare, keeping a devious enemy on the move, making it difficult for them to muster in sufficient strength to pose a significant threat. There was also a need for a 'hearts and minds' campaign to gain the support of the uncommitted rural dweller, on the lines of the successful campaign mounted by the British Army in Malaysia.

Unfortunately, counter-insurgency operations in such difficult terrain are intensive in manpower. This was one reason why the South Vietnamese were unable to counter the guerrillas, since it takes upwards of six or seven defending soldiers to counter one guerrilla, never knowing where they will strike next, or when. After an armistice in January 1973, the Americans abided by the agreement, while the Soviet Union continued to supply their North Vietnamese clients.

The Vietnam War had to be fought, but the strategy adopted was flawed.

THE WINTER WAR: BATTLING OVER THE FALKLANDS, 2 APRIL–15 JUNE 1982

On 2 April 1982 Argentinian troops invaded the Falkland Islands, a British colony in the South Atlantic long claimed by Argentina as its own, despite the fact that the local residents were all of British descent. The initial invasion was resisted by the small force of thirty or so Royal Marines, the sole garrison on the islands, who managed to shoot down a helicopter with an anti-tank missile before bowing to the inevitable and surrendering. The British Government immediately raised a task force for the recovery of the islands, and of South Georgia, some distance further south, which had also been seized by Argentinian forces.

The difficulties of retaking the Falklands after the Argentinian invasion can be clearly seen from this map. (IWM FKD2304)

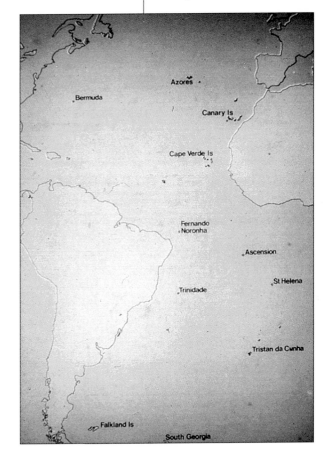

It took just three days to prepare the core element of the task force for the recovery of the islands, based on the aircraft carriers *Hermes* and *Invincible*. The task force had to be seaborne, given the difficulty of moving heavy loads over almost 4,000 miles which separated the Falklands from the nearest available air base on Ascension Island. The RAF was to find mounting bombing raids from Ascension difficult.

OPERATION BLACK BUCK: STRATEGIC BOMBING AND THE FALKLANDS, 30 APRIL–12 JUNE 1982

The naval operation was hindered by the lack of significant bomber capability and airborne early warning aircraft, having to rely on the British Aerospace Sea Harrier, which proved itself to be extremely versatile, and a small number of RAF Harriers.

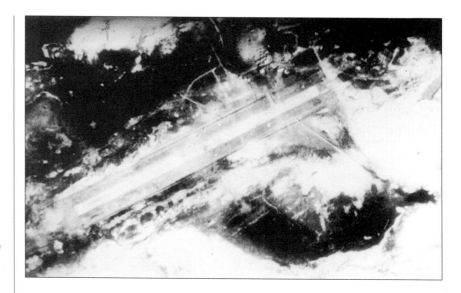

Poor weather made good reconnaissance difficult, as this photograph of the runway at Port Stanley, taken from a Fleet Air Arm Sea Harrier, shows. (IWM FKD2316)

This shows the damage done to the runway by the Vulcan bomber raids. The runway would still have been usable by aircraft such as the Pucara. (IWM FKD872)

The Aircraft

The Avro (later Hawker Siddeley) Vulcan was the world's first delta-wing jet bomber when the prototype first flew in August 1952. The aircraft was the second of the trio of British heavy jet bombers, known as the V-bombers, designed to carry the UK independent nuclear deterrent. The prototype used four Rolls-Royce Avon turbojets, but production models used the more powerful Bristol Siddeley Olympus when deliveries of the BMk1 started in mid-1956. The BMk2, with modified aerodynamic surfaces, first flew in August, 1958, and deliveries to the RAF started in mid-1960. The Vulcan was able to carry up to twenty 1,000 lb bombs or Blue Steel air-to-surface missiles. Four 20,000 lb thrust Bristol Siddeley (later Rolls-Royce) Olympus 301 turbojets gave a maximum speed of 640 mph and a range of up to 5,000 miles, depending on the warload.

Given the long range over which operations had to be conducted, the Vulcans had to be refuelled by the third of the V-bomber trio, the Handley Page Victor, which had been converted to the tanker in-flight refuelling role after the earlier Vickers Valiants (themselves converted V-bombers) had to be retired due to metal fatigue. First flown in December 1952, the BMk1 version of the Victor had used four Armstrong-Siddeley Sapphire turbojets, and deliveries started in 1958. These aircraft were eventually replaced by the BMk2, with four 20,600 lb thrust Rolls-Royce Conway turbojets and larger but thinner wings. The Victor was easily identified by its 'T' tail and large, crescent-shaped wing. The bombload could be carried internally and on under-wing strongpoints. After conversion to the tanker role, in-flight refuelling points were fitted to the wingtips and to the tail.

One of the RAF Vulcans used to attack the airfield. (IWM FKD1198)

The Action

At the time of the Falklands conflict, the RAF's Vulcan force had been reduced to just three squadrons, Nos 44, 50 and 101, all due to have disbanded by June 1982. The crews had not used air-to-air refuelling for many years. Ten aircraft were selected to have their in-flight refuelling probes brought up to operational standard, and five crews were chosen, two from 50 Sqn, one each from 44 and 101 Sqns, and one from the recently disbanded 9 Sqn. Five aircraft received updated navigational equipment. On 29 April two aircraft were flown to Wideawake Airfield on Ascension Island. The sorties from Ascension Island were given the code-name BLACK BUCK.

To help refuel RAF Harriers being positioned to the Falklands, and to refuel bombing sorties by some of the last few remaining Vulcans, the Victor tankers of the RAF's 57 Sqn were deployed to Wideawake Airfield, 4,400 miles from the UK, the Falklands being almost 4,000 miles further on.

The first sortie took off around midnight on 30 April/1 May, both aircraft taking off with the 11 Victor tankers at one-minute departure intervals in complete darkness with navigational lights turned off. The plan was for the second Vulcan to return to base once the first had completed its first air-to-air refuelling. The crew were unable to pressurize the aircraft because the pilot's direct vision window refused to seal, so the second Vulcan took over the mission, captained by Flt Lt Martin Withers.

On the way to the Falklands four Victors refuelled the Vulcan at 840 miles out, two more after a further 300 miles, and a third refuelling took place at 1,900 miles. The fourth and final transfer took place at 2,700 miles, in a tropical storm. The first tanker had not been able to top itself up due to a broken fuel probe, meaning that the reserve tanker which then took over had itself to refuel on the homeward leg to avoid having to ditch in the Atlantic.

The Vulcan ascended to 10,000 ft for its bombing run over the airport at Port Stanley, while the ships of the task force and the Fleet Air Arm's Sea Harriers were ordered to adopt the 'weapons tight' procedure. The aircraft dropped its 21 1,000 lb bombs diagonally over the end of the runway, transmitting the code word 'Superfuze' at 07.46 to indicate success. The raid was a complete surprise to the Argentinians, whose Skyguard fire control radar was jammed by the Vulcan's ALQ-101 pod. The mission took almost 15 hours.

A second raid, BLACK BUCK 2, on 3–4 May, failed to cause any damage. BLACK BUCK 3 was cancelled. BLACK BUCK 4 was an anti-radar mission, the aircraft being fitted with Shrike missiles, on specially prepared under-wing strongpoints. The aircraft set off at midnight on 28/29 May, but had to return because of technical problems with the lead Victor tanker. Eventually BLACK BUCK 5, flown by Sqn Ldr Neil McDougall, launched two Shrike missiles against the Argentine radar shortly after 08.45 on 31 May. One missile struck the ground some 10–15 yd from the radar aerial, causing minor damage, while the other did not fall close enough. The Argentinians switched off the radar, convincing the British that the raid had been a success.

BLACK BUCK 6, also flown by Sqn Ldr Neil McDougall, was armed with four Shrike missiles for its raid on 2/3 June. The aircraft had to loiter for around 40 minutes waiting for the radar to be switched on. Eventually, two Shrikes were launched, destroying the Skyguard radar which was providing fire control for AA batteries, and killing four soldiers. The aircraft continued to loiter, hoping for another radar to be turned on, but eventually had to return due to its parlous fuel state. On attempting to refuel, the tip of the refuelling probe broke off and forced the crew to divert to Rio de Janeiro.

The final BLACK BUCK mission, No. 7, was mounted by Flt Lt Martin Withers on the night of 11/12 June, again using conventional bombs.

Comment

The idea behind the BLACK BUCK missions was to demonstrate to the Argentinian authorities that they were not out of reach of the RAF, but infrequent visits by a solitary aircraft could be no more than a token gesture, and if anything, underlined the relative weakness of the British position. While the RAF's Vulcan force was being wound down at the time, the lack of experience in in-flight refuelling seems to have been the result of a premature reduction in training, doubtless to cut costs. It seems highly unlikely that the in-flight refuelling demands of a significant force of aircraft could have been met unless the bombload was cut substantially, possibly in favour of air-to-surface weapons.

Certainly, the damage done did not justify the effort. Lt Cdr (later Cdr) Nigel 'Sharkey' Ward, in command of the Royal Navy's Sea Harriers, was convinced that four of his aircraft could have done as much damage as the Vulcan's first sortie, while one of his fellow officers, with Vulcan operational experience, estimated that it must have taken ten tankers to refuel the aircraft, equivalent to using 1.1 million lb of fuel, enough for

260 Sea Harrier sorties taking 1,300 1,000 lb bombs to Port Stanley. In fact, eleven Victors were needed, including tankers to top up some of the tankers.

The British were paying the price of excessive cuts in defence capability, and most importantly, given the distances from available airfields, of cutting their once impressive carrier force, which just twenty years earlier had totalled seven ships, two of them commando carriers, and the remainder able to operate a mixture of fighters and bombers. Each of the five carriers would have been able to operate at least as many combat aircraft as were available to the entire task force, and the larger ships, *Eagle* and *Ark Royal*, twice as many.

Lt Cdr (later Cdr) Nigel 'Sharkey' Ward commanded Invincible's *801 Naval Air Squadron during the Falklands campaign. (IWM FKD541)*

THE ARGENTINIAN ATTACK ON HMS ARDENT, 21 MAY 1982

Throughout the Falklands Campaign, the ships of the task force were subjected to intense air attack by aircraft of both the Argentinian Air Force, the Fuerza Aerea Argentina, and the Argentine Navy, the Comando de Aviacion Naval. Once landed, ground forces were also often subjected to heavy aerial attack, most conspicuously at Bluff Cove, when the Welsh Guards were being landed. In contrast to the performance of the ground forces, the Argentinian pilots acquitted themselves well, but suffered heavy casualties, nine aircraft being lost on 21 May alone. The British lost four warships, a landing ship and a container ship taken up from trade for the operation.

The Aircraft

The aircraft used in the attack on the frigate *Ardent* was a McDonnell Douglas A-4 Skyhawk (see p. 237).

The Action

The attack on the Type 21 frigate *Ardent* on 21 May 1982 was led by Captain Alberto Philippi of the Argentinian Navy's Fleet Air Arm, flying a Douglas A-4 Skyhawk. He was based ashore at the Rio Grande air station. He recalls:

We took off in two sections, a total of six planes, and headed for the islands at 27,000 feet. As soon as we approached enemy radar range we dipped down to sea level and headed for the south-western entrance to San Carlos Bay. We were flying very low and the weather was breaking . . . the visibility was so reduced that my wingman had to pull up very close beside me. This is something you should never do, because it produces a bigger signature on the enemy radar and therefore you are an easier target.

*An Argentinian Dassault Mirage 5
attack aircraft used in attacks
against the British Task Force.
(FAAM FALK/240)*

Visibility was down to a mile, which was also dangerous because a frigate on picket-duty would detect us at about fifteen miles, launch its missiles at a distance of about five miles, and still we would not be able to see her.

As we came in from the south there was no ship to attack so we continued towards the designated alternative target . . . ships in the port of San Carlos itself. We swerved in at maximum speed and minimum height and at that moment we saw a frigate and immediately deployed into attack formation. Normally we wouldn't attack so low because it is quite dangerous – you feel a sort of vertigo when you are flying at fifty feet. I had my altimeter set at thirty feet and the alarm went off several times. When you are doing all this at 450 knots you feel you're on the edge.

. . . She began to move at high speed so that we knew that she had detected us . . . a direct attack was no longer possible . . . so we circled to the right hugging the terrain . . . to attack the ship from behind. We attacked diagonally from starboard.

We each carried four bombs and as we started on the run-in we fired at the frigate with everything we had to reduce its anti-aircraft fire. We had studied silhouettes of all the British ships . . . I knew exactly what kind of ship it was . . . The frigate was reacting very well. She had increased speed . . . There is no doubt that the skipper . . . knew his job.

As I escaped I heard my wingman saying over the radio: 'Very good sir,' which meant that at least one of my bombs had exploded, so I could forget about everything else and concentrate on the evasive manoeuvre. I thought I might have a missile on my tail. The frigate threw everything at us . . . I could see little fireballs rushing past . . . I heard another wingman say: 'Another one has hit', which told me that we had struck the ship with at least two bombs. That was a good percentage . . .[3]

As the Skyhawks made their return to base, Capt Phillipi heard his No. 3 call out 'Harriers, Harriers', and he ordered them to drop their fuel tanks ready for a dogfight. He then started to manoeuvre, before feeling an impact on his tail, followed by a loud explosion. The plane wouldn't respond to the controls, the rudders seemed not to be working, as he saw another Sea Harrier approaching. He ejected, and was knocked out by the force of the ejection. He came to while descending in his parachute before landing in the water. After trying to inflate his dinghy without success, he had to swim more than 600 ft to the shore. He was so exhausted on coming ashore that he couldn't stand. He spent four nights and three days walking south before being discovered by a Falkland islander, who gave him hot food and a bath before notifying the Argentinian authorities.

Comment

There could be no doubt that this was a successful attack – a classic 'hit and run' by a small force of skilled airmen, while the frigate was at a disadvantage in the confines of San Carlos Water.

The fears about being caught on the radar of a frigate were real enough, but the other great absentee from the Royal Navy at the time was the airborne-early-warning (AEW) radar cover following the retirement of the Fleet Air Arm's Fairey Gannets with the rundown of the conventional carrier fleet. Good AEW cover is the best guarantee against a surprise attack.

CHAPTER ELEVEN

THE GULF WAR
AND THE
KOSOVO CRISIS

I raq invaded the neighbouring state of Kuwait on 2 August 1990, after having laid claim to the small desert kingdom for more than thirty years. An earlier attempt at invasion in 1961 had been thwarted by the timely intervention of British forces, led by the commando carrier *Bulwark*, followed by the aircraft carrier *Victorious*.

Faced with the overwhelming might of Iraq's armed forces, and having little room in which to fight and delay the invasion, Kuwait's own armed forces were soon overwhelmed. The international outrage over the invasion came after the collapse of the Soviet Union, and this meant that for just the second time in its history, the UN was able to play a significant role in resisting an invasion, with the armed forces operating under the UN banner. In practical day-to-day terminology, the forces gathered initially for the defence of Saudi Arabia and then for the liberation of Kuwait were referred to as the 'Coalition Forces'. In addition, the essential command and control mechanisms vital to creating an effective operational force out of so many different national forces were based on the tried and tested systems NATO. The backbone of the combined air, land and sea operation was provided primarily by the USA, but with strong support from the UK and France. Other nations also provided forces, including a number of the Arab states, although many of these were hampered to some extent by lack of manpower.

The two stages of the operation were known as DESERT SHIELD, protecting Saudi Arabia, and DESERT STORM, the campaign to liberate Kuwait. The British armed forces referred to their role as OPERATION GRANBY. To military historians, the conflict has become known as 'The Second Gulf War', recognizing the earlier prolonged conflict between Iraq and Iran throughout the 1980s as 'The First Gulf War'. This earlier conflict was widely believed to have weakened the armed forces of both countries, but as events proved, any weakness was exaggerated.

Although forces started arriving in Saudi Arabia and offshore in the Gulf within days of the invasion, the need to assemble substantial ground forces with heavy armour and to stockpile substantial quantities of munitions, fuel and spares meant that it took some time before the conflict could start. The war started with Coalition air attacks on 17 January 1991, preparing for the start of the ground war on 23 February. This was a short but violent conflict, which ended on 26 February.

The air war started with a strike by eight AH-64 Apache attack helicopters of the US Army's 1st Battalion, 101st Aviation Brigade. These destroyed Iraqi air defence radar, creating a corridor between two Iraqi radar stations.

USAF F-111 ATTACKS AGAINST IRAQI AIRFIELDS, 17 JANUARY 1991

The priorities for the Coalition air forces were to neutralize Iraqi airfields, thus gaining air supremacy, and then attack other strategically important targets. The first wave of attacks was at night, and despite the large number of targets available, the air attacks had to be staggered, partly to avoid the problems of congestion with so many aircraft available to the Coalition, partly to maintain steady pressure on the Iraqi Air Force around the clock, and last but by no means least, to avoid IFF (identification, friend or foe) hazards with so many different types of aircraft from a wide number of air forces and air arms.

The Aircraft

The General Dynamics F-111 was the mainstay of the USAF's bomber force in the Gulf, although complemented by cruise missile-carrying Boeing B-52s. The conflict was to see this aircraft, which had first entered combat during the Vietnam War, in its last operational role as a strike aircraft.

Originally developed by General Dynamics to meet the USAF's TFX two-seat tactical fighter-bomber design competition in 1962, the aircraft was the world's first production variable-geometry aircraft. Early versions suffered from teething troubles, but these were resolved with modified engine air intakes on the F-111E. Twin 21,000 lb Pratt & Whitney TF30-P-3 turbofans with reheat gave the aircraft a maximum speed in excess of mach 2, and a range of up to 3,300 miles. Eight air-to-surface missiles could be carried in a fuselage weapons bay and on under-wing strongpoints. The aircraft had an unusual side-by-side seating configuration for the two-man crew, and an ejectable cockpit module.

The Action

At the outset of the air war in the Gulf, the USAF's 48th Tactical Fighter Wing launched 53 General Dynamics F-111Fs in formations of 4 or 6 aircraft against a dozen individual targets, including the airfields at Balad, Jalibah, Ali Al Salem and Ahmed al-Jabar, H-3, Salman Pak and Ad Diwaniyah. The last three included chemical weapons storage bunkers.

At this early stage in the war, many of the Coalition aircrew felt that there was an atmosphere of unreality, as if their attacks were unexpected. This was far from the conditions of total blackout experienced during the Second World War when flying over enemy-occupied Europe. Lt Dave Giachetti, the WSO (Weapons Systems Officer) in one of the aircraft, recalls:

I thought it was kind of eerie, because outside everything was so calm and so quiet. We went in at low level on TFR [terrain-following radar]. In the built-up areas everyone had their lights on, the street lights were on. On the way in we flew parallel to a road for some time, there were cars moving with their lights on. We were flying at 400 feet at 540 knots towards our target and I thought, 'Man, they don't even know we're coming!'[1]

Six of the F-111Fs attacked the airfield at Balad in Iraq. Two of the aircraft launched GBU-15 electro-optical guided bombs at the airfield's maintenance complex, while the remaining four dropped CBU-89 cluster weapons at the ends of the runways and amongst the aircraft shelters – in common with the British JP233, the CBU-89 package included area-denial mines. Laser-guided bombs were used against the airfield at H-3, some 270 miles to the west, attacked by 6 F-111Fs, which were followed by 4 RAF Tornado GR1s attacking the airfield's runways.

The F-111F attack at H-3 was led by Capt Mike Buck:

We didn't do very well that time, most of the bombs missed because of the threat reactions. There were [Iraqi] fighters up, some of the guys got tapped [had radars lock on to them], a couple of guys got missiles shot at them. I got tapped a couple of times, I didn't see anything come my way but I reacted to the threat. The AWACS was calling the threats, so I had to honor the calls.[2]

In addition to the F-111s and the B-52Gs, the USAF sent its F-117A Stealth fighters for the first time, 40 aircraft being deployed, including 18 of 415 Tactical Fighter Sqn. These aircraft used their stealth characteristics by concentrating on what the USAF described as 'high value, heavily defended targets', which they attacked with laser weapons, scoring success rates as high as 80–85 per cent, compared to 30–35 per cent in Vietnam, usually against small targets such as windows or ventilation shafts. The sense of being invisible to radar encouraged pilots to loiter, making sure that their weapons hit the target.

Comment

Although the threat of war had been around for some time, the Iraqis did not know exactly when the Coalition air forces would strike, so there was an element of surprise. Attacking on such a broad front also hampered Iraqi attempts at defence, but posed the threat of small groups of aircraft having heavy AA defences concentrated upon them. The greater use of 'smart' or stand-off weapons by the USAF also helped to ensure both accuracy and lower aircraft and aircrew losses.

RAID ON THE AIR BASE AT AR RUMAYLAH, 17 JANUARY 1991

The first RAF combat sorties were launched at 01.30, with Tornado GR1s taking off with extra-large drop tanks and a pair of JP233 runway denial weapons, giving them an all-up weight of 30.5 tonnes. They operated under the protection of three E-3 Sentries, with CAP provided by USAF and RSAF F-15 Eagles, and RAF and RSAF Tornado F3s, while defence suppression was by F-4G 'Wild Weasel' Phantoms, with radar-jamming by USAF EF-111A Ravens and USN EA-6B Prowlers. The Tornados in the first strike included aircraft from 31 and 15 Sqns from Dhahran and Bahrain respectively – four and eight aircraft. At Tallil, the Tornados raced across the airfield at 180 feet, each scattering two JP233s (a container carried under the aircraft's fuselage which distributes concrete-piercing bomblets and delayed action mines, which make repair of the runway difficult), along the two parallel runways and the taxiways.

Elsewhere, at Tabuk, 16 Sqn sent its Tornados against the airfield at Al Asad, the JP233 aircraft being overtaken by the lighter ALARM missile-equipped aircraft which were able to fly direct to the target, arriving at 03.50, five minutes in advance of the JP233-carrying Tornados to suppress the enemy defences. At Al Taqaddum, a wave of 4 Tornados visited the airfield, and 3 of them managed a successful attack with the JP233s despite having no ALARM missiles to suppress Iraqi radar.

The following night 27 Sqn at Muharraq deployed 4 aircraft to Shaibah and 8 to Ubaydah bin al Jarrah, the latter taking off at midnight. At Ubaydah bin al Jarrah, the formation of 8 Tornados, which had refuelled at 10,000 ft before crossing into Iraqi territory, flew at 200 ft for thirty minutes across the desert. Five minutes away from the target, they could see heavy anti-aircraft defences. As they flew into the target, Flg Off Ingle

The RAF's 617 Sqn was operational again during the Gulf War, but this time using Panavia Tornado GR1s, while the squadron's personnel unofficially changed their name from 'Dam Busters' to 'Saddam Busters'! (RAFM P020739)

After the war, this was Flt Lt John Peters's new aircraft, another Tornado GR1. (IWM CT1312)

and Flt Lt McKernan felt a bump, and assumed that they had been hit. They had difficulty in controlling their aircraft, but with the others, flying in a card-four formation a mile apart and with the pairs separated by ten seconds, they pressed home their attack. The first two aircraft dropped their JP233s' contents at one-fifth and three-fifths along the length of the runway, and the other two at two-fifths and four-fifths. Returning home, Ingle found that he could not control his aircraft at more than 350 kt, and could only refuel at an angle of 45°. Nevertheless, he nursed the damaged aircraft back to Muharraq safely, where the damage was found not to be an AAA hit, but a birdstrike which had removed a large section of the port wing's leading edge.

Another unit deployed to the Gulf was the RAF's 15 Sqn (often referred to as 'XV'), which operated the Panavia Tornado GR1. The squadron had been based at RAF Laarbruch in Germany, as part of the British contribution to NATO. Its move to Bahrain meant more than just a change of base, or even of a change of camouflage for the aircraft to 'desert pink'. The squadron had to practise air-to-air refuelling from the RAF's Handley Page Victor tankers, an essential element for operations over the wide expanses of the Middle East, but not considered necessary for the attacks against Warsaw Pact forces in central Europe for which the squadron had been trained.

The Tornado squadrons were also trained for night attack, flying low in the poor visibility of northern Europe on their hi-lo-hi missions, which meant that the aircraft were supposed to fly under the net of the defending radars, hoping to escape detection until the last minute. When the air campaign started, it used air power to crush the enemy air defences and then the enemy ground forces, establishing both air supremacy and softening up the ground forces in a strategy which had served the British and the Americans well since the Second World War. No. 15 Sqn was supposed to be in the second wave of attacks. It would have been impossible to have sent every Coalition aircraft in one single wave. Normally, 15 Sqn's Tornados would have used a variety of weapons against enemy airfields, including the JP233 runway denial weapon. As time passed and the raid became one which would be conducted in daylight, the JP233 was impractical, since the dispensing aircraft had to fly straight and level while using the weapon. Instead, on this occasion, the Tornados were to carry eight 1,000 lb bombs each.

The Aircraft

Originally conceived as the Anglo-German-Italian Multi-Role Combat Aircraft, the Panavia Tornado was one of a number of European collaborative ventures initiated in the late 1960s. Unusually, both bomber and interceptor variants were produced, known respectively to the RAF as the GR1 and F3, the most obvious difference between the two being the longer and sharper nose of the fighter variant.

Both variants of the aircraft have two-seat (pilot and navigator) cockpits, variable-geometry wings, and use two tri-national Turbo-Union RB.199 turbofans of 9,113 lb dry thrust, and on the IDS bomber/interdictor variant this is increased to 16,020 lb with reheat. Unrefuelled combat radius is 875 miles.

The Action

Since the Second World War, military commanders have come to understand that the priority at the outset of any conflict is to neutralize the enemy's air power. In this case, the target for the Tornados of 15 Sqn was the airfield at Ar Rumaylah in southern Iraq. This was a heavily defended target with extensive AA, or AAA, guns as well as SAM-3 and SAM-6 anti-aircraft missiles. Effectively, the Iraqis tried to ensure that attacking aircraft had to fly through a curtain of flak, augmented by the missiles.

Flt Lt John Peters was the pilot and Flt Lt John Nichol was the navigator of a Tornado from 15 Sqn in a four-aircraft formation led by Sqn Ldr Pablo Mason. They took off shortly after daylight on 17 January. Peters' aircraft was loaded with two Hughes AIM-9L Sidewinder air-to-air missiles (nicknamed 'Limas' by the RAF), for defence against Iraqi fighters, with a Marconi Skyshadow ECM pod under one wing, and under the other a 'Boz' pod to disperse chaff and flares, the first to confuse the tracking systems of enemy radars and the second to foil heat-seeking missiles. The two 27 mm Mauser cannon in the nose of the Tornado were supplied with 340 rounds of high-explosive armour-piercing (HEAP) ammunition, although this wouldn't have provided more than a quick burst for the cannon, which could fire 1,700 rounds per minute. All this was in addition to their warload of eight 1,000 lb bombs.

Departure from Bahrain was less orderly than either of the two men would have wished. A technical fault with their aircraft led to a last-minute scramble to find another aircraft and then repeat the pre-flight checks. As the formation took off just after dawn, one of the four aircraft had to abort with a fault, unable to get its Skyshadow to work. En route to the target, the formation, now just three aircraft, refuelled from Victor tankers, dropping away from the tankers just 30 miles or so short of the Iraqi frontier, which they crossed at 10,000 ft, in clear view of Iraqi defence radars, although the key installations had been destroyed at the outset of the conflict by US Army Apache helicopters.

Peters noted how different the attack was from operations in Europe. RAF bomber pilots are taught to use the terrain, keeping their aircraft below the hilltops, making it more difficult for the defences. Here in Iraq, they were flying low across the flat desert. They were being protected by a top cover of USAF McDonnell Douglas F-15 Eagles, although these aircraft flying CAP covered an area, rather than protecting any specific attacking force. US Navy McDonnell Douglas F-18 Hornets had attacked earlier using HARM missiles to take out the airfield's defending radar.

The Tornados were to 'loft' their bombs at the target, the airfield's taxiways, which entailed pulling the aircraft up sharply as they approached, and then releasing the bombs, before racing away to safety. As they approached and completed their pre-attack checks, Peters could see the heavy flak from the airfield:

My thumb jammed hard down on to the commit button, the red arming switch on the sticktop I must hold down for the bombs to come off, a final chance to ensure we were attacking the correct target . . . the computer would do the rest. But I could not see it. There was no bright dot to follow . . . This was a disaster, there was no bloody dot, the bombs would not come off. They must! This was our first attack!

. . . confusion was now king. I was still pulling up, already through 1,500 feet, the bombs had not come off and every bloody Iraqi tracking system for miles around was busily acquiring and shooting at us since we had popped up into general view. John . . . was feverishly scanning his switches to make sure that he had selected the correct weapons package . . . he confirmed, 'Eight 1,000-pound bombs at eighty metres spacing'.[3]

The aircraft continued to climb, but slowly with its heavy warload. Normally, the aircraft would not go above 1,700 ft after a loft attack before dropping down for the run home, and yet it was already at twice that altitude, presenting a good target. Against their training, the crew, anxious to succeed on their first mission of the war, considered re-attacking. They quickly realized that this would be foolhardy, and prepared to jettison their bombs, Peter Nichol hitting the jettison button beside him:

I felt a huge 'Doosh!' as the bombs came off safely, thudding harmlessly into the desert . . . The Tornado lurched upwards as the weight came off.

By now we were way behind the other two aircraft, having spent so much time over the target . . .[4]

While John Nichol pushed out flares and chaff, John Peters concentrated on getting the aircraft back on course. They briefly considered a strafing run against an Iraqi communications centre, but the aircraft was not lined up for it:

> . . . suddenly there was an almighty 'Whump!' and my teeth rattled. The Tornado jumped across the sky like a scalded cat . . . the right engine's dying, the stick's gone dead, the fire warning is blaring out: we've been hit by a SAM!
>
> In peacetime, a crew would very likely eject from an aircraft with a fire in one engine. In time of war, especially over enemy territory, it can be better to fly on, in the hope that the fire will simply burn itself out. This is not quite so insane as it sounds: each of the Tornado's engines sits inside a titanium shell, which should contain the fire, allowing it to burn out – in theory . . . We knew we would never be able to refuel in the air with the problems we had, but we thought we might be able to make it to a reserve airfield or 'bang out' – eject from the aircraft – over friendly Saudi territory.[5]

But worse was to follow.

> At that moment a quadruple-barrelled 23-millimetre gun opened up . . . Four of its shells peppered the AIM-9L Sidewinder missile nestling on our right inboard wing pylon, igniting the Sidewinder's rocket propellant. White hot, the fuel began burning up through the top of the slender white missile, the airflow fanning it back in a die-straight, incandescent line. The Sidewinder had become a giant oxy-acetylene torch, slowly but surely severing the Tornado's wing.[6]

The crew ran through their cockpit checks, noting that the fire in the right engine hadn't gone out as they had hoped, but instead was getting worse. Peters again:

> I glanced up. A bright orange glow in the rearview mirrors made me twist backwards sharply in the narrow seat. It wasn't just the wing; the back of the aircraft had disappeared. There was no sign of the Tornado's massive tailplane. In its place a huge fireball was devouring the fuselage whole. Already it was halfway along the aircraft's spine, just behind the UHF aerials – about three feet from where John sits. But it was the wing he was worried about . . . John called up the formation leader again. 'Ejecting, ejecting', he transmitted.
>
> No one ever received the message.[7]

The two men ejected safely, although John Peters received an injury to his face around his left eye, something which the Iraqi guards and interrogators were to aggravate during the seven weeks as PoWs which were to follow. Throughout their imprisonment, they were beaten and tortured, kept short of food and water, with no facilities for washing. They were also displayed on Iraqi television where they were 'interviewed', all in complete disregard of the Geneva Convention.

Comment

Sending such a small force against a heavily defended target ignored all the lessons of war – allowing the enemy to concentrate their fire on just the three aircraft which reached the target. There is nothing new about technical failures, which delayed their departure and possibly also impeded their efficiency as they approached the target, and having bombs 'hang up' is nothing new either.

To ensure safety when flying over friendly territory, jettisoned bombs would not explode, but such sophistication was a drawback under genuine combat conditions. The suspicion has to be that too much of the wrong sort of technology was available, and not enough of the right kind. Given the small size of the attacking force and the heavy defences of the target, stand-off weapons were the only viable option.

ABOARD THE USS KENNEDY

The US Navy was the only one to deploy aircraft carriers during the Gulf War – the Royal Navy not sending any of its Invincible-class carriers, ostensibly because these were designed for a different kind of war, but the limited range of the Sea Harrier would have meant that these ships would have had to be within range of Iraqi missile attack. In any event, they weren't needed, since sufficient ground bases were available.

The Aircraft

The LTV A-7 Corsair II was covered in the section on Vietnam (see p. 239).

The Action

Capt Warren of the USS *Kennedy* sent A-7E Corsair IIs and A-6 Intruders against Iraqi targets. The A-7Es were on their last operational sorties, with *Kennedy* having the last two A-7E squadrons, VA-46 and VA-72. These were the only aircraft not to receive any damage when used in the first strikes against Iraq on 17 January. Warren recalls:

> I really enjoyed watching the A-7s get out there and participate in what would be their last war. It was a pleasure having them on the deck because they were so agile and so consistently up and ready . . . They were always ready and easier to get to the catapults than larger aircraft . . . We launched 18 loaded A-7s in one launch, nine per squadron. [They had 12 planes per squadron.] It was incredible! Two major strikes per day on the average.[8]

Comment

Large size isn't always better, especially in the confines of an aircraft carrier deck. A rugged, relatively simple aircraft such as the A-7 has considerable appeal. Note too that the US Navy was sending more substantial numbers of aircraft against its targets.

ATTACK ON THE AIRFIELD AT AHMED-AL-JABAR, KUWAIT, 17 JANUARY 1991

While the vast bulk of the forces deployed were from the USA, strong contingents were provided by the UK and Saudi Arabia, and by France. The first stage in the conflict was the air war, designed to weaken Iraq's defences, and in particular, eliminate the Iraqi Air Force as an effective fighting machine. Fighting started at 02.30 on 17 January 1981.

The Aircraft

The Sepecat Jaguar was a joint venture between the British Aircraft Corporation (a predecessor of British Aerospace) and the French Breguet concern, later absorbed by Dassault. The aircraft was designed as both an advanced jet trainer and a strike aircraft for both the RAF and the Armée de l'Air, entering service during the early 1970s.

In strike form the aircraft was normally single-seat. Twin 6,750 lb thrust Rolls-Royce/Turbomeca Adour turbofans with reheat provided a maximum speed of 1,120 mph and a range of up to 1,900 miles. A single fuselage and four under-wing strongpoints could accommodate a load of up to 10,000 lb, while two 30 mm cannon were also fitted.

The Action

One of the first French units in the conflict was the 11th *Escadre de Chasse* of the Armée de l'Air, equipped with twenty-four Sepecat Jaguars, based at Al Ahsa, near Dhahran. Twelve of the squadron's aircraft were sent to attack the Iraqi base at Ahmed-al-Jabar, in Iraqi-occupied Kuwait, 18 miles south of Kuwait City itself. The aircraft were given the task of destroying the airfield's SAMs and communications, and a Scud missile store. To help them in this task, McDonnell Douglas F-4G Wild Weasels were deployed to suppress the Iraqi radar, with AGM-45 Shrike and AGM-88 HARM missiles, while top cover was provided by Lockheed F-16C Falcons of the USAF. For the attack, the Jaguars were carrying 500 lb bombs, Belouga cluster bombs and laser-guided AS-30L missiles.

The unit's aircraft took off at 05.30, as part of the second wave of attacks on Iraqi military installations. The Wild Weasel attack worked well. Then it was the turn of the Jaguars. A pilot recalled:

Half an hour after leaving the runway, in pairs and heavily loaded, we crossed the Kuwait frontier. Already lines of tracer were coming up towards us, and in the distance I noticed a refinery belching huge clouds of black smoke. We were approaching the target at an altitude of 150 feet, while the US fighters kept watch above us. The triple-A was suddenly all around us; 23mm ZSU cannon and SAM-7 light missiles had been massed all round the airfield. Strangely, over the target itself there was a moment of relative calm. At last, ahead of us, we saw the buildings which housed the Iraqi missiles.

The first AS-30 left the aircraft, and detonated. There was no time to enjoy the spectacle. To relieve my tension I opened up with my 30mm cannon. That's a bit less weight to carry home . . . Behind me the other guys released their cluster bombs over the runways: what a firework display! Finally everyone was clear of the target area, and we set course for base. I looked at my watch and found that we had been over Kuwait for just six minutes.[9]

All the Iraqi bases proved to have strong AAA. In this case, four of the French aircraft were damaged, and one pilot was slightly injured after his canopy was hit. Two of the others had taken damage in their engines, and diverted to make emergency landings at the USAF base at Al Jubayl.

A further operation was mounted by this unit the following morning, again with 12 Jaguars, but on this occasion to attack the munitions depot at Ras-al-Quilayah. This depot, also on Iraqi-occupied Kuwaiti territory, was 1,000 yd long and 750 yd wide. Flying without top cover because of the early successes against Iraqi missiles and radar, the aircraft carried the same mix of weapons as on the previous day. For the individual aircraft, this meant either four 500 lb bombs or two Belougas, and four aircraft carried an AS-30L missile under one wing, balanced by a 260 gallon drop-tank under the other wing. The aircraft with bombs dived on to the target, while the missile-carrying aircraft fired their missiles from a range of 3 miles, aiming at the reinforced concrete hangars of the munitions depot. The operation was repeated the following day, but on 20 January bad weather disrupted operations, making missile-aiming difficult.

The munitions depot was seen as being particularly important because it included the Kuwaiti Navy's stock of Exocet sea-skimming anti-ship missiles, used to such devastating effect by Argentinian forces during the Falklands conflict.

One item in the Armée de l'Air's armoury which was especially effective was the Durandal anti-runway missile. This was launched against runways, using a braking parachute to induce an angle of attack of 30°, when a rocket motor fired driving the missile downwards at 800 ft per second so that it could penetrate 15 in of concrete before exploding.

Comment

This was a rare instance of the Jaguar being used in combat – the aircraft has had a charmed life from its introduction to service, especially considering that its service life has since been prolonged due to delays in developing its successors.

Once again, aircraft were operating in small numbers, and often with small bombloads, doubtless to enhance manoeuvrability. The use of 'smart' weapons such as the Durandal against runways reduced the risk of having aircraft shot down as they flew straight along the runway to deliver runway denial weapons such as the JP233, although a simple hole in a runway is easier to repair than the damage inflicted by a denial weapon.

BOMBER TWILIGHT IN THE BALKANS
24/25 MARCH–10 JUNE 1999

The Kosovo crisis shared with the Gulf War the distinction of being a 'post-Cold War' conflict, but there were differences as well. Instead of being a United Nations-sponsored operation, the Balkan campaign was mounted purely by the North Atlantic Treaty Organisation, NATO, with opposition to the policy from both Russia and China. The operation was also mounted with different aims. In the Gulf War the objective, if not simple, was at least clear cut: the removal of Iraqi forces from Kuwait and the restoration of that sovereign state's legitimate government. In Kosovo the political background was far more complex, since Kosovo was not an independent state, but had been an autonomous province of Serbia, itself formerly a part of the Yugoslav Federation.

Although the crisis had its origins in the collapse of Yugoslavia following the death of the dictator President Tito, leading to demands for independence from Belgrade by many of the constituent parts of the nation, in fact the roots of the problem dated back more than six hundred years. Yugoslavia had been a surprisingly successful multi-cultural society which had managed to suppress ethnic rivalries between the mainly Roman Catholic Croatians, the Orthodox Serbs and the Muslims, who dwelt mainly in Bosnia and Kosovo, and were a substantial minority in what had been the Yugoslav state of Macedonia.

During the mid-1990s mainly British, American, Canadian and French forces had formed the core of a UN force deployed under NATO command to halt ethnic cleansing by Serb forces in Bosnia, a conflict ended by the deployment on the ground of Croatian forces. Troops from the NATO countries ensured that supplies were provided for refugees, and once a cease-fire agreement had been reached, policed this.

The Kosovo crisis followed an attempt by Serbia to integrate Kosovo fully into that country, which led to demands for independence and the formation of a Kosovo Liberation Army, the KLA. The NATO powers attempted an agreement at Rambouillet, near Paris, under which Kosovan autonomy would be restored, but this was rejected by both sides. Criticism of the operation came from those who argued that it was an illegal intervention in a civil war, while others pointed out that if this wasn't the case, and the constitutional make-up of the former Yugoslavia had indeed been dismantled, then it was illogical for NATO to be pressing for autonomy rather than for full independence for Kosovo.

One feature that the Gulf War and the Kosovo crisis had in common was what effectively amounted to the final operations of the traditional bomber, with a large aircraft carrying substantial munitions in a bomb bay. In both conflicts the huge Boeing B-52 Stratofortresses were deployed, not on conventional bombing missions but as launch aircraft for cruise missiles, augmenting those missiles fired by surface vessels and, off Kosovo, submarines. Increasingly, bombing raids became the preserve of interdictor or strike aircraft, carrying their war load on underwing and under-fuselage strongpoints, as with the Panavia Tornados of the RAF, with increasing use as 'bombers' of fighter, strike and ground attack aircraft, including the British Aerospace Harrier GR7, Lockheed F-16 Falcon and Boeing (formerly McDonnell Douglas) F/A-18 Hornet.

Such changes have been inevitable, with the role of the strategic heavy bomber being taken over by the submarine-launched intercontinental ballistic missile, and air forces increasingly being restructured to operate over a shorter radius of action. It is clear that such a reduced role means that limitations have to be accepted in what an air force can do in conventional warfare when operating over longer distances, even if the Falklands campaign was an extreme case better suited to carrier operations. The paradox is that both the RAF and USAF, whose strategic bombing campaign amounted to so much during the Second World War, are now in the position of the wartime Luftwaffe and Soviet Air Force, effectively being able to do little more than provide *blitzkrieg* support for ground forces.

The Aircraft

The aircraft used in the air actions over the former Yugoslavia included the Boeing B-52H Stratofortress, the Panavia Tornado, including both the GR1/GR4 series of the RAF and the Luftwaffe's similar Tornado IDS, the British Aerospace Harrier GR7, the USN's Boeing F/A-18 Hornet, and the USAF's Lockheed F-117A Nighthawk 'stealth' fighter-bomber, Lockheed F-16 Falcon and Fairchild OA-10 Thunderbolt II or 'Warthog'.

Of these only the B-52, equipped with Boeing AGM-86 conventional air-launched cruise missiles, fits the traditional image of a bomber, with its huge bomb-bay and eight Pratt & Whitney TF33 turbojets. The F-117A, which was a star of the Gulf War and embodies 'stealth' technology to make detection difficult, rather spoilt its image by being one of the few aircraft to be shot down by Serbian forces, although a helicopter-borne combat rescue team managed to snatch the pilot from behind Serbian lines.

In this case we are concerned with the British Aerospace Harrier GR7, or Harrier II, a joint venture between BAe and McDonnell Douglas, now Boeing, in the United States. The Harrier IIs for the RAF embraced both the upgraded GR5 and its development, the GR7, capable of night attack. As with the original Harrier, the GR7 uses a single Rolls-Royce Pegasus turbofan, in this case the Mk105 of 95.63kN, or 21,517 lb dry thrust (the Pegasus is not available with reheat). This gives the aircraft a maximum

Operations over the former Yugoslavia by the RAF were conducted by a wide variety of aircraft, few of which really fitted the traditional description of a bomber. Mainstay of the British contribution were the Harrier IIs. (© British Crown Copyright/MoD)

speed of 585 knots, or Mach 0.87, and a warload of up to 4,175 kg, or 9,185 lb, using short take-off and vertical landing techniques. The war load compares well with that of many Second World War heavy bombers!

A sign of the times, and of changes in tactical air power, was the arrival of 24 Boeing AH-64 Apache attack helicopters of the United States Army for close air support, although two of them were lost in accidents within the first two weeks of their deployment.

The Action

The RAF's Harriers of 1 Sqn were deployed at the Italian Air Force's base at Gioia del Colle in southern Italy. Initially just eight aircraft were available when operations started on the night of 24/25 March 1999, but as the momentum of the operation was increased this force was reinforced by a further four Harriers and eight Tornados.

In contrast to the Gulf War, most sorties were flown at an altitude of 15,000 ft, making bombing difficult when low cloud obscured the target. Operations started with no more than 50 sorties on the first night, and the number of sorties by all the air forces involved during the first twelve days did not exceed that of the first twelve days of the Gulf War. It soon became plain that the American and British leadership of the operation had expected that a relatively small-scale campaign would persuade the Serbian leadership to cease operations against Kosovan civilians in a programme of ethnic cleansing, but in fact the campaign had the opposite effect. While accuracy remained far higher than during the Second World War, accurate bombing by the Harrier required either clear visibility or targets to be marked by special forces deployed behind Serbian lines and using lasers.

Overall, the NATO air forces, primarily American, British, French, Canadian and German, managed some 20,000 sorties during the first 50 days of the conflict, destroying 29 out of 31 bridges across the River Danube, and 70 per cent of Serbian fuel stocks and upwards of 50 per cent of their ammunition. Power supplies were disrupted both by direct attacks on power stations and by the use of new graphite bombs, which effectively short-circuited electricity transmission. Unfortunately, civilian casualties (generally known as 'collateral damage') are inevitable in any conflict and NATO forces accidentally hit a passenger train, a bus crossing a bridge that had been targeted, and a hospital close to a Serbian barracks, as well as at least one convoy of Kosovan refugees. Accuracy was affected by orders to fly high and avoid low level operations to minimize NATO casualties, and possibly also by a growing shortage of munitions, especially 'smart' weapons.

A BBC correspondent reported on a typical day's operations, noting that just before dawn the aircraft were prepared, with 1,000 lb bombs, and at 0630, 'as daylight seeps through, the Harriers scream down the runway'.[10] In an interview with a Harrier GR7 pilot, who had to be anonymous for security reasons, in case he was shot down and taken prisoner by the Serbs, the pilot reported: 'The operation is now settling into a steady rhythm. The first mission we did out there was extremely exciting and worrying and scary, but now when we go out there we are a lot more, not so much confident, but we know what the threat is like out there, so we can go in with a degree of experience and deliver the weapons with confidence because we have that much more experience and trust in what we are doing.'[11]

On this occasion the Harrier crews set off on their mission, but had to return with their bombs as poor visibility over the target made an attack difficult, and carried the risk of collateral damage.

Keeping the operation going proved hard work, not least for the ground crews, rostered to work twelve hours on and twelve hours off, seven days a week, reflecting both the intensity of operations and the scant resources spared for the conflict. An armourer working on the Harriers, WO John Macrae, explained: 'We have got to bear in mind now that human beings can only go on for so long, so we are now working in time off.'[12]

Comment

The decision over whether or not to mount this campaign was entirely in NATO's hands. The political decision to press ahead when there were too few aircraft in the area and, no less importantly, after declaring that ground troops would not be used unless agreed by the Serbian authorities, meant that success was difficult to achieve. During the Gulf War the air war did not start until ground troops and their equipment had been assembled in the area, ready to attack once the air campaign had softened up the Iraqi ground and air forces. At the outset of the air campaign in the former Yugoslavia, there were few ground troops deployed, with little or no heavy equipment, and in fact barely enough to help the authorities in Albania and Macedonia to cope with the influx of refugees from Kosovo.

The outcome of the campaign, started after NATO had increased its membership to 19 with the admission of Poland, Hungary and the Czech Republic, and during which NATO celebrated its fiftieth anniversary, may well be the need for NATO to reappraise its role as a defensive alliance, and the way in which it responds to a challenge.

NOTES

CHAPTER ONE

1 C.G. Grey, *Bombers*
2 Maj Raymond H. Fredette, *The Sky On Fire: The First Battle of Britain 1917–18*
3 Anon., *War Birds: Diary of an Unknown Aviator*
4 Geoff D. Copeman, *Bomber Squadrons at War*
5 Ibid.
6 Ralph Barker, *The Royal Flying Corps in France: From Bloody April, 1917, to Final Victory*
7 Ibid.
8 Ibid.

CHAPTER TWO

1 The Smuts Report (July 1917)
2 Basil Liddell Hart, *The Defence of Britain*
3 Sir Arthur Harris, *Bomber Offensive*
4 Dudley Saward, *'Bomber' Harris: The Story of Marshal of the Royal Air Force*
5 Ibid.
6 Ibid.
7 Jesus Salas Larrazabal, *Air War Over Spain*
8 Ibid.
9 Ibid.

CHAPTER THREE

1 Giulio Douhet, *The Command of the Air*
2 Max Hastings, *Bomber Command*
3 Address to meeting of Gauleiters, 6 October 1943
4 Janusz Piekalkiewicz, *The Air War: 1939–45*
5 Alfred Price, *Blitz on Britain 1939–45*
6 Ibid.
7 Piekalkiewicz, *The Air War*
8 Price, *Blitz on Britain*
9 Ibid.
10 Ibid.
11 Ibid.
12 Ibid.
13 *Front Line: The History of the London Fire Brigade*
14 Price, *Blitz on Britain*
15 Ibid.
16 Ibid.
17 Piekalkiewicz, *The Air War*
18 Price, *Blitz on Britain*

CHAPTER FOUR

1   Bruce Lewis, *Aircrew: The Story of the Men Who Flew the Bombers*
2   Ibid.
3   Imperial War Museum Sound Archive
4   Ibid.
5   Ibid.
6   John Bushby, *Gunner's Moon*
7   Wg Cdr Guy Gibson, *Enemy Coast Ahead*
8   Ibid.
9   Imperial War Museum Sound Archive
10 Gibson, *Enemy Coast Ahead*

CHAPTER FIVE

1   Public Record Office document
2   Geoff D. Copeman, *Bomber Squadrons at War*
3   Ibid.

CHAPTER SIX

1   Imperial War Museum Sound Archive
2   *Daily Telegraph*, 22 October 1993
3   *Daily Telegraph*, 20 May 1998
4   Gordon Prange with Donald M. Goldstein and Katherine V. Dillon, *God's Samurai*
5   Brian Johnson, *Fly Navy*
6   Janusz Piekalkiewicz, *The Air War: 1939–45*
7   Geoffrey Brooke, *Alarm Starboard: A Remarkable True Story of the War at Sea*
8   US Navy Liaison Officer aboard HMS *Indefatigable*
9   Ryuji Nagatsuka, *I Was a Kamikaze*
10 Ibid.

CHAPTER SEVEN

1   Charles Messenger, *'Bomber' Harris and the Strategic Bombing Offensive, 1939–45*
2   Public Record Office, Air
3   Wg Cdr Guy Gibson, *Enemy Coast Ahead*
4   Edward Smithies, *War in the Air*
5   Gibson, *Enemy Coast Ahead*
6   Ralph Barker, *Strike Hard, Strike Sure*
7   John Bushby, *Gunner's Moon*
8   Michael Renaut, *Terror By Night*
9   Letter from Sgt E.A. Manson dated 5 June 1942, RAF Museum, Hendon, DC74/81/1
10 Public Record Office, Air
11 Imperial War Museum Sound Archive
12 Gibson, *Enemy Coast Ahead*
13 Ibid.
14 Ibid.
15 Ibid.
16 Ibid.
17 Wilbur H. Morrison, *Fortress Without a Roof*
18 Ibid.
19 Ibid.

CHAPTER EIGHT

1   Charles Messenger, *'Bomber' Harris and the Strategic Bombing Offensive, 1939–45*
2   Ibid.
3   Wilbur H. Morrison, *Fortress Without a Roof*
4   Alfred Price, *Battle Over the Reich*
5   Imperial War Museum Sound Archive
6   Edward Smithies, *War in the Air*
7   *Goebbels' Diaries*
8   Ibid.
9   Ibid.
10 Robert S. Raymond, *A Yank in Bomber Command*
11 Messenger, *'Bomber' Harris and the Strategic Bombing Offensive*
12 *Statistics of Armaments Production of the Technical Office*, 15 February 1945
13 John Sweetman, *Operation Chastise – The Dams Raid: Epic or Myth?*
14 Wg Cdr Guy Gibson, *Enemy Coast Ahead*
15 Ibid.
16 Ibid.
17 Ibid.
18 Ibid.
19 Albert Speer, *Inside the Third Reich*
20 Norman Longmate, *The Bombers*
21 Ibid.
22 *Goebbel's Diaries*
23 Speer, *Inside the Third Reich*
24 Ibid.
25 Ibid.
26 Dudley Saward, *'Bomber' Harris: The Story of Marshal of the Royal Air Force*
27 Janusz Piekalkiewicz, *The Air War: 1939–45*
28 Ibid.
29 Ibid.
30 Adolf Galland, *The First and the Last*
31 Speer, *Inside the Third Reich*
32 Alfred Price, *Blitz on Britain 1939–45*
33 Ibid.
34 Imperial War Museum Sound Archive
35 Air Cdre John Searby, *The Bomber Battle for Berlin*
36 Ibid.
37 Edward Smithies, *War in the Air*
38 Ibid.
39 Imperial War Museum Sound Archive
40 Edward Smithies, *War in the Air*
41 Imperial War Museum Sound Archive
42 Imperial War Museum Sound Archive
43 Imperial War Museum Sound Archive
44 Imperial War Museum Sound Archive
45 Imperial War Museum Sound Archive
46 Geoffrey S.C. Bishop, *The Battle: A Tank Officer Remembers*
47 *News Chronicle*
48 Geoff D. Copeman, *Bomber Squadrons at War*
49 Imperial War Museum Sound Archive
50 Imperial War Museum Sound Archive
51 *RAF Official History*
52 Alexander McKee, *Dresden, 1945*
53 Michael Renaut, *Terror By Night*

CHAPTER NINE

1 Edwin P. Hoyt, *Japan's War*
2 Ibid.
3 Chester Marshall, *B-29 Superfortress*
4 Ibid.
5 Ibid.
6 Russell Braddon, *Cheshire VC*
7 Ibid.
8 Ibid.

CHAPTER TEN

1 Cdr John B. Nichols and Barrett Tillman, *On Yankee Station: The Naval Air War Over Vietnam*
2 Ibid.
3 Michael Bilton and Peter Kosminsky, *Speaking Out: Untold Stories of the Falklands War*

CHAPTER ELEVEN

1 Stan Morse, *Gulf Air War Debrief*
2 Ibid.
3 John Peters and John Nichol, *Tornado Down*
4 Ibid.
5 Ibid.
6 Ibid.
7 Ibid.
8 Morse, *Gulf Air War Debrief*
9 Eric Michelette, *Air War Over the Gulf*
10 BBC television news
11 Ibid.
12 Ibid.

BIBLIOGRAPHY

Anderson, William, *Pathfinders*, Norwich, Jarrolds, 1946

Anon., *War Birds: Diary of an Unknown Aviator*, London, Hamish Hamilton, 1927

Barker, Ralph, *Strike Hard, Strike Sure*, London, Pan, 1974

Barker, Ralph, *The Royal Flying Corps in France: From Bloody April, 1917, to Final Victory*, London, Constable, 1995

Bilton, Michael and Kominsky, Peter, *Speaking Out: Untold Stories of the Falklands War*, London, André Deutsch, 1989

Bishop, Geoffrey, S.C., *The Battle: A Tank Officer Remembers*, published privately

Boyle, Andrew, *Trenchard*, London, Collins, 1962

Braddon, Russell, *Cheshire VC*, London, Odhams, 1956

Brooke, Geoffrey, *Alarm Starboard: A Remarkable True Story of the War at Sea*, Yeovil, Patrick Stephens, 1982

Boiten, Theo, *Nachtjagd, The Night Fighters versus Bomber War Over the Third Reich, 1939–45*, Ramsbury, The Crowood Press, 1997

Burden, Ronald A., *Falklands – The Air War*, British Aviation Research Group, 1986

Bushby, John, *Gunner's Moon*, London, Ian Allan, 1972

Clarke, Ronald, *Rise of the Boffins*, London, Harrap

Clarke, Ronald, *Battle for Britain*, London, Harrap, 1965

Clostermann, Pierre, *The Big Show*, London, Chatto & Windus, 1951

Collier, Basil, *History of Air Power*, London, Weidenfeld & Nicolson, 1974

Copeman, Geoff D., *Bomber Squadrons at War*, Stroud, Sutton, 1997

Craven, Wesley Frank, and Cate, James Lea, *The Army Air Forces in World War II*, Chicago, University of Chicago Press, 1953

Davies, R.B., *Sailor in the Air*, London, Collins, 1967

Douhet, Giulio, *The Command of the Air*, London, Faber & Faber, 1921

Freeman, Roger, *The US Strategic Bomber*, London, MacDonald & Jane's, 1975

Fredette, Maj Raymond H., *The Sky on Fire: The First Battle of Britain 1917–18, and the Birth of the Royal Air Force*, New York, Rinehart & Winston, 1966

Galland, Adolf, *The First and The Last*, London, Methuen, 1955

Gibson, Wg Cdr Guy, *Enemy Coast Ahead*, London, Michael Joseph, 1946

Grey, C.G., *Bombers*, London, Faber & Faber, 1941

Harris, Sir Arthur, *Bomber Offensive*, London, Collins, 1947

Hastings, Max, *Bomber Command*, London, Michael Joseph, 1979

Haddow, G.W. and Grosz, Peter M., *The German Giants, The Story of the R-Planes, 1914–19*, London, Putnam, 1969

Hoyt, Edwin P., *Japan's War*, London, Hutchinson, 1987

Inoguchi, Capt Rikkei, and Nakajima, Cdr Tadashi, *The Divine Wind: Japan's Kamikaze Force in World War II*, London, Bantam, 1978

Johnson, Brian, *Fly Navy*, Newton Abbot, David & Charles, 1981

Kay, C.E., *The Restless Sky*, London, Harrap, 1964

Larrazabal, Jesùs Salas, *Air War Over Spain*, London, Ian Allan, 1969

Lewis, Bruce, *Aircrew: The Story of the Men who Flew the Bombers*, London, Leo Cooper, 1991

Liddell Hart, Basil, *The Defence of Britain*, Greenwood Press, 1980

Longmate, Norman, *The Bombers: The RAF Offensive Against Germany 1939–45*, London, Hutchinson, 1983

Lucas, Laddie, *Five Up*, London, Sidgwick & Jackson, 1978

Marshall, Chester, *B-29 Superfortress*, Motorbooks International, 1993

McKee, Alexander, *Dresden, 1945*, London, Souvenir Press, 1982

Messenger, Charles, *'Bomber' Harris and the Strategic Bombing Offensive*, London, Arms & Armour Press, 1984

Micheletti, Eric, *Air War Over the Gulf*, Windrow & Greene, 1991

Morrison, Wilbur H., *Fortress Without a Roof*, London, W.H. Allen, 1982

Morse, Stan, *Gulf Air War Debrief*, London, Aerospace Publishing, 1991

Nagatsuka, Ryuji, *I Was a Kamikaze*, Abelard-Schuman, 1973

Nichols, Cdr John B. and Tillman, Barrett, *On Yankee Station: The Naval Air War Over Vietnam*, Naval Institute Press, 1987

Peters, John and Nichol, John, *Tornado Down*, London, Michael Joseph, 1992

Piekalkiewicz, Janusz, *The Air War: 1939–45*, London, Blandford, 1985

Prange, Gordon, with Donald M. Goldstein and Katherine V. Dillon, *God's Samurai*, Dulles, VA, Brassey's

Price, Alfred, *Battle Over the Reich*, London, Ian Allan, 1973

Price, Alfred, *Blitz on Britain 1939–45*, London, Ian Allan, 1977

Raymond, Robert S., *A Yank in Bomber Command*, Newton Abbot, David & Charles, 1977

Renaut, Michael, *Terror by Night*, London, Kimber, 1982

Saundby, Robert, *Air Bombardment*, London, Chatto & Windus, 1961

Saward, Dudley, *'Bomber' Harris: the Story of Marshal of the Royal Air Force*, London, Cassell, Buchan & Enright, 1984

Searby, Air Cdre John, *The Bomber Battle for Berlin*, Shrewsbury, Airlife, 1991

Smithies, Edward, *War in the Air*, London, Viking, 1990

Southworth, Herbert Rutledge, *Guernica, Guernica!*, University of California Press, 1977

Speer, Albert, *Inside the Third Reich*, London, Weidenfeld & Nicolson, 1970

Sweetman, John, *Operation Chastise – The Dams Raid: Epic or Myth?*, London, Jane's, 1982

Webster, Sir Charles and Frankland, Noble, *The Strategic Air Offensive Against Germany, 1939–40*,

Winfield, Dr Roland, *The Sky Shall Not Have Them*, London, Kimber, 1976

INDEX

Page numbers in *italics* indicate illustrations.